Rural Economic Development, 1975–1993

Rural Economic Development, 1975–1993

An Annotated Bibliography

Compiled by
F. Larry Leistritz
and
Rita R. Hamm

Bibliographies and Indexes in Economics and Economic History,
Number 16

Greenwood Press
Westport, Connecticut • London

Library of Congress Cataloging-in-Publication Data

Leistritz, F. Larry.
    Rural economic development, 1975–1993: an annotated bibliography
/ compiled by F. Larry Leistritz and Rita R. Hamm.
       p.   cm.—(Bibliographies and indexes in economics and
economic history, ISSN 0749-1786; no. 16)
    Includes indexes.
    ISBN 0-313-29159-4 (alk. paper)
    1. Rural development—Bibliography. I. Hamm, Rita R. II. Title.
III. Series.
Z7164.C84ZL435 1994
[HN49.C6]
016.3071′412—dc20   94–6778
British Library Cataloguing in Publication Data is available.

Library of Congress Catalog Card Number: 94–6778
ISBN: 0-313-29159-4
ISSN: 0749-1786

First published in 1994

Greenwood Press, 88 Post Road West, Westport, CT 06881
An imprint of Greenwood Publishing Group, Inc.

Printed in the United States of America

The paper used in this book complies with the
Permanent Paper Standard issued by the National
Information Standards Organization (Z39.48–1984).

10 9 8 7 6 5 4 3 2 1

CONTENTS

ACKNOWLEDGMENTS

We could not have completed this work without the support, encouragement and assistance of numerous persons and agencies. The Department of Agricultural Economics, the Institute for Business and Industry Development, and the North Dakota Agricultural Experiment Station at North Dakota State University all provided support for this effort and receive our sincere appreciation. We also extend appreciation to the Cooperative State Research Service of the U.S. Department of Agriculture for providing partial financial support for the effort, and to Dr. Richard Stuby from that agency for his personal encouragement.

In accessing the works included in this book, the Interlibrary Loan staff at the North Dakota State University library made an invaluable contribution. We particularly thank Deborah Sayler, Lorrettax Mindt, and Donna Graber for their help in securing hundreds of documents. Without their help and the cooperation of other libraries, we could not have produced such an extensive and complete book.

Every project of this magnitude needs a person with a multitude of skills, organizational ability and good humor; we were fortunate to have such a person to help with this project, JoAnn Thompson. Our highest level of appreciation is extended to JoAnn, who served as our research assistant and word processing specialist. Her many trips to the library were exceeded only by the many hours she spent inputting and formatting the material.

Finally, we thank Kathryn Theresa Smudge, who in spite of her busy schedule, always managed to be here to help edit and proofread this manuscript.

OVERVIEW

The past decade has been a period of economic restructuring nationwide, but the effects of economic change have been particularly severe in nonmetropolitan areas of the United States. Nonmetropolitan areas are often characterized by dependence on one or a few key economic sectors and therefore are quite vulnerable to adverse changes in one of their basic industries. In recent years, many rural areas of the United States and in other industrialized nations as well have shown this vulnerability. The restructuring of the manufacturing sector in the Midwest and South, depressed markets for the agricultural products of the Great Plains and Corn Belt states, retrenchment of the energy industry in the Rocky Mountain states and in Appalachia, and environmental and market constraints on the forest products industry in the Northwest all have led to economic stress for many rural areas and, in some cases, for entire states. Similar problems have been experienced in rural areas of other industrialized nations, including Canada, Australia, New Zealand, the United Kingdom and many Western European nations.

One result of the economic restructuring that has been occurring in rural areas has been a widening economic gap between metropolitan and nonmetropolitan areas. (In this work, the terms *rural* and *nonmetropolitan* are used interchangeably.) Since 1979, per capita income in rural counties in the United States has fallen relative to that of their urban counterparts, and by the early 1990s, rural per capita income was less than 75 percent of that in urban areas. Further, these patterns of widening rural disadvantage prevailed regardless of the county's dominant economic base; counties with primary economic dependence on farming, manufacturing, and mining all recorded major declines in relative income, while those primarily dependent on retirement and tourism had smaller losses. Rural counties also recorded substantial declines in earnings per capita compared to metropolitan counties during the 1980s, and rural unemployment rates have risen, in both relative and absolute terms.

Worsening economic conditions in rural areas have led to substantial migration flows from rural to urban areas. By the end of the 1980s, rural areas in the United States were experiencing a net loss of almost 500,000 residents annually. Rural counties that are not adjacent to metropolitan areas have been hit particularly hard by outmigration. For example, in the Great Plains states, more than 80 percent of the rural counties lost population during the 1980s. Such population outflows can be detrimental to future growth prospects of rural communities since the migrants are primarily an area's younger, better educated, and more highly skilled residents.

Significant losses of population and purchasing power through outmigration can seriously impair the ability of a community to mobilize its residents and resources to address its problems. Faced with declining income and population in their trade areas, local retail businesses and service firms may be forced to make severe adjustments, and local governments may find it difficult to remain solvent and to maintain services. Social effects also occur in an economically declining area. The sense of despair and helplessness felt by many individuals and families as they experience the loss of their livelihood and social ties has become prevalent. Continuing economic decline and outmigration can lead to a degradation of the overall social and institutional fabric of a community.

While the relative decline of rural areas has been attributed to a variety of factors, a major underlying cause is the inability of nonmetropolitan economies to adapt to global economic changes. Rural areas have been buffeted by economic, technological, and political forces beyond their control, and the cumulative impact of these forces has been the deterioration of the competitive advantage of nonmetropolitan areas. Among the forces leading to rural disadvantage is the fact that the principal basic industries of many rural areas are particularly subject to foreign competition (e.g., agriculture, mining, and labor-intensive manufacturing). During periods when the U.S. dollar is strong, as it was during much of the 1980s, export markets are lost to foreign competitors (e.g., agricultural products) or imports from abroad increase (e.g., textiles). Deregulation in U.S. financial markets and in the transportation and communications industries also may have worked to the disadvantage of rural areas. Meanwhile, productivity increases in such primary sector industries as agriculture and manufacturing, while important for long-run competitiveness, have often decreased employment opportunities in rural areas even though production grew.

Much of rural America is now confronted with the problems associated with economic restructuring and community decline. Consequently, there is a new awakening of interest in rural economic development. The rekindled interest in the economic revitalization of rural communities might at first appear to be merely a reincarnation of the rural development movement of the 1960s and early 1970s. However, a number of new emphases have appeared within the past decade. Perhaps the most important of these has been the changing roles of various levels of government in the economic development process, with state and local governments assuming a more active role as the federal role has diminished. Other topics which have been receiving increased attention include (1) retention and expansion of existing firms as a development option--rather than a total focus on attracting new industry, (2) the process by which new enterprises are created, commonly referred to as *entrepreneurship*, and (3) the efficacy of alternative economic development strategies that states and/or localities might pursue.

In addition, the economic problems of many rural areas are increasingly seen as an extension of the difficulties that certain sectors have encountered nationwide. In particular, some manufacturing sectors have suffered greatly from offshore competition, and international market forces also have severely affected some types of mining. Increasing the global competitiveness of our manufacturing industries has become a national policy concern, and a substantial number of programs have been initiated to provide technical assistance to manufacturers. Some of these programs attempt to create linkages between manufacturing sectors, universities, and the state, similar to the agricultural research and extension system.

While rural economic development is the basis for a growing research and public policy emphasis in recent years, progress is hampered by the difficulty inherent in identifying and accessing relevant works in the area. This difficulty stems in part from the multidisciplinary nature of the subject, which results in articles appearing in a wide variety of journals and report series. An additional problem for those seeking an understanding of the process of economic development and the economic forces affecting rural areas is that, although some of the literature is found in readily available professional journals or commercially published texts, many of the most relevant works in the field consist of special reports prepared by economic development organizations or by agricultural experiment station or extension service personnel, proceedings from conferences, or papers presented at such conferences. Such documents can be very difficult to identify. Thus, scholars and policymakers alike could benefit from a reference work that would help them readily identify key works related to specific issues.

The authors have previously completed two bibliographies and an edited book related to, but not encompassing, this topic (see items 40, 45, and 652 in this book). Readers may find these bibliographies on the interdependence of agriculture and rural communities and on rural community decline and revitalization and the book on the farm crisis in the United States to be useful as they evaluate rural economic development options. Only a few of the works from these previous efforts are included here.

The *purpose* of this book, then, is to bring together the salient works on the process of economic development and economic revitalization strategies that are applicable to nonmetropolitan areas. The literature represented examines (1) the forces affecting various economic sectors (such as manufacturing, tourism, and services) and the potential of these sectors to contribute to economic development in rural areas, (2) the forces affecting various types of firms (for example, new firms, small firms, and high-tech firms) and the potential of these types of firms to contribute to rural economic development, (3) contextual factors, such as markets, business climate, and technological change, and (4) economic development policies and strategies that could be employed by various levels of government.

The book is an attempt to meet the needs of (1) students of economic and community development, regional and agricultural economics, community and regional planning, rural sociology, and related disciplines; (2) teachers and researchers in the academic community; and (3) policymakers and economic development practitioners in both public and private sectors. The specific elements of its focus and scope are discussed below.

Scope

The focus of the bibliography is on the processes of economic growth and change in rural areas and economic development strategies applicable to such areas. The book covers the problems of economic development and revitalization within the world's industrialized countries, concentrating on North American and European literature written in English. The time frame is 1975 to the present with concentration on the period since 1980. Since our earlier works (mentioned above) dealt with related topics during the period prior to 1988, special attention has been given to the period 1988-1993. The bibliography covers professional journals, books, university research reports, extension reports, conference proceedings, government documents, and selected unpublished papers and theses. Unpublished works are included only if they are accessible to the general public.

Methodology

A thorough search of socioeconomic and governmental indexes and of pertinent professional journals yielded a rich body of literature that was considered for inclusion in this book. In addition, computer bibliographic searches were conducted utilizing the DIALOG system of computer databases. This system allowed us to search many databases such as Dun & Bradstreet, PREDICASTS, PROMPT, AGRICOLA, the Economic Literature Index, and CAB (Commonwealth Agricultural Bureau, a worldwide producer of rural economic development information). Because of the need to limit the length of this book and maintain its focus, not all works revealed in our literature search are annotated here. Criteria for inclusion of works included methodological, empirical, or policy contribution, as well as timeliness and availability. In addition, only English language publications are included.

Organization

The bibliography proper is organized into four broad categories: (1) economic sectors, the forces affecting them, and their potential contribution to economic development; (2) type of business/firm, including discussion of the unique problems encountered by new and/or small firms and the respective contributions to economic development of firms of different types; (3) contextual factors, including markets, business climate, technological change, and cultural factors; and (4) economic development policies and strategies. Many of these categories are further subdivided. The works within categories and subdivisions are organized alphabetically by author.

Much care was taken to provide the reader with a well-indexed book. The author index includes all authors and/or editors. The geographic index lists the citations which pertain to a specific geographical area. The final index, the subject index, was difficult to construct because of the seemingly endless opportunity to cross reference topics. Many cross references are provided, however, to help the reader wade through the abundance of similar topics. The reader should also note that *the indexes use citation numbers and not page numbers* when referring to location in the book.

ECONOMIC SECTORS

OVERALL

1. Bender, Lloyd D., Bernal L. Green, Thomas F. Hady, John A. Kuehn, Marlys K. Nelson, Leon B. Perkinson, and Peggy J. Ross. 1985. *The Diverse Social and Economic Structure of Nonmetropolitan America*. Rural Development Research Report No. 49. Washington, D.C.: USDA, Economic Research Service.

    Identifies seven distinct types of rural counties according to their major economic base, presence of federally owned land, or population characteristics. The types are farming dependent, manufacturing dependent, mining dependent, government functions, persistent poverty, federal lands, and retirement settlements. Seven U.S. maps by county are included.

2. Bowler, I. R., C. R. Bryant, and M. D. Nellis, eds. 1992. *Contemporary Rural Systems in Transition: Volume 2, Economy and Society*. Wallingford, Oxon, U.K.: CAB International, 314 pp.

    Consists of papers first presented at a 1991 international conference on the rapid and significant transition of rural areas in the developed countries over the previous decade, a transition sometimes referred to as the "restructuring" of rural economy and society. In Volume 2, 20 chapters address 5 major aspects of the rural economy and society: (1) the emergence of new socioeconomic issues, (2) changes in the structure of rural society, (3) trends in countryside recreation and tourism, (4) the changing employment structure, and (5) development strategies for rural communities. Each chapter discusses broad processes and structural changes that are common to all rural systems in developed countries; however, different geographical contexts (in Canada, the U.K., and the

U.S.) are used to illustrate the uneven development of those systems under the contemporary transition of rural areas.

3. Connaughton, John E., and Ronald A. Madsen. 1990. "The Changing Regional Structure of the U.S. Economy." *Growth and Change* 21(3):48-60.

Utilizes newly available industry-specific historical measures of Gross Regional Product to highlight the changing regional structure of the U.S. economy between 1963 and 1986. During this period, the percentage of U.S. output produced in eight different regions shifted substantially. The largest changes were in the Great Lakes (-3.65 percent), Mideast (-3.32 percent), and Southeast (+3.64 percent). Four major industry sectors (Agriculture, Mining, Construction, and Government) declined in relative importance in all eight regions. Somewhat surprisingly, manufacturing output expanded for the U.S. as a whole and for six of the eight regions.

4. Deller, Steven C., and David L. Chicoine. 1989. "Economic Diversification and the Rural Economy: Evidence From Consumer Behavior." *Regional Science Perspectives* 19(2):41-55.

Extends previous analyses of the implications of farm sector performance for rural economies by presenting more detailed descriptions of economic activity and changes in economic activity by size of place and type of local rural economy (e.g., agriculture, manufacturing) and analyzing factors associated with the level of overall economic activity in rural communities between 500 and 20,000 in population. The authors measure the economic activity of a community by the total taxable sales that occur within the community during one year. Descriptive data are for Illinois for 1977 and 1986. The analysis uses 1981 expenditure data.

5. Dillman, Don A., and Daryl J. Hobbs, eds. 1982. *Rural Society in the U.S.: Issues for the 1980s.* Boulder, CO: Westview Press, 437 pp.

Contains forty-one articles that define and clarify problems facing rural America in the 1980s. Topics include the reversal of nonmetropolitan migration loss, energy, technology, rural-urban differences, rural families, youth, elderly, minorities, women, poverty, public services, transportation, employment, education, housing, recreation, community development, needs assessment surveys, indicators of well-being, impact assessment, the structure of agriculture, part-time farming, and natural resources.

6. Economic Research Service. 1987. *Rural Economic Development in the 1980's: Preparing for the Future.* ERS Staff Rpt. No. AGES 870724. Washington, D.C.: USDA, Economic Research Service, 410 pp.

    Reports that structural change in the economy is causing economic stress in rural America, in sharp contrast with the 1970s, when growth and economic vitality were the dominant rural themes. The papers in this volume provide up-to-date information on changes in the structure and performance of the rural economy and on alternative policies to facilitate the adjustment of displaced people and their communities.

7. Farness, Donald H. 1989. "Detecting the Economic Base: New Challenges." *International Regional Science Review* 12(3):319-328.

    Reports that a growing and significant share of the economic base of many communities is comprised of output consumed within the region by nonresidents or by residents who expend externally derived funds. That output poses problems for analysts attempting to identify basic activity. This conceptual article assesses the discriminating power of the bifurcation techniques employed in economic base studies. It is intended to make users and builders of macro regional models more aware of the problem.

8. Jones, Warren, ed. 1990. *Research in Rural Issues: An Annotated Bibliography.* Macomb, IL: Western Illinois University, Illinois Institute for Rural Affairs, 315 pp.

    Contains extensive annotated entries dealing with the following topics: agriculture and agribusiness, banking and financial intermediaries, economic development, education, health, local government, social services, and transportation. Literature directly related to rural Illinois is included in each section of the bibliography, but all go beyond the local literature to include national and international materials as well.

9. Lall, Betty G., ed. 1985. *Economic Dislocation and Job Loss.* Ithaca, NY: Cornell University, Extension and Public Service Division, 275 pp.

    Contains 28 papers originally presented at a National Conference on Economic Dislocation and Job Loss held in Washington, D.C. in April, 1984. The book is divided into four parts. Part I includes six papers focusing on the causes and impact of the economic dislocation and resulting massive unemployment which began in the 1970s but greatly accelerated in the early 1980s. Part II contains employment projections for the period 1982-1995 for three major economic sectors: manufacturing, "high-tech" industries, and the service sector. Part III contains several papers which discuss measures to ameliorate dislocation problems. Among the options discussed are incubators for beginning businesses, an industrial extension service, employee ownership, new forms of labor-management cooperation, and efforts by communities to finance and nurture new enterprises. The final section deals with the experiences of Western Europe with problems of unemployment and industrial change.

10.   Marsden, Terry, Philip Lowe, and Sarah Whatmore, eds. 1990. *Rural Restructuring: Global Processes and Their Responses.* London: David Fulton Publishers, 197 pp.

Arises out of the perceived need for international debate and dissemination of on-going empirical and theoretical research associated with rural areas in advanced societies. Rural areas, their residents, and agencies are now facing rapid social, economic, and political change. The balance between production, amenity, mobility and development is readjusting as economic activities and their dependent relations become relocated. This first volume of a series contains seven chapters which address the broad theme of rural restructuring, looking particularly at the nature of rural-related responses to global processes of change. The volume is intended to attract a wide audience associated with international comparative research.

11.   Porterfield, Shirley L., and Thomas L. Cox. 1991. "The Export Decision of Selected Services-Producing and Manufacturing Industries." *Growth and Change* 22(3):66-85.

Provides a comparative analysis of factors influencing the out-of-state export decisions of establishments within selected groups of service producing and manufacturing industries. Data were gathered through a mail survey of establishments located in both rural and urban areas of five Midwestern states. The proportion of sales exported was specified as a function of establishment and location characteristics and estimated using Tobit analysis. Results of the study indicate that both establishment and location characteristics are important predictors of the export decision and confirm that establishments in some services-producing industries are able to enter and compete in out-of-state export markets. Similar factors were found to influence the export decisions of services-producing and manufacturing establishments. The results suggest that services-producing establishments may not be footloose with respect to location choices.

12.   Shepard, John C.   1993.   "The New Economy of the Great Plains: Implications for Economic Development." *Economic Development Quarterly* 7(4):403-410.

Reports that communities across the Great Plains are adapting successfully to the new economy. The author highlights some of these efforts in innovation, agriculture, small business, technology, trade, and tourism. Economic restructuring is changing how towns and cities work and interact, leading to the emergence of a "community of networks," as old economic and social ties are broken. Of increasing importance are quality of life factors as more people discount economic factors and incorporate a "sense of place" into their location decisions. Implications point toward needed changes in economic development and growth strategies. Finally, suggestions are made for further research.

13.   Smith, Stephen M., and Cosette M. Gibson.   1988.   "Industrial Diversification in Nonmetropolitan Counties and Its Effect on Economic Stability." *Western Journal of Agricultural Economics* 13(2):193-201.

Tests the hypothesis that employment is more stable in a more diverse economy by applying indexes of economic instability and industrial diversification to Idaho's 43 nonmetropolitan counties. While results support the hypothesis, other aspects of a county's economic structure are just as influential. Indiscriminate diversification will not necessarily bring economic stability.

14.   Summers, Gene F., Francine Horton, and Christina Gringeri.   1990. "Rural Labour-Market Changes in the United States," pp. 129-164 in *Rural Restructuring: Global Processes and Their Responses*, T. Marsden, P. Lowe, and S. Whatmore, eds.   London: David Fulton Publishers.

Summarizes U.S. economic trends of the 1980s as they pertain to the conditions and performance indicators of labor markets situated in rural areas. Then, the authors review theoretical interpretations of trends in labor markets in the U.S., especially those that have addressed changes in rural labor market areas. In the final section, they argue that it is increasingly necessary to link directly the mainstream theoretical arguments with rural labor market changes.

AGRICULTURE

15.   Aldinger, Lori, William J. Owings, Gene A. Futrell, and Larry D. Trede.
        1988. *A Feasibility Study of Egg Production in Iowa.* Ames, IA:
        Iowa State University, Agricultural Experiment Station, 37 pp.

        Reports that in the past 35 years Iowa fell from the number one position
        in egg production to its current rank of 15th. With the advent of large
        poultry operations much of the industry had become concentrated in the
        South and East. However, due to the current state of the layer industry
        Iowa may be in a good position to produce eggs competitively. Iowa is
        found to have an advantage in feed costs and poultry processing labor
        costs, compared to other midwestern states.

16.   Babb, Emerson M., and Burl F. Long. 1988. "Alternative Enterprises for
        Strengthening Southern Agriculture," pp. 344-357 in *The Rural
        South in Crisis: Challenges for the Future*, L. J. Beaulieu, ed.
        Boulder, CO: Westview Press.

        Focuses on providing information that can be useful to agencies advising
        farmers about the transition to alternative enterprises. The authors use the
        term, "alternative agriculture," to refer to a mix of products and services
        that involve nonconventional crops and animals, access to various uses of
        land and water, and integrated farm and off-farm activities. They
        examine the potential market for these products and services, obstacles to
        success, and activities which can help reduce these obstacles.

17.   Bangsund, Dean A., and F. Larry Leistritz. 1993. *Economic Impact of
        Expanded Calf Backgrounding and Expanded Irrigation:
        Applications of the Value-Added Agricultural Impact Assessment
        Model.* Agricultural Economics Report No. 300. Fargo, ND: North
        Dakota State University, Department of Agricultural Economics, 98
        pp.

        Discusses a modeling system designed to estimate the direct and
        secondary impacts of various agricultural scenarios. The modeling system
        is composed of two major components: (1) a Regional Assessment Model
        (RAM) designed to trace changes in resource use, enterprise levels, and
        economic activity, that result from a departure from traditional or current
        production combinations to alternative production combinations and (2)
        a Secondary Impact Model (SIM) designed to use many of the outputs
        from the RAM to estimate secondary economic, demographic, and fiscal
        impacts of various agricultural development scenarios. The potential

applications of the modeling system include (1) changes in existing enterprises, (2) adoption of new enterprises, (3) assessment of the effects of policy changes, and (4) analysis of the effects of changes in resource use. Two applications were chosen to illustrate the model: (1) analyzing the effects of expanded feeder calf backgrounding and (2) assessing the impacts of expanded irrigation.

18.   Barkema, Alan, and Michael L. Cook. 1993. "The Changing U.S. Pork Industry: A Dilemma for Public Policy." *Economic Review* (Federal Reserve Bank of Kansas City) 78(2):49-65.

Considers the changes underway in the U.S. pork industry today and what they suggest in the years ahead. The first section reviews the structural changes taking place in the industry. These include concentration of pork production in the hands of fewer, larger producers and processors and increasing integration of the industry. The second section describes the causes underlying this structural evolution. Three related factors appear to be driving the pork industry toward a more compact market structure: (1) growing discrimination of consumers which challenges the food industry to tailor food products for more precisely defined market niches, (2) new technology that gives the industry the means to tailor its products, and (3) a more compact market structure that improves the flow of information between consumers and producers. The final section examines the dilemma the changing pork industry poses for public policy.

19.   Barkema, Alan D., and Mark Drabenstott. 1990. "A Crossroads for the Cattle Industry." *Economic Review* (Federal Reserve Bank of Kansas City) 75(6):47-66.

Reports that a decade of mergers, buyouts, and declining cattle numbers has brought the nation's cattle industry to a crossroads as it enters the 1990s. One road would continue the path toward a smaller, more concentrated industry; the other would change direction and allow some expansion. Which road the industry takes will depend on consumers and their willingness to purchase beef instead of other meats. The future course of the industry will have a great impact on the farm economy of the region. Cattle account for nearly $15 billion in farm income in the seven states of the Tenth Federal Reserve District (Colorado, Kansas, Missouri, Nebraska, New Mexico, Oklahoma, and Wyoming). The economic activity associated with beef processing is even greater.

20.   Barkema, Alan D., Mark Drabenstott, and Julie Stanley. 1990. "Processing Food in Farm States: An Economic Development

Strategy for the 1990s." *Economic Review* (Federal Reserve Bank of Kansas City) 75(4):5-23.

Examines steps farm states can take to encourage food processing activity in the 1990s. First, the seven farm states with the greatest potential to expand food processing activity are identified. These are Arkansas, Idaho, Iowa, Kansas, Minnesota, Nebraska, and Wisconsin. Then, the authors examine how these states can develop food products to encourage growth in food processing and identify four food products best suited to the seven states. The article concludes that a successful food processing strategy will depend on investments in emerging food technologies that could offset the distance separating the farm states from major consumer markets.

21.   Barkley, David L., and Paul N. Wilson.   1992.   "Is Alternative Agriculture a Viable Rural Development Strategy?" *Growth and Change* 23(2):239-253.

Examines the potential of alternative agriculture as a means of enhancing rural area jobs and income. The authors define this nontraditional agricultural activity as new crops or products to an area, industrial uses of agricultural products, value-enhancement activities, and urban agricultural activities. The potential for new agriculturally related activities is summarized. The long-term rural economic and development potential, through new income and jobs, is assessed. Next, five case studies are provided to illustrate alternative agriculture successes, limited successes, and failures (Guayule, Jojoba, Muscadine grapes, market windows for fresh fruit and vegetables, and aquaculture). The authors conclude that alternative agriculture may be viable in select rural areas. However, total employment generation potential is too small and diffused to provide significant rural development impacts.

22.   Beaulieu, Lionel J., ed. 1988. *The Rural South in Crisis: Challenges for the Future.* Boulder, CO: Westview Press, 384 pp.

Contains 24 chapters which reflect the thoughts and views of leading scholars of rural society in the United States and the South. The purpose of the volume is fourfold: (1) to articulate the dimensions of the agricultural/rural community crisis in the South, (2) to examine current socioeconomic issues that are of critical importance to the well being of agriculture and rural communities in the region, (3) to assess the impacts of past agriculture/rural development policies on the South and to delineate the directions that such policies might take in the future, and (4) to identify opportunities for vitalizing the rural South.

23.   Bowler, I. R., C. R. Bryant, and M. D. Nellis, eds. 1992. *Contemporary Rural Systems in Transition: Volume 1, Agriculture and the Environment.* Wallingford, Oxon, U.K.: CAB International, 272 pp.

Based on papers presented at a 1991 international conference on the rapid and significant transition of rural areas in developed countries over the previous decade, a transition sometimes referred to as the "restructuring" of rural economy and society. Volume 1 contains 18 chapters on agriculture and the environment, divided into five sections: (1) developing organizational structures in the food supply system, (2) changing farm business structure, (3) the environmental impact of modern agriculture, (4) emerging agricultural policy issues, and (5) the growing concern with "sustainable agriculture." Each chapter discusses broad processes and structural changes that are common to all rural systems in developed countries; however, different geographical contexts are used to illustrate the uneven development of those systems under the contemporary transition of rural areas.

24.   Buttel, Frederick H. 1987. "Biotech Trade-offs in the Rural Economy." *Rural Development Perspectives* 3(3):11-15.

Argues that biotechnology's benefits to rural America may come chiefly in expanded demand for raw materials necessary for industrial-biotechnological production. Its drawbacks may include declining farm numbers and the displacement of rural workers in chemical and pharmaceutical facilities rendered obsolete by the new technology.

25.   Christy, Ralph D., and John M. Connor. 1989. "Economic Forces Influencing Value-Added Food Industries: Implications for Southern Agriculture." *Southern Journal of Agricultural Economics* 21(1):13-22.

Has three objectives which are (1) to discuss the economic forces shaping the U.S. value-added food industry, (2) to evaluate regional differences in U.S. food industries and predict future growth trends, and (3) to suggest an expanded role for Land Grant-supported research in food distribution and manufacturing sectors.

26.   Commins, Patrick. 1990. "Restructuring Agriculture in Advanced Societies: Transformation, Crisis, and Responses," pp. 45-76 in *Rural Restructuring: Global Processes and Their Responses*, T. Marsden, P. Lowe, and S. Whatmore, eds. London: David Fulton Publishers.

Argues that, conceptually, agricultural restructuring must be understood as a set of dynamic changes determined by the reciprocal relationships among (1) the macroeconomic forces of capitalist development, (2) the nature of socioeconomic structure that conditions the relative power of different interests to influence change, and (3) the role of government intervention. Empirically, the analysis examines several structural trends and their outcomes in the transition from a "productionist" to a "post-productionist" agriculture in developed countries. A general conclusion is that current policy responses to the problems of agricultural restructuring will consolidate the distinction between farms that produce quality food efficiently and those farms that will serve other functions for modern society.

27.   Deseran, Forrest A., and Ann Z. Dellenbarger. 1988. "Local Labor Markets in Agricultural Policy Dependent Areas of the South." pp 170-180 in *The Rural South in Crisis: Challenges for the Future*, L. J. Beaulieu, ed. Boulder, CO: Westview Press.

Explores the effects of industrial composition and location of local labor markets on part-time farm households in the South. The authors' research goes beyond previous efforts in several respects: (1) they employ a unique data set of local labor markets derived from community-to-work patterns of residents, (2) their analysis encompasses the family (in this case, the married couple), and (3) they compare farm with nonfarm members of the labor force.

28.   Drabenstott, Mark. 1991. "Developing the Farm-Dependent Rural Economy: The Policy Choices," pp. 91-103 in *The Future of Rural America: Anticipating Policies for Constructive Change*, K. Pigg, ed. Boulder, CO: Westview Press.

Examines steps state and local policy makers can take to improve the rural economic outlook of farming regions. The first section of the chapter reviews economic changes that have occurred in farm-dependent rural areas. The second section describes the new rural economic reality that will constrain policy makers in the 1990s. The third section considers policy steps to boost rural economic growth where possible and to encourage adjustment where growth is not possible.

29.   Farris, Paul L., Richard T. Crowder, Reynold P. Dahl, and Sarahelen Thompson. 1988. "Economics of Grain and Soybean Processing in the United States," pp. 315-348 in *Economics of Food Processing in the United States*, C. O. McCorkle, ed. San Diego, CA: Academic Press, Inc.

Focuses on major agribusiness industries that process wheat, rice, corn, barley, and soybeans. The major processing industries examined are flour milling, rice milling, corn wet milling, corn dry milling, manufactured feeds, barley malting, and soybean processing. Basic dimensions examined are (1) grain production and utilization, (2) procurement, pricing, storage, and transportation of grain, and (3) type, size, and organization of major grain industries.

30. Germer, Henry A., Jr., and Stephen H. Replogle. 1988. "A Study of Factors Critical to Poultry Industry Location." *Arkansas Business and Economic Review* 21(4):1-11.

Undertakes to develop a basic understanding of the poultry industry, to identify critical factors relating to locational aspects of the poultry industry, and to suggest a method by which these critical factors may be used to evaluate the suitability of particular areas for the poultry industry. The scope of the study was limited to broiler and turkey production. The analysis of critical location factors is organized around three key groups or operations: (1) growers, (2) feed processors, and (3) poultry processors. Critical location factors were identified for each group and then prioritized by industry representatives. Overall, the analysis points to the advantage of locating the poultry operation as close as possible to a grain source.

31. Goe, W. Richard, and Martin Kenney. 1991. "The Restructuring of the Global Economy and the Future of U.S. Agriculture," pp. 137-155 in *The Future of Rural America: Anticipating Policies for Constructive Change*, K. Pigg, ed. Boulder, CO: Westview Press.

Contends that, due to its tight linkages with the larger industrial economy, the future of U.S. agriculture will be shaped by forces of change that are propelling the current restructuring of the global economy. The first section briefly examines ways in which U.S. agriculture was shaped by and integrated into the larger U.S. industrial economy in the postwar period. The second section outlines several important facets of global restructuring and how they are likely to influence the future of U.S. agriculture. Finally, the implications of these dimensions of change are discussed.

32. Golz, Theresa K., Joel T. Golz, Delmer L. Helgeson, and Timothy A. Petry. 1990. *Preliminary Economic Feasibility of Broiler Production in North Dakota*. Ag. Econ. Rpt. No. 261. Fargo, ND: North Dakota Agricultural Experiment Station, 80 pp.

Examines the potential for competitive broiler production in North Dakota. The authors review (1) national, regional, and state production patterns, (2) types of broiler diseases and their preventative measures, and (3) national trends in consumption of beef, pork, fish, and broiler meat over a 30-year period. The major forms in which broilers are sold, the trend in the broiler market, and the major marketing channels for broilers are analyzed. The level of industry integration and resulting impact on industry participants is analyzed using a historical data base. Trends in broiler exports were analyzed and the major export markets identified. The potential domestic broiler market available to North Dakota was determined using a linear programming transportation model. The potential Canadian export market available to North Dakota was estimated by presenting surplus and deficit production by province. Plant investment for an integrated broiler producing complex was estimated by referencing previous studies.

33.   Henderson, David, Luther Tweeten, and Dean Schriener.   1989. "Community Ties to the Farm." *Rural Development Perspectives* 5(3):31-35.

Reports on a study of the three counties of the Oklahoma Panhandle over the period 1969-84. The authors found that, as farm structure in the area changed, the smallest towns in the region suffered the greatest exodus of businesses. The farm trade previously served by small-town businesses apparently shifted to businesses in the larger towns; the largest town in the area managed to grow while the smaller towns were shrinking.

34.   Kearl, W. Gordon. 1988. *Opportunities for Economic Development and Potential for Value Added in Wyoming Production Agriculture.* P-898.18.   Laramie, WY: University of Wyoming, Agricultural Experiment Station, 61 pp.

Presents information on economic development opportunities and potential for creating added value in production agriculture. The researcher identifies underutilized resources and opportunities in crop and livestock production.

35.   Kenney, Martin. 1987. "Biotechnology: Industrial Growth in a Period of Crisis." *Economic Development Quarterly* 1(3):293-300.

Is a review article that evaluates the written documents on the development of the biotechnology industry so that people unfamiliar with the industry will be able to identify documents useful to their needs. The review pays special attention to those documents referring to the social, economic, and political aspects of biotechnology. The role of the university in biotechnology is examined in depth.

36. Kliebenstein, James, et al. 1988. *The Iowa Pork Industry: Competitive Situation and Prospects.* STF1. Ames, IA: Iowa State University, 76 pp.

Includes five major sections that examine (1) trends in pork supply and demand, (2) competition in the hog slaughter industry, (3) current location, demographics, and characteristics of Iowa and U.S. hog industries, (4) hog production efficiency, returns, and costs, and (5) other factors affecting Iowa's competitive position in the hog industry. A comparison of production costs between the typical Iowa swine operation and a group of competitors who operate large, intensively managed facilities was made. The large operations are located primarily in the Atlantic coastal region and the midsouth. The top 20-25 percent of Iowa producers had production costs on par with the competition.

37. Korsching, Peter F., and Judith Gildner, eds. 1986. *Interdependencies of Agriculture and Rural Communities in the Twenty-first Century: The North Central Region.* Ames, IA: North Central Regional Center for Rural Development, Iowa State University, 230 pp.

Collects papers from a conference on the nature of changes occurring in agriculture and rural communities. Two major questions were addressed at the conference: What is the role of the agricultural sector in a program of rural development? How can rural development programs improve both the agricultural and nonagricultural sectors of rural America?

38. Lansford, Notie H., Jr., and Lonnie L. Jones. 1988. *Impact of the Changing Farm Economy on Rural Communities.* SRDC No. 110. Mississippi State, MS: Southern Rural Development Center, 50 pp.

Develops the capability to quantitatively analyze the impacts of changes in agricultural activity on the economies of rural communities. Data from 48 rural, agricultural counties in Texas were used to estimate equations to predict (1) total agricultural sales, (2) total county employment, and (3) total county income. The estimated equations that predict intracommunity linkages among sectors were integrated into an interactive computer model to foster the use of the research findings. Examples of model applications are provided.

39. Lawrence, Geoffrey. 1990. "Agricultural Restructuring and Rural Social Change in Australia," pp. 101-128 in *Rural Restructuring: Global Processes and Their Responses*, T. Marsden, P. Lowe, and S. Whatmore, eds. London: David Fulton Publishers.

Seeks to identify the structural changes occurring in Australia, including the ways technological change and deregulation have combined to force a reduction in the number of rural producers, and more indirectly to cause the erosion of the economies of many smaller country towns. The author attempts to link theoretically the technological dynamic of Australian agriculture, the activities of international corporate capital, the changing role of the state, and the social impact of economic changes occurring in rural Australia.

40. Leistritz, F. Larry, and Brenda L. Ekstrom. 1986. *Interdependencies of Agriculture and Rural Communities: An Annotated Bibliography.* New York, NY: Garland Publishing, 200 pp.

Contains nearly 600 items on socioeconomic changes in rural communities, the role of shifts in agricultural structure and technology in stimulating such changes, and the role of the local economy in influencing farm organization and the life-styles of farm families. Many of the annotated works review the economic, demographic, public service, fiscal, and social changes in rural communities over the past several decades and describe the effects of the current economic crisis in agriculture on farm families, agribusiness, and rural communities.

41. Logan, Samuel H., Lisa J. Steinmann, and Donald E. Farris. 1988. "Economics of Meat Processing in the United States," pp. 241-277 in *Economics of Food Processing in the United States*, C. O. McCorkle, ed. San Diego, CA: Academic Press, Inc.

Provides a description and analysis of the U.S. meat processing industry. The authors review overall trends in production and consumption, prices and demand, industry organization and structure, futures trading, and processed products. They then examine the industry's major subsectors: beef, pork, lamb, and poultry.

42. Lopez, Rigoberto A., and Nona R. Henderson. 1989. "The Determinants of Location Choices for Food Processing Plants." *Agribusiness* 5(6):619-632.

Examines the determinants of location choices for new food processing plants using the results of a telephone survey of 56 firms in the Mid-

Atlantic states (New Jersey, Pennsylvania, New York, Delaware, and Maryland). Six categories of business climate factors (market, infrastructure, labor, personal, environmental regulation, and fiscal policy) containing 41 specific location factors are considered. Findings indicate that plant location choices are driven by market and infrastructural factors. Fiscal policies such as tax and development incentives are insignificant.

43.   McCorkle, Chester O., ed. 1988. *Economics of Food Processing in the United States.* San Diego, CA: Academic Press, Inc., 449 pp.

Contains 11 chapters dealing with various aspects of the U.S. food processing industry, in addition to an extensive overview section. Topics addressed by specific chapters include factors influencing consumption and production of processed foods, changing technical processes in the industry, marketing and market structure, regulation of the industry, the food processing industries and the national economy, and industry dynamics and economic policy. The authors also examine five major segments of the food processing industry: fruit and vegetable processing, meat processing, dairy processing, grain and soybean processing, and the wine industry. Most of the contributing authors are associated with Land-Grant universities or with the food industry.

44.   Mjelde, James W., J. Richard Conner, Jerry W. Stuth, James Jensen, Chia-Cheun Chang, and James B. Jones. 1992. "The Emerging Exotic Ungulate Livestock Industry: A Survey of Current Producers." *Agribusiness* 8(5):473-484.

Presents survey responses concerning the general aspects of current exotic operations and attitudes of current producers. The survey provided 99 responses from producers in the U.S. and Canada, about 54 percent response. About 50 percent of the respondents resided in Texas. Fallow deer was the most prevalent species owned with blackbuck a distant second, but the respondents indicated a wide diversity of livestock operations. Respondents were on average well educated and in high gross income brackets. Overall, the responses could be characterized as coming from producers involved in an industry in the introductory stage. Limited information and lack of knowledge concerning marketing issues were the major concerns indicated by the respondents regarding the development of the exotic venison industry.

45.   Murdock, Steve H., and F. Larry Leistritz, eds. 1988. *The Farm Financial Crisis: Socioeconomic Dimensions and Implications for Producers and Rural Areas.* Boulder, CO: Westview Press, 205 pp.

Is an attempt to address the need for more comprehensive analyses of the socioeconomic impacts of the farm financial crisis of the 1980s. The authors examine the socioeconomic context, the impacts, and the long-term consequences of the crisis, emphasizing how these affect agriculturally dependent rural areas. In addition to a survey of the base of empirical data available by the late 1980s, the results of the editors' own extensive analyses of the impacts of the crisis on the producers, former producers, business operators, former business operators, employees of rural businesses, and other rural residents are used.

46.   Reich, Robert B. 1988. "The Rural Crisis, and What To Do About It." *Economic Development Quarterly* 2(1):3-8.

Points out that America's rural economy has been heavily dependent on agriculture and raw materials production and that the broad decline in world prices of primary commodities during the 1980s has had a depressing effect on the rural economy. The author asserts that the way to revitalize the U.S. rural economy is not to preserve primary commodity production by heavily investing in rural America, but rather to ease the transition of the rural economy out of an almost exclusive dependence on primary commodities and into more competitive, more specialized production. The author identifies four key barriers that must be overcome in order to enable rural America to make the transition. These are (1) rural transportation, (2) rural communications, (3) rural technology extension and (4) rural training and retraining.

47.   Sommer, Judith E., Fred K. Hines, and Mindy Petrulis. 1993. "Agriculture Still Key to Economic Health of the Rural Great Plains." *Rural Development Perspectives* 8(2):28-36.

Reports that the nonmetro population of the Great Plains has declined 16.2 percent since 1980. Job losses in agriculture and boom-bust cycles in the energy sector have contributed to this decline. Although farm numbers are declining, the Plains still produces a large portion of the nation's agricultural products. The future ability of the nonmetro Great Plains to retain population depends on its ability to attract new industries to diversify the economic base and on the viability of its farming and energy sectors.

48.   Torok, Steven J., Richard A. Ahlschwede, Diane I. Hambley, and Sam M. Cordes. 1988. *Value-Added Agribusinesses in Wyoming-- Characteristics, Problems, and Barriers.* B-898.10. Laramie, WY: University of Wyoming, Department of Agricultural Economics, 88 pp.

Provides information on the specific characteristics of, and problems and barriers encountered by Wyoming's value-added agribusinesses. Data are drawn from a survey of 115 agribusiness firms. The firms were involved in a wide variety of agricultural processing activities, the most numerous of which were livestock slaughter-meat processing, feed milling, and leather processing or manufacturing. The firms were primarily oriented toward the Wyoming market; over 62 percent indicated that Wyoming was their primary shipping destination for their largest single customer. About 67 percent employed 10 or fewer workers. Among the problems and barriers reported were those related to labor (wages and/or availability), finance, and transportation.

49. Torok, Steven J., Richard A. Ahlschwede, Diane I. Hambley, and Sam M. Cordes. 1988. *Former Value-Added Agribusinesses in Wyoming-- Characteristics and Reasons for Suspending Operations.* B-898.11. Laramie, WY: University of Wyoming, Department of Agricultural Economics, 28 pp.

Reports on the characteristics of and reasons for suspending operations of Wyoming's former value-added agribusinesses. A survey of 20 former businesses provided the data base for the study. Most of the firms had suspended operations between 1981 and 1985. The number of years the firms had operated varied greatly, ranging from 3 years to more than 50. The number of employees also ranged widely; 40 percent of the firms had 5 employees or less while 5 percent had more than 100. About one-fourth felt that technical assistance would have been helpful in sustaining their businesses.

50. Torok, Steven J., Dale J. Menkhaus, Vincent Colombel, and Edward B. Bradley. 1990. "Analysis of Sales Problems of Small Value-added Agricultural Processors." *Journal of Agribusiness* 8(2):97-106.

Analyzes survey data to identify technical or educational assistance needs that may help small value-added agricultural processors in increasing their sales. The authors also examine policy alternatives suggested by the data and management strategies that may aid firms in increasing their sales. Data were obtained from 115 Wyoming firms that process agricultural products.

51. Trede, Larry D., William J. Owings, Gene A. Futrell, and Lori Aldinger. 1986. *A Feasibility Study of Broiler Meat Production in Iowa.* PS-243. Ames, IA: Iowa State University, Cooperative Extension Service, 56 pp.

Assesses the potential for expanded broiler production in Iowa. Factors favoring Iowa as a site for expanded production include prices for corn and soybean meal that are generally lower than in the major broiler producing states. This feed cost advantage is offset in part, however, by a disadvantage in housing investment costs.

52. Van Duren, Erna, and Larry Martin. 1992. "Assessing the Impact of the Canada-U.S. Trade Agreement on Food Processing in Canada: An Analytical Framework and Results for Poultry, Dairy, and Tomatoes." *Agribusiness* 8(1):1-22.

Assesses the impact of the Canada-U.S. Trade Agreement (CUSTA) on food processors in Canada. The authors examine the interaction between Canada's agricultural marketing boards and changes to domestic and border regulation resulting from CUSTA on processors in the poultry, dairy, and tomato processing industries. The results vary by the processed product but suggest that the chicken industry needs to make the biggest adjustment, while the tomato industry is best positioned to make the change required to become competitive.

53. Wagner, Michael J., Roger J. Beck, Phillip R. Eberle, and Bill Goodman. 1989. *A Feasibility Study for an Integrated Broiler Producing Industry in Southern Illinois*. Carbondale, IL: Southern Illinois University, 96 pp.

Examines the potential for a successful integrated broiler producing complex in southern Illinois by comparing advantages and disadvantages that the southern Illinois area would exhibit when compared with northwest Arkansas. Southern Illinois has an overall net advantage over Arkansas in broiler production, processing, feed cost, and transportation of 1.36 cents per pound of meat produced. However, Illinois showed a disadvantage in labor costs and property taxes. The authors conclude that there are no major economic constraints that would inhibit the industry from becoming established in Illinois.

54. Williams, Gary W., ed. 1989. *Value-Added Research Investments: Boon or Boondoggle?* TAMRDC Special Series Rpt. No. SS-1-89. College Station, TX: Texas A&M University, Department of Agricultural Economics, 51 pp.

Reports that adding value to agricultural products is often seen as a means to dispose of raw commodity surpluses and to add jobs, boost incomes, and otherwise promote rural economic development. A major component of this development strategy has been federal and state investments in research intended to boost the production, marketing, and distribution of value-added agricultural products. This monograph is the proceedings of a symposium that explored the economic rationale and implications of such research investments.

55.   Wilson, Paul N. 1993. "Nontraditional Agriculture: An Economic Development Alternative," pp. 185-204 in *Economic Adaptation: Alternatives for Nonmetropolitan Areas*, D. L. Barkley, ed. Boulder, CO: Westview Press.

Analyzes the economic feasibility of nontraditional agriculture as an employment generation alternative for rural areas. The author defines nontraditional agriculture as crop and livestock production and related processing and marketing services, that are in some sense unusual or atypical, at least for that part of the country. Nontraditional agriculture includes income enhancement and value-added programs. Income enhancement is a broad concept that implies augmenting rural incomes through a variety of production, processing, and service activities. Value-added activities create new uses for traditional crops or create additional jobs by further processing local agricultural products in rural areas. The paper concludes with a discussion of the necessary conditions for successfully promoting nontraditional agricultural activities as employment generation activities for rural America.

MANUFACTURING

56.   Ahlbrandt, Roger S., Jr. 1988. "Adjusting to Changes in Traditional Markets: The Problems of Small Manufacturers in Older Industrial Regions." *Economic Development Quarterly* 2(3):252-264.

Based on a study carried out in the Pittsburgh metropolitan area, this article examines the experiences of smaller manufacturing companies in adjusting to new market circumstances. Many of these companies, job shops in particular, are experiencing difficulties because they do not have the marketing and product development expertise required to recapture lost markets or to identify new ones. For many, outside assistance may be necessary to help them with the transition, and programs to provide this help should become part of a region's overall approach to economic development.

57.   Ahlbrandt, Roger S., Jr.   1991.   "Technical Assistance for Small
       Manufacturing Companies: Management Issues for Nonprofit
       Providers." *Economic Development Review* 9(1):29-33.

Points out that many states have created business assistance programs to
help startup companies and small and medium-sized firms address a
variety of business needs. The author discusses one of these programs,
the Industrial Resource Centers Program of the state of Pennsylvania and
describes the first year of activities of the Southwestern Pennsylvania
Industrial Resource Center. The discussion covers a number of important
implementation issues that managers of technical assistance programs face
as they go through a startup phase.

58.   Ahlbrandt, Roger S., Jr.   1992.   "Helping Small Manufacturing
       Companies   Become   More   Competitive: A   Model   and   an
       Evaluation." *Economic Development Review* 10(1):67-71.

Reports that small manufacturing companies are facing increased
competitive pressures. To respond they need to take a longer term view
of what is required to compete successfully in a marketplace that requires
greater attention to improved quality, increased reliability, on time
delivery, continuous product improvement, and the like. Many small
firms lack the in-house expertise to accomplish what is necessary, but
could with some outside assistance. The author describes one such
successful effort. It shows that management assistance can be an
important component of a strategy to improve the competitiveness of the
small manufacturing sector.

59.   Atkinson, Robert D. 1992. "The Impact of the Defense Build-Down on
       State and Local Economies." *Economic Development Review*
       10(4):55-59.

Examines the potential economic impacts of reductions in national
defense spending. The author concludes that, while national defense
money is spent in all 50 states and thousands of American communities,
the number of areas seriously distressed by a decrease in defense
spending is not likely to be great. The fate of those communities that do
depend on defense for their economic vitality will depend to a great
extent on how well the U.S. economy performs. Well funded and
designed economic development programs also can help many affected
communities.

60.   Barkley, David L. 1993. "Manufacturing Decentralization: Has the Filtering-Down Process Fizzled Out?" pp. 29-48 in *Economic Adaptation: Alternatives for Nonmetropolitan Areas*, D. L. Barkley, ed. Boulder, CO: Westview Press.

Reviews recent and historic changes in metro-nonmetro growth patterns in an effort to understand current reurbanization phenomena and to predict the consequences for rural areas. The focus is on manufacturing employment, a leading sector in many nonmetro counties. The author begins with a summary of political and economic forces that initially fostered an urban concentration of manufacturing activity. Next, explanations of the post-World War II dispersal of this activity are provided. A review of factors associated with past concentration and decentralization movements provides insights into the potential impacts of current structural changes. Finally, recent manufacturing employment trends are reviewed, and four theories are proposed for the slowing of manufacturing decentralization. Alternatives for maintaining a viable manufacturing base in small towns are provided in the concluding section.

61.   Barkley, David L., and Sylvain Hinschberger. 1992. "Industrial Restructuring: Implications for the Decentralization of Manufacturing to Rural Areas." *Economic Development Quarterly* 6(1):64-79.

Indicates that traditional methods of industrial organization and production are giving way to smaller, more flexible and specialized operations. This industrial restructuring increases the importance of localization economies relative to internal economies, and thus, the attractiveness of rural locations is reduced. Analysis of spatial employment data for 106 metalworking industries for 1981 to 1986 supports the restructuring/agglomeration hypothesis. Industries experiencing marked shifts toward specialization and reduced size (vertical disintegration) were less likely to relocate employment from metro to nonmetro areas. However, the relationship between industrial restructuring propensities and agglomeration was weak after controlling for industry growth rates and technological sophistication.

62.   Battelle. 1992. *Identification of Key Technologies and Industries for the State of Iowa*. Des Moines, IA: The Wallace Technology Transfer Foundation and the Iowa Department of Economic Development, 163 pp.

Identifies technology/industry targets for the state of Iowa and recommends an action agenda. The authors examine the characteristics and needs of current and projected future Iowa industries, giving preference to industries that have the greatest potential to create or retain quality jobs in Iowa. The authors recommend that the Iowa technology strategy be based on highly focused investments. A near-term, employment-based strategy must be built around maintaining and enhancing the economic competitiveness of Iowa's manufacturing base. The primary investment target should be a specific field of manufacturing. Specific industries identified for attraction, retention, and expansion include (1) packaging and sanitary paper products, (2) drugs and pharmaceuticals, (3) computers and related products and services, (4) instruments and related products, (5) communication services, and (6) insurance and commercial banking. The technologies critical to the competitive success of Iowa's existing and future growth industry groups are broadly defined as manufacturing, materials, computer and information services, and electronics.

63.   Bernat, G. Andrew, Jr.   1992.   "Manufacturers' Restructuring in Nonmetro Areas Contributes to Lagging Pay, Job Instability." *Rural Development Perspectives* 8(1):32-33.

Points out that restructuring in the nonmetro manufacturing sector over the past 20 years has important implications for nonmetro employment and earnings. Manufacturing is the only major sector in which employment grew faster in nonmetro areas than in metro areas between 1970 and 1988. In 1988, manufacturing accounted for over 17 percent of all nonmetro wage and salary employment and over 23 percent of nonmetro earnings. During the 1980s, 11 of 21 nonmetro manufacturing sectors added jobs, with only 3 sectors (motor vehicles, printing, and rubber) accounting for half the jobs created, while 10 of the 21 sectors lost jobs and 4 (apparel, machinery, primary metal, and leather) accounted for 53 percent of the job losses. Nonmetro manufacturing employment has shifted into durable goods sectors, but this shift has not been accompanied by higher pay per job as in the past. Also since 1970, changes in manufacturing employment have constituted a disproportionate share of the year-to-year fluctuations in total nonmetro employment.

64.   Best, Michael H.   1990. *The New Competition: Institutions of Industrial Restructuring.*   Cambridge, England: Polity Press, 296 pp.

Is an analysis of the causes of industrial decline and the possibilities for industrial policy. The starting point is the presumption that industrial policy has no chance of success unless it is anchored by an understanding of the underlying principles of production and business organization, principles that cannot be found in either conventional economic analysis or the business press. The author develops a framework incorporating the business enterprise, strategic decision-making, and sector regulation. He then uses this framework to examine the effects of industrial policy on the forces that influence the prosperity of a community or nation. A goal is to integrate a theoretical analysis of the business enterprise with extra-firm concepts of markets, competition, regulation, and planning.

65. Blair, John P., Carole Endres, and Rudy Fichtenbaum. 1990. "Japanese Automobile Investment in West Central Ohio: Economic Development and Labor-Management Issues," pp. 117-135 in *The Politics of Industrial Recruitment: Japanese Automobile Investment and Economic Development in the American States*, E. J. Yanarella and W. C. Green, eds. New York, NY: Greenwood Press.

Reports that the Honda automobile facility near Marysville, which produces Civics and Accords, is the brightest star in a constellation of Japanese automobile-related facilities in West Central Ohio, a region on the leading edge of the internationalization of the American economy. The authors examine the decisions made since 1977 which have created the West Central Ohio, Honda-centered automobile complex. They first examine the reasons for the emergence of the West Central Ohio automobile complex. Particular attention is given to the role of state government and to local economic and quality of life factors. The second section provides a detailed examination of labor-management issues. The final section extracts some lessons for public and private policy makers.

66. Bollard, Alan, and David Harper. 1986. "Employment Generation and Establishment Size in New Zealand Manufacturing." *International Small Business Journal* 4(4):10-28.

Reports on an investigation of the process of employment generation in New Zealand's manufacturing industry during the period 1980-84. The authors investigate how rates of employment change differ by size of establishment and which establishments have provided the most employment growth over the period. They find that firm birth and death rates are generally higher for smaller units and that the rates of job growth in new establishments and of employment decline in contracting or closing establishments are higher for smaller units. When the employment expansion and contraction effects are aggregated, however, the outcomes are less clear-cut. In the sample, medium-small and very large units generated net jobs while the smallest units lost them.

67.   Carlsson, Bo. 1989. "The Evolution of Manufacturing Technology and
       Its Impact on Industrial Structure: An International Study." *Small
       Business Economics* 1:21-37.

Shows that plant and firm size in manufacturing, and especially in
engineering industry, in several Western industrial countries has declined
since the early 1970s. Two hypotheses explaining the decline are
advanced. One is "de-glomeration" or specialization, which is the
divestiture of noncore businesses in order to free scarce resources
(particularly management time) to defend and nurture core business
activities. The second hypothesis is that the emergence of new computer-
based technology has improved the quality and productivity of small-and
medium-scale production relative to standardized mass-production
techniques which dominated previously.

68.   Daugherty, Scott R. 1992. "Rural Entrepreneurship: The Role of
       Institutions of Higher Learning in Fostering Job Creation and
       Economic Development in Rural America," pp. 105-120 in *Local
       Initiatives for Job Creation: Businesses and Jobs in the Rural
       World.* Paris, France: Organisation for Economic Co-operation and
       Development.

Explores the growing role of institutions of higher education in support
of job creation and economic development initiatives in rural areas of the
United States.

69.   Dunne, Timothy, Mark J. Roberts, and Larry Samuelson. 1989. "The
       Growth and Failure of U.S. Manufacturing Plants." *The Quarterly
       Journal of Economics* 104(4):671-698.

Examines the patterns of postentry employment growth and failure for
over 20,000 plants that entered the U.S. manufacturing sector in the 1967-
1977 period. The postentry patterns of growth and failure vary
significantly with observable employer characteristics. Plant failure rates
decline with size and age as do the growth rates of nonfailing plants. The
expected growth rate of a plant, which depends on the net effect of these
two forces, declines with size for plants owned by single-plant firms but
increases with size for plants owned by multiplant firms.

70.   Ersenkal, Caryl R., and B. L. Dillman. 1984. "The Product Cycle and
       Shifts in the Location of Manufacturing." *Regional Science
       Perspectives* 14:30-39.

Examines whether industrial growth in South Carolina can be explained by its ability to attract industries in the later stages of the product life-cycle. Specific hypotheses examined were that (1) a positive relationship exists between the change in value added for an industry in South Carolina and the change in the relative proportion of production workers in the same industry and (2) a positive relationship exists between the change in value added in an industry in South Carolina and the change in relative capital intensity in the industry. Empirical analysis clearly suggests that the state is attracting industries in the mature phase. The rate of change in the proportion of production workers employed in the state's industries, relative to the nation, is positively related to industrial growth. The results concerning the relationship between change in relative capital intensity and industrial growth are somewhat less conclusive.

71.   Esparaza, Adrian. 1990. "Manufacturing Decline and Technology Lags in Nonmetropolitan Illinois." *Growth and Change* 21(4):19-32.

Examines the causes of manufacturing decline at the substate level within Illinois. The author evaluates whether the impact of factors influencing decline varies according to the size and location of medium- and small-sized cities in Illinois. Survey data from surveys of economic development organizations in cities between 3,000 and 50,000 population and loglinear modeling methods are used in the empirical analysis. The results indicate that the impact of technology lags in substate areas varies significantly by the size of cities. The effects of technology, the regional shift of manufacturing, and federal trade policies are influenced by the relative location of cities.

72.   Fox, William F. 1990. "Japanese Investment in Tennessee: The Economic Effects of Nissan's Location in Smyrna," pp. 175-187 in *The Politics of Industrial Recruitment: Japanese Automobile Investment and Economic Development in the American States*, E. J. Yanarella and W. C. Green, eds. New York, NY: Greenwood Press.

Reports that in October 1980 an announcement was made that Nissan would locate its U.S. light truck production facility in Smyrna, Tennessee. Many states had sought to attract the plant and its expected economic and fiscal benefits. After the announcement, there was speculation regarding the incentives offered and the potential effects of population inmigration on the area's housing and public services. The author examines the effects of Nissan with the benefit of eight years of retrospect. The first section places the Nissan investment in context by evaluating the overall level of Japanese investment in Tennessee. The next two sections address the magnitude of Nissan's investment and the reasons behind the choice of Smyrna. The public sector's role in attracting Nissan is considered, and the economic and fiscal effects are identified.

73.   Gertler, Meric S. 1986. "Regional Dynamics of Manufacturing and Non-
       manufacturing Investment in Canada." *Regional Studies* 20(6):523-
       534.

Seeks to determine the changing importance of manufacturing versus non-manufacturing investment in local and regional economies. The focus is on two interrelated questions: (1) how prominent are manufacturing and nonmanufacturing sectors in particular locations and how has this relative importance changed over time and (2) how consistently does manufacturing investment drive capital accumulation in other sectors of the local/regional economy? An empirical analysis is performed for 10 provinces and 15 metropolitan areas in Canada over the period 1955-1983. Manufacturing continues to contribute a major proportion of total private capital accumulation and consistently leads investment in other sectors of metropolitan economies. This implies that technological change has involved the replacement of labor with capital over time.

74.   Giaoutzi, Maria. 1988. "Regional Dimensions of Small and Medium-
       Sized Enterprises in Greece," pp. 264-281 in *Small and Medium Size
       Enterprises and Regional Development*, M. Giaoutzi, P. Nijkamp,
       and D. Storey, eds. London: Routledge.

Examines the role of small and medium-size enterprises (SMEs) in the Greek regional context along with the policy framework in support of SME development.

75.   Giaoutzi, Maria, Peter Nijkamp, and David J. Storey, eds. 1988. *Small
       and Medium Size Enterprises and Regional Development*. London:
       Routledge, 314 pp.

Contains 16 chapters that address the role of small and medium-size enterprises (SMEs) in regional economic development, primarily in the context of the European Economic Community. The compilers report that the SME sector has become a focal point of scientific and policy interest because it is believed to contain the rejuvenation potential necessary for revitalizing the industrial and service sectors of stagnating economies. SME firms are also regarded as important vehicles for regional development planning. The book examines both the spatial economic theoretical basis and the empirical evidence concerning the regional development potential of small and medium-sized enterprises from a broad cross-national view.

76.   Glasmeier, Amy, and Norman Glickman. 1990. "Foreign Investment Boosts Rural Economies." *Rural Development Perspectives* 6(3):19-25.

Reports that rural firms accounted for about 10 percent of all foreign investment in U.S. manufacturing firms through 1986. About two-thirds of that represented the construction of new facilities, which represented new money coming into a community and new jobs. Almost half (46 percent) of rural foreign investments in manufacturing were in the South, followed by the Midwest (28 percent). Eighty percent of these manufacturing investments have occurred since 1980.

77.   Glickman, Norman J., and Douglas P. Woodward. 1988. "The Location of Foreign Direct Investment in the United States: Patterns and Determinants." *International Regional Science Review* 11(2):137-154.

Reports that the internationalization of the U.S. economy over the past 15 years has had a discernible impact on regional development. The authors analyze the regional effects of inward foreign direct investment, a particularly dynamic component of the internationalization process. Foreign direct investment dispersed over time, with the locations of foreign operations becoming more like those of U.S. firms. Regression results demonstrate that the location of foreign-owned property, plant, and equipment can be explained by variables representing energy costs, infrastructure and transportation, and labor climate.

78.   Gunn, Thomas G. 1987. *Manufacturing for Competitive Advantage: Becoming a World Class Manufacturer.* Cambridge, MA: Ballinger Publishing Co., 224 pp.

Reviews some of the causes for the decline in competitiveness of U.S. manufacturing and why executives have been slow to turn it around. The focus of the book, however, is on ways to move U.S. manufacturers to a more competitive position in the global economy. A major focus is on computer integrated manufacturing and its potential role in making U.S. manufacturers more competitive.

79.   Hansen, Niles. 1993. "Endogenous Growth Centers: Lessons From Rural Denmark," pp. 69-88 in *Economic Adaptation: Alternatives for Nonmetropolitan Areas*, D. L. Barkley, ed. Boulder, CO: Westview Press.

Reviews the endogenous rural development experiences in Europe, with particular attention to peripheral Jutland in Denmark. The author briefly considers historical and contemporary European evidence concerning the emergence of endogenous development in peripheral areas. Next, the nature and spatial implications of modern flexible production systems are examined in some detail. Economic development in rural Denmark, and especially peripheral Jutland, is then discussed in terms of the historical and cultural background and the relatively recent growth of small manufacturing firms characterized by flexible production and, frequently, by rich interactions among localized networks of firms producing similar products.

80.   Healey, M. J., and D. Clark. 1985. "Industrial Decline in a Local Economy: The Case of Coventry, 1974-1982." *Environment and Planning A* 17:1351-1367.

Reveals the process of industrial decline in Coventry and the effects on the nature of industry in the city through an analysis of both net change in manufacturing employment and of the components of change between 1974 and 1982. The results are compared with those for other U.K. localities. Coventry has suffered far more from in situ decline of manufacturing establishments than other industries. It lost relatively few jobs through exits but gained relatively less from the indigenous growth and the in-movement of industry. The implications of these differences for explanations of urban change and for policy are discussed.

81.   Hekman, John S. 1982. "What Are Businesses Looking For? Survey of Location Decisions in the South." *Economic Review* (Federal Reserve Bank of Atlanta) (June):6-19.

Reports results of a survey of manufacturing firms which had built or expanded plants in the Southeast during the last five years, examines these companies' preferences, and relates regional growth trends to the region's changing industrial structure. States included in the study are Alabama, Florida, Georgia, Louisiana, Mississippi, North Carolina, South Carolina, Tennessee, and Virginia.

82.   Hitoma, Katsundo. 1989. "Non-mass, Multi-product, Small-sized Production: The State of the Art." *Technovation* 9:357-369.

Points out that non-mass, jobbing and intermittent (small-batch) production is more important than single-product mass production. Statistics indicate that mass production is only 15 percent of total output, the other 85 percent being production volumes of less than 50. This is because many individuals wish to possess special goods different from those of other people, and the demand for special ordered products has increased, while the life cycle of the product has decreased. This tendency results in a wide range of low-volume production. This article is focussed on the subset of low-volume production described as non-mass, multi-product, small-sized production. The meaning and characteristics of this type of production are mentioned, and then the present state of the art and the effective techniques to overcome difficulties are explained.

83. Holmes, John. 1986. "The Organization and Locational Structure of Production Subcontracting," pp. 80-106 in *Production, Work, and Territory: The Geographical Anatomy of Industrial Capitalism*, A. Scott and M. Storper, eds. Boston, MA: Allen and Unwin.

Reports that a resurgence of subcontracting in both emerging and declining economic sectors has led to the recognition that subcontracting is not an anachronism, but rather one of a range of possibilities open to firms in organizing production. The author identifies several different types of production subcontracting generated by different causal mechanisms. Factors related to the nature of product markets, the technical organization of the labor process, and the structure of labor markets which encourage the development of subcontracting are discussed.

84. Howland, Marie. 1988. "Plant Closures and Local Economic Conditions." *Regional Studies* 22:193-207.

Tests the hypotheses that plant closures are influenced by local production costs, local rates of unionization, changes in local production costs, and local and national market growth. Using data on three of the three-digit Standard Industrial Code industries of metalworking machinery, electronic components, and motor vehicles for SMSAs, the study finds that local economic conditions have little impact on plant closures. The only variables to consistently predict the probability a plant will close is the plant's status as a branch, subsidiary, headquarters, or independent, and for independents, the firm's age. The likelihood of a branch plant or subsidiary closing is much higher than that of an independent or headquarters. New firms are more likely to close than more mature ones, and for two of the industries, small establishments exhibited a higher probability of closures than larger ones.

85.   Howland, Marie. 1990. "Plant Closures: Are Local Conditions Responsible?" pp. 17-21 in *Plant Closures and Community Recovery*, J. E. Lynch, ed. Washington, D.C.: National Council for Urban Economic Development.

Examines the causes of job loss, plant closure, and relocations in the three manufacturing industries (machinery manufacturing, electronic components, and motor vehicles). The author concludes that (1) plant closures within these three industries occur at even rates across all regions of the U.S. and across central cities, suburbs, and nonmetropolitan areas; (2) areas experiencing slow employment growth in these industries do so because of low rates of plant startups and expansions, rather than because of high rates of plant closures and relocations; (3) local economic conditions, including wages, utility costs, taxes, changes in costs, and labor force unionization in a local economy do not influence the probability that a plant in that locale will close; (4) branches and subsidiaries close at much higher rates than headquarters and independent facilities; and (5) there is some evidence that out-migration is more likely from economies with a unionized labor force, although the out-migration of plants plays a very small role in regional job loss.

86.   Johne, Frederick A. 1986. "The Adoption of New Technology in Manufacturing Firms," Vol. 1, pp. 141-162 in *Advances in Business Marketing*, A. G. Woodside, ed. Greenwich, CT: JAI Press.

Reports that many theoretical perspectives have been used in business marketing and related studies to examine why some manufacturing firms adopt particular types of technology faster than others. After reviewing the main strands of this literature, the paper examines the proposition that the speed with which new component technology is bought depends on the use to which it is put in adopter firms. The results of an empirical investigation show that user firms which are active product innovators (1) buy advanced components earlier than firms which are less active product innovators and (2) purchase such components in quite a different way. The findings suggest new ways for macro and micro market segmentation.

87.   Johnson, Merrill L. 1988. "Labor Environment and the Location of Electrical Machinery Employment in the U.S. South." *Growth and Change* 19(2):56-74.

Focuses on the location of electrical machinery manufacturing in South Carolina, Georgia, Mississippi, and Alabama, and the degree to which this industry is associated with labor environments attractive to firms in the late stage of the product cycle. Labor-environment variables were selected from published sources and then collapsed into principal components. County-level component scores were then correlated with selected electrical machinery employment variables. The analysis suggests that, with the possible exception of electronic components manufacturing, there has been no widespread locational response by electrical machinery manufacturing in these states to labor environments attractive to firms in the late stage of the product cycle.

88. Kale, Steven R. 1984. "U.S. Industrial Development Incentives and Manufacturing Growth During the 1970s." *Growth and Change* 15(1):26-34.

Discusses changes in manufacturing employment for regions and states during the 1970s and the relationship of industrial incentives to these changes. Incentives offered by the states as of 1977 are weighted based on a survey of industrial facility planners. Growth rates in manufacturing employment were found to have little relationship to states' incentive scores when analyzed nationwide.

89. Kale, Steven R., and Richard E. Lonsdale. 1987. "Recent Trends in U.S. and Canadian Nonmetropolitan Manufacturing." *Journal of Rural Studies* 3(1):1-13.

Has three objectives (1) to review the results of previous research on nonmetropolitan manufacturing in the U.S. and Canada, (2) to analyze recent changes in employment for nonmetropolitan manufacturing in the two nations, and (3) to discuss factors contributing to recent trends in nonmetropolitan manufacturing on both sides of the border. The authors find that the recession of the early 1980s led to absolute and relative declines in manufacturing employment in nonmetropolitan areas on both sides of the border, and nearly every state and province experienced employment declines. Impacts were greatest in the Northwest and Midwest in the U.S. and in the Atlantic provinces, Quebec, and British Columbia in Canada. Job losses were especially significant in several states and provinces where nonmetropolitan areas accounted for a large proportion of total manufacturing employment.

90. Karlsson, Charlie. 1988. "The Role of Small and Medium-Sized Manufacturing Plants in Regional Employment--A Swedish

Perspective," pp. 181-199 in *Small and Medium Size Enterprises and Regional Development*, M. Giaoutzi, P. Nijkamp, and D. Storey, eds. London: Routledge.

Assesses the role of small and medium-sized manufacturing firms for regional employment in Sweden. The first section gives an overview of changes in the employment structure at a sectoral level in Sweden and in the region of Värmland, the county with the second highest unemployment rate in Sweden. The next section provides a more detailed examination of employment in the manufacturing sector. Then, a cross-sectional view of how the size structure of the manufacturing sector varies among different regions in Sweden is provided. The author next analyzes changes in the employment structure of the manufacturing sector over time in Sweden and in Värmland. Changes in total employment in different size categories are then described, and the growth potential of plants of different sizes in Värmland is examined.

91.　　Kotabe, Masaaki. 1991. "Development of a Systematic Approach to the Promotion of Missouri Manufacturing Exports," pp. 110-132 in *Missouri Policy Choices*, K. L. Kempf, J. F. Springer, G. R. Stephens, and D. J. Webber, eds. Columbia, MO: University of Missouri Extension.

Is intended to provide guidance concerning means to increase the export of Missouri's products. The author identifies the types of export-related expertise that are utilized by the managements of Missouri firms, variation is observed depending on how involved the firm is with exportation. The problems typically encountered at each stage of export involvement and the types of government assistance desired by these firms are discussed. Procedures to overcome difficulties with current policies are suggested.

92.　　Lamberson, Morris, and Clint Johnson. 1992. "Financing Experiences of Small Manufacturers in Arkansas: Survey and Analysis." *Economic Development Review* 10(2):62-66.

Presents an analysis of the startup and expansion capital financing experiences of 140 small manufacturers in Arkansas. Small firms were observed to make greater use of equity capital when beginning operations, while greater use was made of debt capital for expansion. New and expanding firms used personal savings as the major source of equity financing and banks as the major source of debt capital.

93.   Leistritz, F. Larry. 1992. "Agribusiness Firms: Location Determinants and Economic Contribution." *Agribusiness* 8(4):273-286.

Assesses factors influencing the location of agribusiness firms and evaluates their economic contribution to the local economy vis-à-vis other types of firms. Data are from a survey of 297 basic-sector firms (70 of which were agribusiness) in the Upper Midwest region. Factors affecting location decisions were found to differ significantly, both between agribusiness and other firms and among agribusinesses of different types (e.g., food processors vs. farm machinery manufacturers). Agribusinesses employed fewer workers directly, but through their higher level of in-state purchases, they generated greater secondary (multiplier) effects, compared to other firms.

94.   Leistritz, F. Larry, and Janet K. Wanzek. 1992. *Rural Manufacturers: Attributes, Intentions, and Needs of Manitoba, North Dakota, and Saskatchewan Firms.* Ag. Econ. Misc. Rpt. No. 162. Fargo, ND: North Dakota State University, Department of Agricultural Economics, 39 pp.

Reports the results of a 1991 survey of manufacturing firms in Manitoba, North Dakota, and Saskatchewan. A total of 333 firms provided data for the study. Durable goods manufacturers dominated the sample, accounting for 65 percent in Manitoba, 66 percent in North Dakota, and 78 percent in Saskatchewan. Many of the firms were relatively new; about 59 percent of the Saskatchewan companies and 44 percent of the North Dakota firms, but only 25 percent of the Manitoba manufacturers, had been established since 1979. Many of the firms also were quite small; about 57 percent of North Dakota companies and 44 percent of those in Canada reported 1990 gross sales of less than $1 million (U.S.). The Canadian manufacturers were more oriented to international marketing and sales than their U.S. counterparts. Another substantial contrast was in the firms' current utilization of their production capacity; North Dakota firms reported an average of 76 percent utilization, Manitoba companies 67 percent, and Saskatchewan firms 57 percent.

95.   Leistritz, F. Larry, and Janet K. Wanzek. 1993. "Rural Manufacturers: Attributes and Technical Assistance Needs." *Economic Development Review* 11(3):55-61.

Describes the firms that make up the manufacturing sector in the predominantly rural state of North Dakota and identifies their needs for support in such areas as financing, worker training, and technical assistance. The firms see marketing skills as critical to their success and are looking for training and educational assistance in marketing and sales and consulting assistance in the preparation of marketing studies, quality assurance, and process improvement.

96.   Lonsdale, R. E., and H. L. Seyler. 1979. *Nonmetropolitan Industrialization*. Washington, D.C.: V. H. Winston and Sons, 195 pp.

Provides a survey and assessment of the growth of manufacturing in nonmetropolitan areas of the United States during the post-World War II period. Major chapters address such topics as trends and patterns in nonmetropolitan industrialization, factors affecting plant location in nonmetropolitan areas, characteristics of branch plants attracted to nonmetropolitan areas, manufacturers' satisfaction with nonmetropolitan locations, and the economic, demographic and social impacts of industrialization. A discussion of policy implications concludes the work.

97.   Lorenz, Edward H. 1989. "The Search for Flexibility: Subcontracting Networks in British and French Engineering," pp. 122-132 in *Reversing Industrial Decline? Industrial Structure and Policy in Britain and Her Competitors*, P. Hirst, and J. Zeitlin, eds. Oxford, U.K.: Berg Publishers, Ltd.

Examines the issues of subcontracting and flexibility from a comparative perspective. Conditions in the Lyons region of France, where subcontracting is used extensively and in novel ways, are contrasted with conditions in the West Midlands region of the U.K., where possibilities remain comparatively unexplored. The author considers whether the West Midlands might benefit from some version of the policies adopted by employers in Lyons. This research is directly relevant to the debate on mass production versus flexible specialization. The key to flexible specialization is seen to be the development of organizational forms that achieve a balance between cooperation and encourage competition on the basis of product and process innovation rather than price.

98.   MacPherson, Alan. 1988. "New Product Development Among Small Toronto Manufacturers: Empirical Evidence on the Role of Technical Service Linkages." *Economic Geography* 64(1):62-75.

Examines the technical linkage arrangements which exist between small Toronto manufacturers and consultants in the service sector. It is suggested that technical inputs from external specialists contribute significantly to the innovation performance of small firms that produce for export. Detailed evidence from a sample of local manufacturers is used to highlight the extent of inter-firm contact networks. While the empirical findings suggest a positive relationship between small firm innovation and backward linkages to producer service units, patterns of subcontracting are found to be less extensively developed than they could be. The paper concludes with a series of broad recommendations for future public policy and industrial strategy design.

99. Markusen, Ann R. 1988. "Planning for Industrial Decline: Lessons from Steel Communities." *Journal of Planning Education and Research* 7(3):173-184.

Points out that economic development planning has weaker tools than does land use planning and is hampered by a great deal of analytical and normative conflict. The author reviews the causes and remedies of industrial decline in the steel industry. At least eight different causal explanations of steel job loss have been offered, and diverse normative objectives have been invoked. This research examines the intergovernmental issues and the politics involved in a number of innovative steel strategies. The paper concludes that this type of controversy is bound to escalate in the coming decades. Therefore, economic development planners will need a broad education in both political economy and institutional and intergovernmental settings, as well as improved skills in conceptualizing and testing causal models of industry evolution.

100. McDowell, Bruce D. 1990. "State and Local Initiatives on Productivity, Technology, and Innovation." *Intergovernmental Relations* 16(1):29-31.

Reviews recent efforts by state and local governments in providing assistance to help U.S. manufacturers obtain and use technologies, modernize their manufacturing processes, and improve their productivity and profitability. The types of assistance provided are broadly categorized as passive information dissemination, brokering services, and hands-on help. Limitations of existing programs are discussed, and a new Clearinghouse for State and Local Initiatives on Productivity, Technology, and Innovation within the U.S. Department of Commerce is briefly described.

101. McNamara, Kevin T., and David L. Barkley. 1993. "Foreign Direct Investment: Prospects for Employment Generation in

Nonmetropolitan Areas," pp. 205-222 in *Economic Adaptation: Alternatives for Nonmetropolitan Areas*, D. L. Barkley, ed. Boulder, CO: Westview Press.

Assesses the potential for and impacts of foreign direct investment (FDI) in nonmetropolitan areas. Of particular interest are the labor and input-product market characteristics of the foreign-owned nonmetropolitan manufacturers and the reasons for selecting a specific location for the facility. First, an overview of FDI in the United States is provided. Next, the locations of foreign manufacturers in nonmetropolitan Georgia and South Carolina are analyzed to determine which types of communities have been successful in attracting these facilities. Locational factors important to rural, foreign-owned manufacturers also are compared to determinants provided by rural, domestic branch plants and metropolitan, foreign-owned facilities. Finally, labor force and market linkage characteristics of foreign and domestic manufacturers are compared to ascertain whether local economic impacts varied by source of ownership. Differences between foreign-owned and domestic plants are summarized and policies to encourage FDI in rural areas are suggested.

102.   McNamara, Kevin T., Warren P. Kriesel, and Brady J. Deaton. 1988. "Manufacturing Location: The Impact of Human Capital Stocks and Flows." *The Review of Regional Studies* 18:42-48.

Reports the results of a manufacturing firm location study that incorporates measures for both human capital stocks and flows into a statistical model of community attributes that were hypothesized to influence firm location decisions. The results indicate the complexity of evaluating the impact of human capital investment on local and regional economic growth.

103.   Miller, James P. 1993. "Small and Midsize Enterprise Development: Prospects for Nonmetropolitan Areas," pp. 89-104 in *Economic Adaptation: Alternatives for Nonmetropolitan Areas*, D. L. Barkley, ed. Boulder, CO: Westview Press.

Addresses small and midsize enterprise (SME) development as an economic development strategy for rural communities. The author reports that programs to foster SME development are seen by many state and local officials as an attractive alternative to recruitment strategies that target branch plants of large companies. These SME development programs include provision of venture capital, enterprise zones, and incubators for small business. The author examines the economic contribution of SMEs in nonmetropolitan areas in terms of the number of jobs created, the quality of those jobs, the cyclical stability of SMEs, and their export orientation. He reports that rural areas face sizeable disadvantages in trying to generate economic development through SMEs. Strategies that rural areas can use to reduce or overcome these disadvantages are discussed in the final section.

104. Nebraska Department of Economic Development. 1988. *Targeted Industries for Nebraska: Report of the Nebraska Industry Targeting Committee.* Lincoln, NE: Nebraska Department of Economic Development, Division of Research, 30 pp.

Identifies 21 manufacturing industries, out of 440 reviewed, to receive priority in future state marketing programs. The process for screening of industries was to (1) identify characteristics of Nebraska which represent advantages and disadvantages for the location of industry, (2) review industry studies completed since 1983, (3) review quantitative industry rankings from a screening model, and (4) prepare a final list.

105. Nelson, Arthur C. 1990. "Regional Patterns of Exurban Industrialization: Results of a Preliminary Investigation." *Economic Development Quarterly* 4(4):320-333.

Reports preliminary results of current research into the changing spatial pattern of manufacturing in the contiguous states. Between 1965 and 1985 total employment in the 48 contiguous states rose about 70 percent, but manufacturing employment grew only 10 percent. During this period employment in exurban counties grew by 86 percent and manufacturing employment by 32 percent. About 61 percent of the new manufacturing jobs created during the period were in exurban counties. Exurban areas are defined here as areas within about one hour's travel time from urban areas (i.e., within 60-80 miles of the outer beltway or 70-100 miles of the central city). The author concludes that manufacturing is moving further away from central cities and their traditional suburbs, but not so far away that goods, workers, and services cannot be shipped easily within a day to nearby urban areas.

106. Nijkamp, Peter, Theo Alsters, and Ronald van der Mark. 1988. "The Regional Development Potential of Small and Medium-sized Enterprises: A European Perspective," pp. 122-139 in *Small and Medium Size Enterprises and Regional Development*, M. Giaoutzi, P. Nijkamp, and D. Storey, eds. London: Routledge.

Analyzes the regional development potential offered by the small and medium-size enterprise (SME) sector. The first section outlines the principles of a multidimensional locational profile analysis. The features and regional relevance of the SME sector are discussed in the next section. Special attention is given to the factors determining the regional production environment of the SME sector. The third section describes the methodology of the study, based on a step-wise multicriteria analysis, in which the attributes of a regional development potential are related to the specific regional importance of a set of SME branches. Finally, a case study, based on 18 regions of the Common Market, is presented.

107.   Norton, R. D. 1989. "Reindustrialization and Economic Development Strategy." *Economic Development Quarterly* 3(3):188-202.

Contends that the United States is in the early phases of an export-led resurgence that will continue through the year 2000. The author examines the one-year period from March 1987 to March 1988 as a "test period" that may help predict patterns of manufacturing growth that might occur during the 1990s. A dominant trend during this period was that manufacturing growth was strongly affected by labor supply. Above-average growth in manufacturing employment was recorded in the (generally labor-surplus) states of the Upper Midwest, Gulf Coast, and Pacific Northwest.

108.   O'Farrell, P. N., and R. Crouchley. 1987. "Manufacturing-plant Closures: A Dynamic Survival Model." *Environment and Planning A* 19:313-329.

Analyzes the phenomenon of industrial closures among new plants which commenced production in Ireland between 1973 and 1981. A major aim of the research is to develop a dynamic survival model of industrial plant closure which permits the introduction of time-constant and time-varying covariates. Results indicate that there is no duration-of-stay effect; that British-owned branches are highly vulnerable; that grant aid reduces the chances of early closure; and that new clothing and footwear plants are more likely to close than are plants in other sectors.

109.   O'Farrell, P. N., and B. O'Loughlin. 1981. "New Industry Input Linkages in Ireland: An Econometric Analysis." *Environment and Planning A* 13:285-308.

Analyzes the input linkages of manufacturing projects in Ireland that had been grant-aided under the New Industries program. The authors investigate both backward linkage and forward linkage effects. The propensity of individual enterprises to purchase inputs is analyzed at two spatial scales: (1) the national economy, and (2) the local areas within a twenty-mile radius of the plant. Econometric methods are used to test a series of hypotheses at the plant level, and implications for industrial and regional policies are discussed.

110. Office of Technology Assessment. 1990. *Making Things Better: Competing in Manufacturing (Summary)*. Washington, D.C.: Congress of the United States, Office of Technology Assessment, 33 pp.

Considers ways to promote the restoration of American leadership in manufacturing technology. Some of the things that most need doing are up to industry--especially in handling people, from managers to engineers to shopfloor workers, and in forming stable, productive relationships between different segments of an industry complex. Government also has a critical role to play. The first essential is to create an economic environment that supports manufacturing and encourages long-term investment in technology. This means higher national savings rates and a declining Federal deficit. Other less traditional activities (at least for the U.S. Government) also deserve consideration--for example, collaboration with industry on supporting R&D for strategic technologies.

111. Owen, C. James. 1990. "Microdemographic Decisions in an Industrial Plant Location: The Fort Wayne General Motors Case." *Economic Development Quarterly* 4(2):137-143.

A study of the specific locational factors involved in a large industrial plant siting decision. The case studied is the General Motors truck assembly plant in Fort Wayne, Indiana. The plant, which became operational in 1986, employs more than 3,500 workers. The decisive factors examined are the land-use permitting, transportation linkages, and utility connections that were required to make the Fort Wayne site a suitable location.

112. Perrucci, Carolyn C., Dena B. Targ, Robert Perrucci, and Harey R. Targ. 1987. "Plant Closings: A Comparison of Effects on Women and Men Workers," pp. 181-207 in *Redundancy, Layoffs, and Plant Closure*, R. Lee, ed. Wolfeboro, NH: Croom Helm Ltd.

Examines effects of a plant closing on male and female workers based on a 1983 survey of 686 blue-collar workers at a television cabinet making plant in Indiana. Data from 328 respondents included work history, union activities, political/social beliefs, and the impact of closing on family, health, and financial situation. Data from blue-collar workers at an ongoing plant that produced roller bearings also allowed for various comparisons. Of the respondents from the closed plant, 71 percent were still unemployed at the time of the survey (eight months after closure), and the percentages were similar for men and women. Both men and women were adversely affected by job loss following plant closing. Those who were re-employed had not recovered their former salaries.

113.   Ponting, J. Rick, and Nigel Waters. 1985. "The Impact of Public Policy on Locational Decision-Making by Industrial Firms." *Canadian Public Policy* 11(4):731-744.

Reports on a survey of the locational behavior of over one hundred firms which at some time during the period 1978-1983, had considered locating in the Prairie Provinces. Included are firms which did and did not decide to locate in this region. The results are compared to other surveys carried out recently in Alberta and the United States. The influence of government incentive and disincentive policies, at various levels, is generally found to be minimal. The policy implications of the survey with respect to environmental protection, transportation, the locational search process, industrial linkages, and governmental responses are considered.

114.   Rees, John, Ronald Briggs, and Raymond Oakey. 1984. "The Adoption of New Technology in the American Machinery Industry." *Regional Studies* 18(6):489-504.

Examines the spread of a number of key production technologies among machinery manufacturers across the United States. Based on a mail and interview survey of over 600 industrial plants across the country, the authors found that adoption rates for these innovations varied by industrial sector, organizational status of plants, age and size of plants as well as by regional and metropolitan characteristics of plants. The findings suggest that policy makers interested in nurturing small businesses should consider technical assistance strategies that encourage the spread of innovation among firms, and that high priority be given to labor training programs in local economic development strategies. At the federal level this study also suggests that the innovation potential of Manufacturing Belt companies should not be overlooked in any new initiatives to encourage economic development.

115. Rosenfeld, Stuart A. 1992. *Competitive Manufacturing: New Strategies for Regional Development.* New Brunswick, NJ: Rutgers University, Center for Urban Policy Research, 400 pp.

Focuses on economic growth in rural America and addresses the problems the United States and other countries face as they adjust from economies based on natural resources and goods-producing processes to economies whose success depends mainly on the quality of human resources and high-performance, market-oriented organizations. The author documents in detail how the viability of the traditional mass-production economy's organizational structure and operating procedures has been eroded by two closely related universal imperatives: technology and international competition. These forces have fundamentally altered the conditions for economic success. In a more competitive environment, firms compete by either reducing cost or improving quality and productivity. The author contends that the strategy used by most American companies, especially in rural areas, has been to follow the low-wage strategy. The alternative that the author recommends, and which is practiced in other countries, is a strategy that emphasizes the competitiveness of industry rather than competition for industry. Competitiveness requires attention to some matters often neglected by mass-production companies: quality, flexibility, and productivity.

116. Rosenfeld, Stuart A., Emil E. Malazia, and Marybeth Dugan. 1988. *Reviving the Rural Factory: Automation and Work in the South.* Research Triangle Park, NC: Southern Growth Policies Board, 152 pp.

Reports results of a study of the automation of rural factories. The authors sought to determine how companies use state and local programs and policies and what barriers they face in attempting to implement new process technologies. Other questions addressed include: what companies need and get from the educational system that helps them operate automated production effectively and innovatively? and what effects do new technologies have on the work force and on communities.

117. Rosenfeld, Stuart, with Philip Shapira and J. Trent Williams. 1992. *Smart Firms in Small Towns.* Washington, D.C.: The Aspen Institute, 93 pp.

Reports that small and medium-sized enterprises (SMEs) are playing an ever-expanding role in the nation's industrial competitiveness and in localities' economic competitiveness. For most of this century, the prevailing management theory has been that large companies, by supporting economies of scale and specialized resources, were more efficient and more competitive than SMEs. Since the late 1980s, however, the benefits of large scale have been questioned, in large part because of trends in both customer demand and technological advances being adopted by competitor nations. The new economic environment in which manufacturers are operating suggests a different approach to regional development. Lowest costs are still factors, but no longer sufficient for comparative advantage. Quality, delivery, reliability, and design have been elevated to importance and now represent the keys to competitiveness. To succeed along these dimensions requires firms to continually innovate and modernize, using state-of-the-art management practices and process technologies. Yet research shows that America's small, rural manufacturers are slow to invest in new technologies and adopt best practices. This book examines state policies and programs aimed at strengthening SMEs.

118. Roura, Juan R. Cuadrado. 1988. "Small and Medium-Sized Enterprises and the Regional Distribution of Industry in Spain: A New Stage," pp. 247-263 in *Small and Medium Size Enterprises and Regional Development*, M. Giaoutzi, P. Nijkamp, and D. Storey, eds. London: Routledge.

Describes those factors characterizing the geographical distribution of industry in Spain over recent decades. The author reports that there has been a process of marked concentration in a number of productive centers, although industry remains well spread throughout the country and a large number of centers have developed significant industrial activity. The leading role in this geographical distribution of industry has been played by the small and medium-sized enterprises.

119. Schroeder, Dean M., C. Gopinath, and Steven W. Congden. 1989. "New Technology and the Small Manufacturer: Panacea or Plague?" *Journal of Small Business Management* 27:1-10.

Summarizes a study of twenty small manufacturers and reports that the relationship between new technology and the ability to compete is not as simple or direct as many managers believe. Both high- and low-performing firms were examined, including both those that used advanced manufacturing technologies (AMTs) and those that did not. In all cases, particular attention was paid to the conditions under which manufacturing technologies offer competitive advantages that lead to improved financial performance. The authors find that while AMT offers many compelling advantages, it can also involve firms in unforeseen and potentially debilitating problems. The implications of these findings are particularly important for small companies because the high costs of new technology may in effect cause these firms to wager their future on the success of a single technology choice.

120. Shaffer, Ron. 1989. *Community Economics: Economic Structure and Change in Smaller Communities.* Ames, IA: Iowa State University Press, 322 pp.

Reviews the economics of smaller communities and is intended primarily as a text for advanced undergraduate (beginning graduate) courses in community economics or related topics. Topics addressed include community economic development theories, location theory, and central place theory; community economic development policies, goals, and objectives; implementing community economic development programs; capital and labor markets; government involvement in community economic development; impacts of community economic development; and economic base and input-output models.

121. Smith, Eldon D. 1990. "Economic Stability and Economic Growth in Rural Communities: Dimensions Relevant to Local Employment Creation Strategy." *Growth and Change* 21(4):3-18.

Examines three issues (1) whether growth in manufacturing industry has stabilized the general employment in the small southeastern Kentucky region under study, (2) whether macro-analyses of the contribution of specific categories of manufacturing industry to employment stability provide reliable guidance for employment creation decisions at the level of small communities (counties and municipalities), and (3) whether the job-creation strategies which have been suggested as means of reducing employment instability have had validity in this rural region. The author finds that aggregate SIC performance and most conventional criteria for judging probable stability appear to provide very limited predictability for individual firm performance. However, manufacturing development appears generally to have desirable effects on community-wide employment stability.

122. Smith, Eldon D., David Freshwater, and David R. Peters. 1992. *Effects of Manufacturing Growth on Employment Instability in a Rural Area: Experience During the Early 1980s in South-Central Kentucky.* Agricultural Economics Research Report No. 56. Lexington, KY: University of Kentucky, Department of Agricultural Economics, 45 pp.

Reports results of a study designed to (1) evaluate the effects of
manufacturing employment on the general stability of employment in a
19-county region in south central and southeastern Kentucky during the
economic recession of the early 1980s and (2) determine how the
characteristics of individual manufacturing establishments, including the
type of manufacturer, affect stability of employment. The report is based
primarily on a survey of individual manufacturing firms. The findings
show that manufacturing has provided a more stable employment base
than coal mining and that manufacturing has offset much of the long-term
decline in employment in coal, farming, and forestry. Counties with the
greatest proportion of manufacturing jobs had the least fluctuation in total
employment, the most favorable employment trends, and suffered least
from the 1980s recession.

123.   Stabler, Jack C., and Pauline J. Molder. 1992. *Rural Manufacturing
       Industry: Products, Markets, and Location Requirements.*
       Saskatoon, Saskatchewan: University of Saskatchewan, Department
       of Agricultural Economics, 85 pp.

Examines the development of the manufacturing industry in rural
Saskatchewan. The authors find that the province's manufacturing
industry has grown steadily, if at a moderate rate, since 1971. This
growth has included a substantial increase in the number of manufacturing
plants in rural areas. Most of the rural manufacturing firms were found
to be small and owned locally but to sell their products into markets
throughout Canada, the U.S., and offshore. Low costs for land and
adequate supplies of labor skilled in the operation, maintenance, and
repair of machinery were found to be the major attractions of a rural
location.

124.   Stafford, Howard A., and Qiutao Wu. 1992. "Manufacturing Plants in
       Ohio: Spatial Changes, 1978-1987." *Economic Development
       Quarterly* 6(3):273-285.

Reports that the numbers of manufacturing plant births and deaths are
both very highly correlated with the total number of manufacturing plants
per county. For the period from 1978 to 1987 there have not been
dramatic absolute changes in the spatial distribution of manufacturing
within Ohio. Spatial variations in opening and closing rates are less
easily explained. About half to three-fourths of the variations in rates are
mainly functions of the economic and social attributes of the counties, of
general levels of economic activity, or are consequences of the inherited
industries and plants. The structural model is generally more powerful

than either the socioeconomic or vitality configurations. Relative change in manufacturing is best predicted by the industrial profile of an area, for example, the sizes and ages of plants and diversity of industrial types, and its classification as a central, suburban, or rural county.

125. Storey, D. J. 1985. "Manufacturing Employment Change in Northern England 1965-78: The Role of Small Businesses," pp. 6-42 in *Small Firms in Regional Economic Development: Britain, Ireland, and the United States*, D. J. Storey, ed. Cambridge, England: Cambridge University Press.

Examines the contribution to manufacturing employment change of small and medium sized enterprises (SMEs) in Northern England--an area which has experienced persistently high rates of unemployment for more than 50 years. The region has also been a recipient of almost every initiative introduced by national government to create employment, but the relative position of the region has remained virtually unchanged during this half century. The author defines a small business as having less than 200 employees; within this group much of the analysis is based on the age of firm. The findings indicate that between 1965 and 1978 the study region experienced a net loss of more than 50,000 manufacturing jobs, or 13 percent of manufacturing employment. Smaller establishments, in aggregate, showed a net increase in employment over the period, but most of these jobs were created by branch plants rather than locally owned firms. The author identifies 1,145 wholly new firms which created a total of 11,857 jobs during the period 1965 to 1978. However, the majority of these firms had less than 10 employees in 1978, while 33.8 percent of the jobs were created by 6 percent of the firms.

126. Thomas, Ian C., and P. J. Drury. 1987. "The Impact of Factory Development on 'Growth Town' Employment in Mid-Wales." *Urban Studies* 24:361-378.

Reports that a central tenet of British government policy in rural areas has been the provision of industrial jobs to counteract the decline in agricultural employment. However, little research has been carried out in Britain on the precise impact of factory development in creating jobs or generating income. The authors use the Mid-Wales region as a case study to assess the direct impact of manufacturing firms in terms of employment generated.

127. Walker, Robert, and Frank Calzonetti. 1990. "Searching for New Manufacturing Plant Locations: A Study of Location Decisions in Central Appalachia." *Regional Studies* 24(1):15-30.

Analyzes the search behavior of manufacturers in Central Appalachia and develops a model of hierarchial decision making under imperfect information. Using data collected from interview surveys of plant managers, regional and local search processes are evaluated. The authors show that the set of factors influencing the decision to undergo a regional search is different from the set of factors influencing the local search. Further, branch plant search behavior may be described by cost minimization objectives whereas the behavior of single-plant establishments is more idiosyncratic. The analysis shows that the comparative advantage of Central Appalachia consists, in part, of low cost electricity.

128. Woodward, Douglas P. 1992. "Locational Determinants of Japanese Manufacturing Start-ups in the United States." *Southern Economic Journal* 58(3):690-708.

Analyzes Japanese-affiliated manufacturing investments in the United States, based on micro data representing individual location choices for 1980-89. The author finds that Japanese direct investment in the United States rose substantially during the 1980s, growing faster than inward investment from other countries. Second, a focus on Japanese investment is germane to the analysis of new plant location because, unlike direct investment from Great Britain and other developed countries, the Japanese often prefer to build factories at greenfield (new) sites rather than acquire existing assets. Also, understanding the spatial behavior of Japanese-affiliated manufacturing will tell us much about location preferences as U.S. production adapts to a different organizational model. Finally, the paper contributes to recent advances in empirical location analysis by clearly separating state and county decisions.

129. Wrigley, Jennifer, and Norman Walzer. 1991. *Flexible Manufacturing Networks*. Rural Research Report Vol. 2, Issue 8. Macomb, IL: Western Illinois University, Illinois Institute for Rural Affairs, 6 pp.

Reports that a flexible manufacturing network is a collection of small firms and supporting organizations that combine resources and skills to provide specialized products and services for manufacturing businesses. The authors report that the benefits that manufacturing networks provide are vital to a small firm's ability to compete, both domestically and globally. The key to successful flexible manufacturing networks is to provide small firms with the support systems and information needed to function as a dynamic competitive force in a particular industry.

130. Yanarella, Ernest J., and William C. Green. 1993. "Community, Labor, and Environmental Participation in Industrial Recruitment: East Asian Automobile Investment in Canada in Comparative Perspective." *Economic Development Quarterly* 7(2):140-159.

Reports that the construction of nine Japanese and one South Korean automobile assembly plants in the North American industrial heartland was a major feature in the transformation of global automobile production in the 1980s. In this article, the authors compare the community, labor, and environmental involvements in and impacts on the Canadian industrial recruitment of four East Asian assembly plants. The authors found that Canadian transplant recruitment has not lived up to its promise to ameliorate local unemployment and generate residential and commercial growth, nor have these transplant sitings in rural communities generated major environmental controversies. Instead they have produced single-issue citizen campaigning, administrative resolution, and elite accommodation. Organized labor represents workers at CAMI, the General Motors-Suzuki joint venture, but its efforts at the three other flexible production facilities will be difficult given Canada's economic woes, the overcapacity problem, and the effects of the North American Free Trade Agreement.

131. Young, Ruth C., and Joe D. Francis. 1991. "Entrepreneurship and Innovation in Small Manufacturing Firms." *Social Science Quarterly* 72(1):149-162.

Summarizes an exploratory study of 123 manufacturing firms that emphasized the process of startup and innovation in high- and low-technology firms. The authors find that in important respects the process is the same in both types of firms, though there are some minor differences. Both types of firms tend to have founders with previous work experience in similar firms and are embedded in networks of manufacturing firms that buy and sell to each other. However, high-tech firms are generally more innovative, have more educated founders and staff, and more often secure some kind of government help.

132. Young, Ruth C., Joe D. Francis, and Christopher H. Young. 1993. "Innovation, High-Technology Use, and Flexibility in Small Manufacturing Firms." *Growth and Change* 24(1):67-86.

Uses data from two surveys of small manufacturing firms in New York and Pennsylvania to study innovation, use of high technology, and flexibility of response to customer needs. These are shown in both surveys to be separate and unrelated concepts. None of the five industry-level classifications of high-technology firms, using SIC codes, predict these concepts on a firm level. Only innovation is related to a sophisticated firm marketing program, and to export from the state.

RECREATION/TOURISM

133.   Anderson, Leslie. 1988. *Tourism and Local Economic Development.*
       Pub. Admin. Series Bibliography #P 2452. Monticello, IL: Vance
       Bibliographies, 12 pp.

Includes case studies, reports by local governments, findings by consulting groups, monographs, and articles that address the potential of tourism to contribute to local economic development. Contains more than 130 entries, mostly to works published since 1980.

134.   Bergstrom, John C., H. Ken Cordell, Gregory A. Ashley, and Alan E.
       Watson. 1990. "Economic Impacts of Recreational Spending on
       Rural Areas: A Case Study." *Economic Development Quarterly*
       4(1):29-39.

Points out that, although researchers, planners, and policymakers are becoming increasingly interested in the rural economic development potentials of outdoor recreation, empirical evidence evaluating this economic development potential is very limited. The article reports results of a study that examined local economic effects of spending associated with outdoor recreation in selected rural areas of Georgia. Recreational expenditures were collected as part of the Public Area Recreation Visitors Survey (PARVS), and economic impacts were estimated using the USDA Forest Service input-output model and data base system (IMPLAN). The results suggest that outdoor recreation may indeed be a viable rural economic development strategy.

135.   Butler, Richard, and Gordon Clark. 1992. "Tourism in Rural Areas:
       Canada and the United Kingdom," pp. 166-183 in *Contemporary
       Rural Systems in Transition: Volume 2, Economy and Society*, I. R.
       Bowler, C. Bryant, and M. Nellis, eds. Wallingford, Oxon, U.K.:
       CAB International.

Explores the development and key issues of rural tourism in Canada and the United Kingdom. Some aspects of rural tourism are strikingly different in the two countries. However, one very clear parallel is the confusion over concepts and definitions that complicates the studies of tourism on both sides of the Atlantic.

136. Cobb, Steven, and David Weinberg. 1993. "The Importance of Import Substitution in Regional Economic Impact Analysis: Empirical Estimates From Two Cincinnati Area Events." *Economic Development Quarterly* 7(3):282-286.

Estimates the magnitude of the import substitution effect that may occur as part of the incremental economic impact of a community-based event. The import substitution effect is simply the spending by local residents that is redirected from imports into the local economy because of the event. Estimates, which are survey based, are for two very different kinds of events in the Cincinnati area: the 1988 Tall Stacks Celebration and the 1990 Travel, Sports, and Boat Show. For both events, the size of the import substitution effect is comparable to that produced from exports, that is, spending by nonlocals in the local economy. As such, the authors believe that ignoring this import substitution effect may significantly understate the true incremental impact of local events.

137. Fagan, Mark, and Charles F. Longino, Jr. 1992. "Migrating Retirees: A Source for Economic Development." *Economic Development Quarterly* 7(1):98-106.

Examines an economic development strategy that many communities may have overlooked--attracting retirees. The authors point out that many older amenity and return migrants have high and generally recession-proof incomes (largely discretionary) and substantial financial assets that they transfer to their community of relocation. Their demand for goods and services stimulates the following industries: real estate, financial, health care, recreational, utilities, insurance, and retail. The community economic impact of these inmigrants is shown to be extremely positive. The authors believe that attracting retirees may be a more efficacious strategy for many communities than attempting to recruit manufacturing industries.

138. Foden, Harry G. 1992. "Destination Attractions as an Economic Development Generator." *Economic Development Review* 10(4):69-72.

Reports that destination attractions and resorts are major assets for areas wishing to achieve a significant share of tourist expenditures. Although traditionally not subjects of attention by economic developers, the favorable economic impact that such attractions can have on a region and the number of jobs directly and indirectly associated with them have led economic developers to examine them more closely. This article discusses the economic benefits of destination attractions and their specialized locational requirements.

139. Frederick, Martha. 1992. *Tourism as a Rural Economic Development Tool: An Exploration of the Literature.* Bibliographies and Literature of Agriculture No. 122. Washington, D.C.: USDA, Economic Research Service, 33 pp.

Presents studies from economics and other social sciences that explore tourism as a rural economic development tool. Topics covered in this annotated bibliography include the tourism industry, measuring and forecasting tourism demand, valuation of tourism resources, effects of tourism, and theories and applications of tourism development. The bibliography contains 113 entries, with emphasis placed on work since 1980. Each entry is annotated. Each annotation contains key words, and the bibliography ends with author and subject indexes.

140. Frederick, Martha. 1993. "Rural Tourism and Economic Development." *Economic Development Quarterly* 7(2):215-224.

Reports that tourism is a popular economic development strategy. The author reviews three diverse books that study tourism from various social science perspectives--economic, sociological, psychological, and anthropological. Despite their different focuses, all three books agree that tourism development has its benefits and costs and that changes to the destination areas are inevitable. Careful planning and marketing can lessen the harmful effects of tourism development.

141. Gibson, Lay James. 1993. "The Potential of Tourism Development in Nonmetropolitan Areas," pp. 145-164 in *Economic Adaptation: Alternatives for Nonmetropolitan Areas,* D. L. Barkley, ed. Boulder, CO: Westview Press.

Examines the implications of adopting tourism development as an explicit strategy in an economic development program. Early discussion focuses on factors promoting an increase in tourism, the institutional setting of tourism programs, and some benefits and liabilities of employing a tourism development strategy. Next, a case study is provided that permits a microscale look at the industries that come together to form the larger tourism industry and the impacts that a tourism industry might have in rural communities. The chapter concludes with a discussion of tourism's role in nonmetropolitan economic development.

142. Green, Bernal, and Mary Jo Schneider. 1989. "Manufacturing or Retirement: A Comparison of the Direct Economic Effects of Two Growth Options." *Arkansas Business and Economic Review* 22(2):1-9.

Address the question, "How does attracting retirees compare with attracting manufacturing jobs as a small area economic growth option?" The authors argue that attracting retirees can offer substantial benefits to small communities. They recommend that state governments, especially in the South, should develop more effective strategies to incorporate retirement into their economic planning. They should focus on ways to attract and retain the more affluent strata of older people from throughout the nation. Private developers and government leaders interested in promoting retirement as an economic option need to be particularly aware of the need to (1) motivate those in farming, manufacturing, and forestry to conduct their operations so as to prevent environmental damage from soil erosion, water pollution, wildlife destruction, and scenic degradation; (2) recognize also that tourism is an expanding source of employment for older workers in many destination-retirement counties; and (3) foster efforts to increase communications between inmigrant retirees and native people.

143. Happel, Stephen K., Timothy D. Hogan, and Elmer Pflanz. 1988. "The Economic Impact of Elderly Winter Residents in the Phoenix Area." *Research on Aging* 10(1):119-133.

Adds to the emerging literature on the seasonal migration of the elderly by considering the economic benefits and costs to a large receiving area. Estimates of the number of "snowbird" households are derived from an annual mobile home and travel trailer park census and a local savings company sample. These estimates are then combined with individual park resident survey results to generate expenditure totals for park snowbirds and all snowbirds during the 1986-87 season. Conflicts between permanent and seasonal residents are considered, and the authors conclude with views about future research needs.

144. Kottke, Marvin. 1988. "Estimating Economic Impacts of Tourism." *Annals of Tourism Research* 15:122-133.

Argues that there is a growing need for economic impact studies by planning officials when making decisions regarding tourism development.

The author presents a linear programming model useful to municipal and regional planners. First, a model representative of a community's tourism industry is formulated. The model is then applied to New London County, Connecticut, to test applicability of linear programming for estimating the potential economic impact of tourism growth. A benchmark situation is created to serve as a basis for comparison. The model is subsequently applied to three different projected growth situations. The analysis demonstrates the effectiveness of linear programming in estimating the number and types of new tourism enterprises that are the most suitable for generating maximum gross income while, at the same time, using limited resources most efficiently.

145. Milman, Ady, and Abraham Pizam. 1988. "Social Impacts of Tourism on Central Florida." *Annals of Tourism Research* 15:191-204.

Investigates Central Florida residents' perceptions of the social consequences and impacts of tourism. A telephone survey of 203 households revealed that residents not only supported the current magnitude of the tourism industry, but also favored its expansion. Respondents also revealed some specific positive and negative impacts that tourism had on their community. The study revealed a relationship between the overall level of support for tourism by residents and their perceptions of the consequences of tourism.

146. Mitchell, Clare J. A., and Geoffrey Wall. 1989. "The Arts and Employment: A Case Study of the Stratford Festival." *Growth and Change* 20(4):31-40.

Examines the impact of the Stratford Festival on employment within the community of Stratford, Ontario. The specific objective was to calculate the secondary jobs created in Stratford per primary job generated at the festival. Results indicate that 1.6 jobs resulted in Stratford for every job generated at the theatre. This finding provides evidence that cultural organizations can contribute positively to the economic base of a community.

147. Patton, Spiro G. 1985. "Tourism and Local Economic Development: Factory Outlets and the Reading SMSA." *Growth and Change* 16(3):64-73.

Presents a case study of a small urban area--Reading, Pennsylvania and the Reading SMSA with its utilization of factory outlets as one facet of a transition and tourism development strategy. The paper begins with a brief overview of the various modes of tourist industry development. A brief sketch of Reading illustrates its qualifications as a transitional area (i.e., one making the transition from manufacturing to services as its principal employment base). Then the specific form of tourism development in Reading is presented, including the results of a study which attempted to pinpoint the economic impact of tourism on the local economy. The paper concludes with some comments on the viability of tourism as a strategy for urban areas such as Reading.

148.   Sastry, M. Lakshminarayan. 1992. "Estimating the Economic Impacts of Elderly Migration: An Input-Output Analysis." *Growth and Change* 23(1):54-79.

Quantifies for the first time the economic impacts of elderly inmigration on the output, earnings, and employment of a receiving state's economy. Data from the Consumer Expenditure Survey and estimates of the total redistribution of income to Florida resulting from elderly inmigration are used to calculate the direct effects by industry. A model for the state of Florida based on the Regional Input-Output Modeling System (RIMS II) is used to estimate the total impacts. The large migration flows and the considerable economic resources of the elderly lead to large, positive total impacts on the Florida economy.

149.   Sem, John. 1989. *Using Tourism and Travel as a Community and Rural Revitalization Strategy.* Proceedings of the National Extension Workshop. St. Paul, MN: University of Minnesota, Minnesota Extension Service, 215 pp.

Summarizes a workshop that documented ideas and resources that small communities can use in developing and expanding business and services for tourists and travelers. The contributors point out that tourism and travel is a major component of the U.S. economy, generating over $300 million annually. A sizeable portion of this industry is based on the attractions of natural resources, much of which is accessed through small rural communities. The authors conclude that the tourism and travel sector can be an important component of rural development if it is approached carefully with a planned approach.

RETAIL

150.   Ayres, Janet S., F. Larry Leistritz, and Kenneth E. Stone. 1992. *Revitalizing the Retail Trade Sector in Rural Communities: Lessons*

From Three Midwestern States. RRD 162. Ames, IA: Iowa State University, North Central Regional Center for Rural Development, 42 pp.

Identifies successful strategies employed by communities and individual businesses to revitalize retail trade. The study included 37 communities with populations of 500 to 5,000 in Indiana, Iowa, and North Dakota. The authors examined the current status of rural retail communities, identified organizational techniques to promote retail sales and businesses, examined effective business funding techniques and recruitment approaches to bring new businesses to the community, identified successful promotional campaigns, and determined the most critical needs of business communities.

151. Ayres, Janet, Larry Leistritz, and Kenneth Stone. 1992. "Rural Retail Business Survival: Implications for Community Developers." *Journal of the Community Development Society* 23(2):11-21.

Identifies strategies employed by rural communities and business proprietors in 37 rural communities in Indiana, Iowa, and North Dakota to enhance the viability of the local retail sector. The authors suggest several possible actions for community development practitioners involved in efforts to improve and sustain rural retail business communities. These actions include (1) assistance to rural communities in building a more diversified economic base, (2) provision of business management training and technical assistance, (3) establishing mechanisms to transfer established business operations to new owners, (4) developing financing mechanisms for new or aspiring businesses, and (5) assisting rural communities in dealing with change and planning for their futures.

152. Bradley, Edward B., and Janice D. Rhodd. 1989. *Cost and Availability of Consumer Goods and Services in Rural Wyoming Towns.* B-922. Laramie, WY: University of Wyoming, Cooperative Extension Service, 17 pp.

Provides information about the comparative prices and availability of goods and services in Wyoming. A survey was conducted in the spring of 1987 in 9 rural and 9 urban Wyoming towns to collect data on availability and price of 304 consumer goods and services. The rural and urban towns were paired; each pair was from a different geographic area of Wyoming. For most of the categories of goods and services examined, prices in rural towns averaged significantly more than among urban towns. Food and personal care items were 6.0 percent and 13.7 percent more, respectively. Prices in the selected rural towns also exceeded urban town prices by 18.1 percent for household supplies and 18.4 percent for clothing. On the other hand, house prices in rural towns averaged 21.2 percent less, and house and apartment rents averaged 23.6 percent less.

153. Gruidl, John, and Steven Kline. 1992. *The Impact of Large Discount Stores on Retail Sales in Illinois Communities.* Rural Research Report Vol. 3, Issue 2. Macomb, IL: Western Illinois University, Illinois Institute for Rural Affairs, 8 pp.

Examines the impact of large discount stores on retail sales in Illinois communities. Fifteen communities in which a large discount store opened between 1986 and 1989 are included in the study. The analysis examines retail trade before and after the opening of a discount store in these communities. The authors examine changes in total sales and sales in seven retail categories: general merchandise, automotive and filling stations, eating and drinking places, apparel, food, furniture and household, and lumber and hardware. The results indicate the effect of the newly opened discount stores on the aggregate drawing power of the retail sector. The results also provide insights as to how existing businesses in specific retail categories, such as apparel, are affected by large discount stores.

154. Henderson, David A., and Fred K. Hines. 1990. "Increases in Rural Income May Not Help Smalltown Retailers." *Rural Development Perspectives* 6(3):31-36.

Uses data from 10 counties in southwestern Minnesota to assess how changes in local income affected retail sales between 1979 and 1986. Increases in income generally led to increased total spending in the larger towns of the area but lower total spending in its smaller towns. The authors believe that with improved income, consumers seem to be more attracted to the greater selection of goods in the larger towns.

155. Henderson, David, and George Wallace. 1992. "Retail Business Adjustment in Rural Hierarchies." *Growth and Change* 23(1):80-93.

Reports that many rural hierarchies are becoming increasingly dominated by a few regional growth centers while the retail sector in adjacent smaller communities either stagnates or declines. This study tests the hypothesis that the rate of adjustment of the retail sector to changing consumer spending patterns is uniform across different ordered communities in a rural hierarchy. Neoclassical investment theory is combined with central place theory to develop a conceptual model of the relationship between the retail sector and investment in a community. A three-tiered 49-community hierarchy is constructed using data from the Minnesota Department of Revenue and the Report of Condition and Income of the Board of Governors of the Federal Reserve System. A cross-section time-series ordinary least-squares regression model is employed to estimate retail coefficients of adjustment. Regional estimates indicate only partial adjustment in the retail sector across the whole hierarchy to shifts in consumer spending patterns. Community estimates indicate that retail businesses in the largest and mid-sized communities adjust totally in one period, but that retail businesses in the smallest communities do not. The faster rates of adjustment by retail businesses in the larger communities to changing consumer spending patterns may augment the development of regional growth centers in rural areas.

156. Leistritz, F. Larry, and Alan V. Schuler. 1992. "Threshold Population Levels for Rural Retail Businesses in North Dakota." *Economic Development Review* 10(4):45-48.

Estimates population levels associated with the presence of 16 specified types of businesses in North Dakota communities with populations of 200 to 10,000 in 1990. The 16 business types examined represent retail establishments frequently found in nonmetropolitan trade centers. The data used to identify the presence of particular types of businesses in a given community were records of sales and use tax permit holders from the North Dakota State Tax Department.

157. Leistritz, F. Larry, Janet S. Ayres, and Kenneth E. Stone. 1992. "Revitalizing the Retail Trade Sector in Rural Communities: Lessons From Three Midwestern States." *Economic Development Review* 10(4):49-54.

Reports that retail trade is undergoing many changes in rural areas. In order to address these changes, the authors document the dynamics of rural retail trade and describe strategies that have been successfully employed by rural communities to revitalize their retail sector. Major findings are grouped into five categories: organizational techniques, business financing, business recruitment, promotional campaigns, and critical needs of business communities.

158. Rochin, Refugio I., and Karen M. Jeter. 1991. *The Availability and Prices of Consumer Goods and Services in Small Towns of Northern California.* Giannini Foundation Information Series No. 91-1. Davis, CA: University of California, Giannini Foundation, 27 pp.

Examines the in-town prices and availability of over 300 consumer goods and services. It compares prices between small towns in northern California with less then 2,500 people and the closest larger city used by small town residents for major shopping. The price comparisons help to determine which items are less expensive, the same, or more expensive in small rural communities. The survey designed for this study also identified several items not likely to be found in small towns. Product "availability" differed between towns and was found to be positively correlated with distance (in miles) to the nearest central city. Small towns located relatively far from larger cities tended to carry most consumer items whereas small towns located relatively near larger cities carried fewer consumer goods and services. This finding and others are then compared to some of the tenets of "central place theory."

159. Stabler, Jack C., M. R. Olfert, and Murray Fulton. 1992. *The Changing Role of Rural Communities in an Urbanizing World: Saskatchewan 1961-1990*. Regina, Saskatchewan: University of Regina, Canadian Plains Research Center, 64 pp.

Reports that Saskatchewan's communities continue to change in the functions they perform, the number of people and businesses they attract, and the way in which they relate to other centers within the province as well as those beyond provincial boundaries. This report traces the evolution of the trade-center system in Saskatchewan between 1961 and 1990, explains the form the consolidation process has taken, and provides an overview of some of the factors which have contributed to the observed changes.

160. Stone, Kenneth E. 1989. *The Impact of Wal-Mart Stores on Other Businesses in Iowa*. Ames, IA: Iowa State University, Department of Economics, 35 pp.

Uses secondary data to assess the impact of the rapidly growing chain of discount department stores (Wal-Mart) on other businesses. Data on total retail sales and sales by major types of stores were obtained from the Iowa Department of Revenue. Pull factors were computed for total sales for all towns in the state for the period 1983-1988. Sales trends were analyzed for 14 towns in which Wal-Mart stores were located, for towns of similar size, and for the largest towns and cities in the state. The author concludes that, when a Wal-Mart store opens in a small-to-medium size town, the trade area tends to expand and some existing firms in town benefit, particularly restaurants and building material firms. However, general merchandise firms, specialty stores, apparel stores, and service firms often had substantial decreases in sales. In towns of similar size but without a Wal-Mart store, substantial losses in home furnishings, service firms, building materials, and apparel could be attributed to the Wal-Mart stores.

161.   Young, Joel J., and Bruce B. Johnson. 1991. *An Analysis of Retail Trade in Nebraska Counties by Major Trade Groupings*. Rpt. No. 165.   Lincoln, NE: University of Nebraska, Department of Agricultural Economics, 55 pp.

Addresses two objectives (1) to trace trends for different retail sales groups in four categories of Nebraska counties and (2) to develop and apply an analytical framework for explaining pull factor variations over time and across geographic space. The four types of counties were agricultural dependent, metropolitan, regional trade, and diverse. County retail sales and service data were collected by store type from *Sales and Marketing Management Survey of Buying Power* data service editions for the years 1975, 1979, 1986, and 1988. The store groups considered were food stores, eating and drinking establishments, general merchandise stores, apparel and accessories stores, furniture and appliance stores, automotive dealerships, gasoline and service stations, building material and hardware dealerships, and drug stores.

SERVICES

162.   Andrianacos, Dimitri, and John Gruidl. 1992. "Services in Regional Employment Change." *Growth and Change* 23(3):303-320.

Examines the role of services in regional employment change in Illinois from 1972 to 1987. The approach applies recent advances in time-series analysis to investigate both the long-term and short-term relationship among employment in three sectors: goods production, export-potential services, and local services. The results indicate that there is not a long-term relation among these variables, i.e., that they do not move together in the long run. In the short term, the evidence is that employment in the service sectors follows employment change in goods production, although the response persists for only six months. The results suggest that a policy of targeting export-potential services is not likely to produce sustained employment growth in the other sectors.

163.   Bailly, A. S., D. Maillat, and W. J. Coffey. 1987. "Service Activities and Regional Development: Some European Examples." *Environment and Planning A* 19:653-668.

Addresses two general issues related to the nature of the service sector. The first concerns the growing interdependence between the secondary and tertiary sectors, largely a function of the increased use of service functions in the manufacturing process. These service inputs may be either internalized or externalized by a manufacturing firm. The second issue concerns the role of the service sector in promoting regional economic development. It is generally acknowledged that, although it may be important for a region to possess a sufficient level of service activity so that its firms are not required to make major service imports, because of externality effects high-order services tend to locate in major cities. The potential for decentralization of service activities is examined both within a conceptual framework and by reviewing the results of certain empirical studies conducted in Switzerland.

164. Beyers, William B. 1991. "Trends in Service Employment in Pacific Northwest Counties: 1974-1986." *Growth and Change* 22(4):27-50.

Reports that the Pacific Northwest has grown more rapidly than the U.S. in recent years, led by the expansion of services employment. However, there have been striking differences in rates of growth of individual counties in the Northwest. These variations in growth rates are shown to be associated with the type of industrial structure found in groups of counties. Their growth is also shown to be related, in part, to changes in the economic base of individual counties, with services contributing a greater share to county exports in 1986 than in 1974.

165. Beyers, William B., and Michael J. Alvine. 1985. "Export Services in Postindustrial Society." *Papers of the Regional Science Association* 57:31-45.

Points out that, although employment in services now dominates the U.S. economy, there still is relatively little understanding of the spatial structure of trade in services. This is in part a legacy of the historical tendency to focus on the markets of the manufacturing and primary production sectors on the theory that they are "basic." However, the great expansion of services employment in the U.S. economy in recent decades means that this assumption needs reexamination. This paper reports the results of interviews with 2,200 service sector firms in the Central Puget Sound region, exploring their degree of export orientation. These interviews show a striking degree of export orientation within these sectors. The study suggests that interregional trade in services is probably extremely important in the economic base of all major metropolitan regions.

166. Blazar, William A. 1992. "Satellite Cities." *Economic Development Commentary* 16(1-2):24-29.

Defines satellite cities as ones that are relatively small (less than 100,000) and freestanding (at least 50 miles from the fringe of a major metropolitan area). Such cities typically have a three-dimensional job base, originating from natural resources, regional services, and export services. Most owe their birth to one or both of the first two dimensions. Their current strength, and in some cases, prosperity, comes from a mix of all three, but most notable for the places discussed in this article, from export services. The author describes satellite cities, focusing on the features of their job base that make them different from and more successful than other rural cities. He also examines development strategies for export service businesses, a vital part of the job base that makes these cities successful.

167. Bohm, Robert A., Henry W. Herzog, Jr., and Alan M. Scholottmann. 1986. "Trade and Service Sector Development in the Rural South: The Case of the Tennessee-Tombigbee Corridor." *The Review of Regional Studies* 16:41-49.

Presents an econometric methodology for identifying trade and service sectors at the county level that possess "development potential" (i.e., appear to be underdeveloped relative to a complete array of local socio-economic conditions). The authors apply the method to counties within the Tennessee-Tombigbee Corridor region of Alabama, Mississippi, Kentucky, and Tennessee. However, the methodology is equally applicable to other multicounty regions of the country, and particularly in situations where state and local planners are asked to make specific recommendations on the preferred industrial composition of a more general trade and/or service development strategy.

168. Coffey, William J., and Antoine S. Bailly. 1991. "Producer Services and Flexible Production: An Exploratory Analysis." *Growth and Change* 22(4):95-117.

Points out that, while the flexible production literature has become increasingly abundant in recent years, the vast majority of it is narrowly restricted to manufacturing activities, entirely ignoring the role that producer services play in modern systems of production. This paper explores the conceptual linkages between the growth and the location of producer services, on the one hand, and the rise of flexible forms of production, on the other. After a brief summary of the flexible production approach, the factors underlying the growth and the increasing externalization of producer services are examined. The appropriateness of employing a flexible production framework in the case of producer services, and the significance of flexible production for understanding the location of producer services are then explored. Finally, the labor force effect of flexibility in the production and use of producer services is considered.

169. Coffey, W. J., and M. Polese. 1987. "Trade and Location of Producer Services: A Canadian Perspective." *Environment and Planning A* 19:597-611.

Introduces elements of a location theory for producer services. The paper is prompted by a perceived need to examine more closely the "technical" processes by which particular services are produced and the modes by which they are "transported." The authors find that patterns of trade and of location are complementary aspects of the same problem. Three distinct channels through which producer services are traded are examined: direct and intra-firm exports by producer-service firms, and intrafirm exports by manufacturing firms. The producer-service location problem may be conceptualized essentially as one of a trade-off between market-pull factors, specialized labor needs and urban externalities. When the location of producer-service activities within the Canadian urban system is examined, these activities are found to be highly concentrated, but not in a simple hierarchial pattern, suggesting the importance of both specialized labor pools and urban externalities.

170. Daniels, P. W. 1985. "Services Industries: Some New Directions," pp. 111-141 in *Progress in Industrial Geography*, M. Pacione, ed. London: Croom Helm.

Reviews selected aspects of the recent work in the geography of service industries with a view to demonstrating the contention that there has been a recognizable diversification of the field of interest in service industry studies. The author suggests, however, that there is still a great deal of scope for more research in which empirical and theoretical approaches could usefully be brought closer together. The chapter concentrates on recent work on office-based and producer services.

171. Davis, H. Craig, and Thomas A. Hutton. 1993. "The Role of Service Activity in Regional Economic Growth." *Economic Development Review* 11(1):54-60.

Reviews the role of services in an economy, using a simple model, and presents empirical evidence of direct service exports for Vancouver, British Columbia. The authors give some suggestions as to how the further development of metropolitan service activities could be stimulated.

172. Doeksen, Gerald, and Joyce Altobelli. 1990. *The Economic Impact of Rural Hospital Closure: A Community Simulation.* Washington, D.C.: U.S. Department of Health and Human Services, 53 pp.

Examines the economic impact of hospital closure on rural communities based on case studies of three towns in Texas. A community-simulation input-output model was used in the analysis in which the closure of each community's hospital is simulated. The relative impacts were greatest for the smallest communities studied.

173. Ekstein, Albert J., and Dale M. Heien. 1985. "Causes and Consequences of Service Sector Growth: The U.S. Experience." *Growth and Change* 16:12-17.

Concludes that the primary factor contributing to employment growth in services has been the dramatic increase in government expenditures, particularly at the state and local levels and for Medicare. Of almost equal importance was the growth in the private components of final demand.

174. Fik, Timothy J., Edward J. Malecki, and Robert G. Amey. 1993. "Trouble in Paradise? Employment Trends and Forecasts for a Service-Oriented Economy." *Economic Development Quarterly* 7(4):358-372.

Reports that the phenomenal growth of Florida's service sector over the past three decades can be largely attributed to the impacts of elderly in-migration and flourishing recreational and tourist industries. The demands of seasonal migrants, a soaring population, and an increasing share of elderly provided the state with an apparent economic boom. Over 40 percent of the state's personal income is derived from interstate income transfers. Although these income flows have undoubtedly helped Florida experience modest gains in many sectors, the ability of these dollars to provide adequate stimulus for further growth remains questionable. As income transfers level off, the growth of Florida's retail and service sectors is likely to slow. Projected structural deficits are likely to offset the benefits of three decades of expansion. State economic development planners must, therefore, seek to promote initiatives aimed at reducing Florida's reliance on transfer income and consumer services.

175. Glasmeier, Amy, and G. Borchard. 1989. "Research Policy and Review 31. From Branch Plants to Back Offices: Prospects for Rural Services Growth." *Environment and Planning* 21:1565-1583.

Examines the potential of service industries as a source of future rural economic development. Recent literature on services is reviewed, and attempts are made to answer the following questions: (1) What are services and how can they be measured accurately? (2) How have rural areas fared with recent growth in services? (3) What are the determinants of rural services growth?, and (4) What affects service industry location and do these factors differ from those for other industries? Policy recommendations about service industry location are also reviewed.

176. Goe, W. Richard. 1991. "The Growth of Producer Service Industries: Sorting Through the Externalization Debate." *Growth and Change* 22(4):118-141.

Explains that the development of a theory for explaining why firms externalize producer services functions is critical to gaining a better understanding of why producer services industries have enjoyed robust growth within the United States, Canada, and the European Community. Scholars of the service economy have attempted to develop explanations for the externalization of producer services functions. These explanations constitute "the externalization debate" since there has been a lack of consistency and agreement as to how and why externalization is taking place. None of the explanations for externalization approach what could be termed a theory of producer services externalization, since they consist of empirical generalizations that are not deductively connected. This paper represents an attempt to move toward the development of such a theory by constructing a more comprehensive and systematic conceptual approach to analyzing the externalization of producer services functions. The motivating factors for externalization that are proposed in the externalization debate are systematically examined. The insights of the transaction cost and production subcontracting literatures are then discussed and the implications of these literatures for producer services externalization are examined. A synthesis of the insights provided by these research literatures is then used to develop a more comprehensive analytical framework for examining producer services externalization.

177. Hall, Peter. 1987. "The Anatomy of Job Creation: Nations, Regions, and Cities in the 1960s and 1970s." *Regional Studies* 21(2):95-106.

Reports that OECD data for four industrial countries (Great Britain, Federal Germany, U.S.A., and Japan) demonstrate a clear shift from manufacturing to service employment, a shift that has been most marked in the U.S.A. There are sharp differences in the degree to which these countries have compensated for manufacturing job losses by gains in the services. Within the U.K., there are also marked differences in these replacement ratios, both between regions and between major cities.

178. Hall, Peter. 1988. "Regions in the Transition to the Information Economy," pp. 137-159 in *America's New Market Geography*, G. Sternlieb and J. W. Hughes, eds. New Brunswick, NJ: Rutgers University, Center for Urban Policy Research.

Describes the shift in employment in the U.S. from industry (construction, mining, and manufacturing) to services. The effects of this shift on broad regions of the U.S. are described. The author finds that in the early 1980s, relative regional performances were dominated first by extraordinary variations in the fortunes of the manufacturing industry and secondly by differences in the rates of information-sector jobs creation.

179. Hamm, Rita R., JoAnn M. Thompson, Randal C. Coon, and F. Larry Leistritz. 1993. *The Economic Impact of North Dakota's Health Care Industry on the State's Economy in 1991*. Agricultural Economics Report No. 296. Fargo, ND: North Dakota State University, Department of Agricultural Economics, 8 pp.

Focuses on the health care industry's far-reaching influence within North Dakota. An input-output model is used to estimate the economic impact of hospitals and long-term care nursing facilities. The analysis shows that nearly 8 percent of the state's total business activity, nearly 10 percent of the state's total retail sales, and nearly 19 percent of the state's total employment in 1991 were attributable to hospitals and long-term care nursing facilities. In addition, these facilities generated nearly $41 million of tax revenues for the state in 1991.

180. Harrington, J. W., Alan D. MacPherson, and John R. Lombard. 1991. "Interregional Trade in Producer Services: Review and Synthesis." *Growth and Change* 22(4): 75-94.

Reviews some of the past decade's studies of producer or intermediate-services exports from local regions. After a discussion of conceptual and methodological problems and inconsistencies, the authors present these studies according to the three basic methodologies: surveys, location quotients, and input-output. Overall, these studies support several conclusions: (1) If intermediate services are defined broadly, certain of these activities have as their major function interregional or international transfer or trade. By nature, these distributive services have widespread clients and benefit from locations with substantial physical and communications infrastructure. (2) Among most business and financial-service activities, most offices are established to serve a local region, but may derive some revenues from beyond this expected zone. (3) The exceptions--activities and establishments that derive much of their revenue beyond such "normal" zones--are particularly specialized, particularly large, or parts of multiregional enterprises. (4) Such firms tend to locate in larger or more specialized urban places, probably because of the labor force, the corporate connections, and the rapid dissemination of ideas, contacts, and information within and among the largest metropolitan areas. These conclusions lead to some general policy recommendations.

181.   Hirschhorn, Larry.   1985.   "Information Technology and the New
        Services Game," pp. 172-188 in *High Technology, Space, and
        Society*, M. Castells, ed.   Beverly Hills, CA: Sage Publications.

Examines the changing nature of service industries that emerges as new technologies bring a competitive and strategic edge to the delivery of old services. Three processes are apparent: (1) a shift from services to marketing, (2) changing boundaries between the provider and the consumer, and (3) the more systematic scrutiny of the service provider's skills. After examining the nature of the modern service industries, the author discusses the impact of new technologies on strategic business units and then examines the resulting tensions and contradictions of the service economy that shape urban economic development. The study draws heavily on case studies of two companies, which in turn were part of a larger research project on the impact of office technologies on job design.

182.   Hirschl, Thomas A., and Samuel A. McReynolds.   1989.   "Service
        Employment and Rural Community Economic Development."
        Journal of the Community Development Society 20(2):15-30.

Addresses two interrelated questions about rural service industries. First, are there significant rural-urban differences in service industry composition? Second, what are the basic income sources associated with service employment concentration in rural areas? An analysis of 382 labor market areas in the contiguous U.S. indicates that rural service concentration is most pronounced in social services and that age-related income from nonwork sources is associated with rural service concentration. The implications for rural community economic development strategies are discussed in terms of capturing more income locally and attracting additional residents.

183. Iannone, Donald T. 1993. "Service and Office Sectors as a Development Opportunity for Canadian Provinces and Communities." *Economic Development Review* 11(1):64-67.

Reports that businesses in the service sector are a development opportunity for Canadian provinces and communities. The service sector is the largest sector in the economy and is projected to grow significantly in the future. This growth is expected to take place mainly in large urban areas, but some has the capability of occurring in smaller communities. Economic developers should consider creating targeted marketing and business development strategies towards this increasingly significant economic sector.

184. Kirn, Thomas J. 1987. "Growth and Change in the Service Sector of the U.S.: A Spatial Perspective." *Annals of the Association of American Geographers* 77(3):353-372.

Reports that, although there is growing recognition that services play a major role in developed economies, knowledge concerning the service sector, including its spatial characteristics, is quite limited. This study examines the spatial structure of the U.S. service sector and change in that structure from 1958 to 1977. It is based on an analysis of service employment and employment change for a sample of U.S. SMSAs and nonmetropolitan areas. Most of the change in service structure that took place during the study period was focused in business and professional services and in finance, insurance and real estate. Many individual industries in these groupings exhibited both downfiltering from larger to smaller places and very strong growth in the South. As a result, the South reversed its relative deficiency in many specialized services. A relationship between total employment growth and both the concentration in and relative growth of business, professional, and financial services was observed. Study results suggest that regional development policies that foster service growth could benefit not only large SMSAs but many smaller places as well.

185. Kirn, Thomas J., Richard S. Conway, Jr., and William B. Beyers. 1990. "Producer Services Development and the Role of Telecommunications: A Case Study in Rural Washington." *Growth and Change* 21(4):33-50.

Examines the potential of information-intensive producer services as a contributor to economic development in rural areas through a case study of a nonmetropolitan community in central Washington. Although producer services constitute one of the fastest growing components of the U.S. economy, the findings indicate that this sector has not been decentralizing to rural Washington. Opportunities for producer services development in rural communities are limited because of the inaccessibility of markets, smaller pools of skilled labor, and the lack of agglomeration economies. Opportunities for producer services are greatest, however, in large rural communities with high quality telecommunications systems.

186. Marshall, J. N., P. Damesick, and P. Wood. 1987. "Understanding the Location and Role of Producer Services in the United Kingdom." *Environment and Planning A* 19:575-595.

Examines the contribution of producer services to the economy and their role in uneven development. The author points out that, although the growth of output and employment in services and their dominance in many local economies have increased academic interest in service activities, questions of definition plague the analysis of services. A definition and classification of producer services is proposed. Existing research on producer services is reviewed and a framework for understanding their location and role is outlined.

187. Moss, Mitchell L., and Andrew Danau. 1987. "Will the Cities Lose Their Back Offices?" *Real Estate Review* 17(1):62-68.

Examines current trends in the location of back offices and explores ways to retain back office operations in central cities. Back office activities are defined as those that usually do not involve direct client contact. Back offices generally perform two basic functions: (1) processing of the firm's transactions and (2) compiling and supplying needed information. The organization of work in back offices has recently undergone dramatic changes, including (1) emergence of data processing centers as distinct units within information-intensive firms and (2) development of new client services. The author points out that the new developments in telecommunications have been permissive rather than determinative factors in office location. That is, technology allows the decoupling of back office operations but does not in itself reduce the desirability of central business district locations. Energy reliability has become increasingly important to computer-intensive firms, as have energy costs. Labor force quality (and an adequate labor pool) is another crucial consideration in choosing a site for a back office operation.

188. Nelson, K. 1986. "Labor Demand, Labor Supply, and the Suburbanization of Low-Wage Office Work," pp. 149-171 in *Production, Work, and Territory: The Geographical Anatomy of Industrial Capitalism*, A. Scott and M. Storper, eds. Boston, MA: Allen and Unwin.

Reports on a locational analysis of "back offices" (large highly automated offices with low extramural contact needs) in the San Francisco Bay area. The author concludes that the distinguishing feature of the outer suburban area attracting this office type is an educated, stable, and nonmilitant female labor supply associated with expanding single family housing districts.   Automated clerical jobs are characterized by high job performance requirements and/or eroded working conditions, increasing the importance of such labor qualities.   Back offices must be located nearby in order to recruit this labor supply, since the journey to work for these women is limited by low clerical wages and by household responsibilities.

189. O'Farrell, P. N., D. M. W. N. Hitchens, and L. A. R. Moffat. 1992. "The Competitiveness of Business Service Firms: A Matched Comparison Between Scotland and the South East of England." *Regional Studies* 26(6):519-533.

Presents a comparative analysis of the competitiveness and performance of matched pairs of business service companies in Scotland and South East England. Several dimensions of performance are investigated for five industries: market research, management consultancy, product design, graphic design, and advertising. Value added per person is one-quarter higher in the English offices and they achieved a much greater degree of export orientation (one-fifth of sales) than the Scottish firms (4%). Possible demand and supply side causes of such differences are reviewed and potential policy responses considered.

190. Patton, Wendy, and Ann Markusen. 1991. "The Perils of Overstating Service Sector Growth Potential: A Study of Linkages in Distributive Services." *Economic Development Quarterly* 5(3):197-212.

Finds that the export potential of services has been assessed without regard to forward and backward linkages. In examining the steel industry, the authors find that regional service sector growth is often associated with (1) the displacement of manufacturing functions into service establishments, (2) the role of marketing manufacturing-displacing imports, and (3) locational shifts toward consumer sites. In addition, service gains may be temporary, associated with cyclical or abnormal business conditions. In the case of steel, service centers grew rapidly in the early 1980s to account for 25 percent of all steel sales. These employment gains were largely attributable to the spin-off of steel manufacturing functions and to opportunities for marketing imported steel. Economic development planners should assess service sector potential in light of such linkages and dynamics.

191.   Peck, John E., and Brian R. Shappell. 1986. "The Income Impact of the Shift to Service Industry: A Case Study." *Economic Development Review* 4(2):11-15.

Examines trends in employment and earnings for the South Bend, Indiana Metropolitan Statistical Area (MSA) to explore the implications of growing service industry employment on earnings and income. The authors find that the assertion that service jobs pay less than jobs in manufacturing stands the test both nationally and in the South Bend area over the 1958-1979 period. However, they also believe that a number of factors mitigate the general conclusion. These include (1) the large number of part-time workers in the service industries, (2) there is a substantial range of pay scales among job types within the services industries, and (3) service employment is less sensitive to the business cycle than manufacturing. In conclusion, the authors indicate that a case can be made for a revitalization policy that calls for attraction of certain service industries, particularly those that are higher paying and are exportable in nature.

192.   Perry, Martin. 1990. "Business Service Specialization and Regional Economic Change." *Regional Studies* 24(3):195-209.

Reports that business services are experiencing rapid employment growth, but there is uncertainty over the interpretation of this trend. This study examines three surveys conducted to assess changes in the demand and supply of business services in the Aukland Region, New Zealand during the period 1983-88. The data indicate that employment growth is "real" in that it is not caused by a transfer of activities that were formerly retained within other industries. Most manufacturing firms have adopted a pragmatic purchasing policy, externalizing and internalizing services on an individual basis with increased internalization dominant for data processing and accounting services. A survey of business service suppliers indicates the greater importance of service exports, demand from other services, and product innovation as the basis for growth.

193. Porterfield, Shirley. 1990. "Service Sector Offers More Jobs, Lower Pay." *Rural Development Perspectives* 6(3):2-7.

Reports that the shift in employment from manufacturing to services in 1981-1986 slowed the increase in the level of average annual pay of U.S. nonagricultural workers. The distribution of jobs among industries in the nonmetro job market changed more than in the metro job market, resulting in a slower increase in annual pay for nonmetro workers.

194. Smith, Stephen M. 1993. "Service Industries in the Rural Economy: The Role and Potential Contributions," pp. 105-126 in *Economic Adaptation: Alternatives for Nonmetropolitan Areas*, D. L. Barkley, ed. Boulder, CO: Westview Press.

Reviews the research that addresses the feasibility of service industries as an alternative rural development strategy. Among the issues addressed are the following (1) should services be included in economic development efforts that seek to recruit industries from other areas; (2) do services play an export base role in rural areas; (3) where do the different types of service businesses locate, and what are the factors that influence this location decision; and (4) what types of employment opportunities are provided by service industries. The author finds that service industries are assuming a large role in rural economies. This is a role that is important in its own right, providing jobs and contributing to the economic base, as well as playing a critical role in supporting the traditional rural economic base.

195. Stabler, Jack C., and Eric C. Howe. 1988. "Service Exports and Regional Growth in the Postindustrial Era." *Journal of Regional Sciences* 28(3):303-315.

Analyzes the change in composition of exports from Canada's four western provinces between 1974 and 1979. The authors observe that service exports increased more rapidly than exports of goods on both a direct and a direct-plus-indirect basis in 88 percent of comparisons. In absolute terms, the gain in service exports was equal to 89 percent of that for goods exports.

196. VanDinteren, J. H. J. 1987. "The Role of Business-Service Offices in the Economy of Medium-Sized Cities." *Environment and Planning A* 19:669-686.

Reports that in The Netherlands over the last fifteen years business-service activities have decentralized towards the intermediate provinces and the regions around the large cities in the west. A mailed survey was conducted to analyze this sector in 13 medium-sized cities in the intermediate provinces. The author concentrates on the role of business-service offices in the urban economy. It is demonstrated that business services are not so reliant on a local market and on the manufacturing sector as has been assumed formerly. However, there are differences among different types of offices. The author concludes with an examination of policy implications and suggests that policy makers need to re-examine the role of business services in the economy.

TYPE OF BUSINESS/FIRM

HIGH TECH

197. Acs, Zoltan J., Lanny Herron, and Harry J. Sapienza. 1992. "Financing Maryland Biotechnology." *Economic Development Quarterly* 6(4):373-382.

   Reports that a well-developed venture capital network is important for launching regional science-based industries. Although these networks are not absolutely necessary for high-technology development, they help facilitate entrepreneurial startups and speed development. The authors examine the degree to which the biotechnology industry in Maryland is supported by the "local" venture capital community. They find that the biotechnology industry is a significant importer of capital, suggesting that Maryland venture capital firms may not be playing an active enough role in economic development. Government policy should be used to strengthen the linkages between the venture capital community and the region's high-technology firms.

198. Barkley, David L., and John E. Keith. 1991. "The Locational Determinants of Western Nonmetro High Tech Manufacturers: An Econometric Analysis." *Western Journal of Agricultural Economics* 16(2):331-344.

   Uses the Tobit estimation procedure to determine the factors which influence the location and size of high technology manufacturers in nonmetro areas in the West. The results indicate that high tech branch plants tend to locate in populous counties adjacent to Metropolitan Statistical Areas (MSAs). Percent of local employment in manufacturing and agriculture was inversely related to branch plant employment, and the stock of human capital was not significantly related to employment. High tech unit plants also exhibited a propensity to locate in the more populous counties. Unlike branch plants, the unit concerns were more likely to develop or locate in communities with a highly educated work force and at greater distances from metro areas. The unit plants better fit the perception of high tech plants selecting high amenity locations with abundant skilled labor.

199. Barkley, David L., Roger A. Dahlgren, and Stephen M. Smith. 1988. "High-Technology Manufacturing in the Nonmetropolitan West: Gold or Just Glitter?" *American Journal of Agricultural Economics* 70(3):560-571.

Utilizes Tobit analysis to determine if employment, occupational, and market-linkage characteristics of nonmetropolitan high- and low-technology manufacturers differed after controlling for selected firm and community characteristics. Data were from a survey of nonmetropolitan firms in the eleven contiguous western states. Results indicate that the average employment of high- and low-technology manufacturers was similar. Nonmetropolitan high-technology manufacturers were more rapidly growing, export oriented, and skilled-labor intensive than low technology firms. However, the low-technology manufacturers maintained stronger backward linkages with the local economy.

200. Barkley, David L., Stephen M. Smith, and Roger H. Coupal. 1991. "High Tech Entrepreneurs in Small Towns." *Journal of the Community Development Society* 22(1):38-55.

Examines new (since 1976), locally owned and locally started high tech manufacturing plants in the rural West. The objective is to provide information on what communities can expect of these firms and to suggest possible strategies to enhance the success of rural entrepreneurs. The founders of the firms in this study were relatively young, self-financed, and experienced as owners, managers, or technicians/engineers. They located in towns because they had lived there previously or liked the natural amenities. Their chosen locations had distinct characteristics-- larger towns near urban centers or areas high in natural amenities and/or near universities. Little activity was found in small, isolated communities with few natural amenities.

201. Braun, Bradley M., and W. Warren McHone. 1992. "Science Parks as Economic Development Policy." *Economic Development Quarterly* 6(2):135-147.

Uses the results of a recent survey of high-technology firms in Orlando, Florida to compare and contrast the characteristics of firms that have located in a university-related research park with high-tech firms that operate in other parts of the metropolitan area. In general, the survey revealed substantial differences between these two categories of high-tech firms, extending across many dimensions of firm structure and development. Additionally, the survey reveals some similarities in the organizational structure of firms located in Orlando's Central Florida Research Park and firms at North Carolina's Research Triangle Park.

202. Castells, Manuel, ed. 1985. *High Technology, Space, and Society.* Beverly Hills, CA: Sage Publications, 320 pp.

Points out that two major phenomena have been taking place in society: a technological revolution of extraordinary proportions and far-reaching implications and a major process of urban-regional restructuring that is reshaping the spatial forms and dynamics at the world level. The simultaneity of these two processes has led numerous observers and policy makers to assume a causal relationship between them, with technology as the leading force of human progress, to whose requirements and logic cities, regions, and nations must adapt. In fact, reality appears to be more complex with a web of interactions between technology and space, mediated by economic, cultural, and political processes. This volume explores such relationships on the basis of a series of 14 original research essays whose common ground is the recognition of the importance of technological change for the evolution of spatial and social forms, together with an emphasis on the need to integrate technology in a broader framework of social relationships to understand the diversity of its effects on people's lives, on institutions, and, ultimately, on spatial forms and processes.

203. Castells, Manuel. 1988. "The New Industrial Space: Information Technology Manufacturing and Spatial Structure in the United States," pp. 43-99 in *America's New Market Geography*, G. Sternlieb and J. W. Hughes, eds. New Brunswick, NJ: Rutgers University, Center for Urban Policy Research.

Points out that in recent years, a growing stream of research has focused on the location of high-technology industries, the factors conditioning their spatial patterns, and the consequences of such patterns for regional development. This paper builds on the results obtained by such empirical research while elaborating a broader analytical framework to integrate what is known about the new industrial space. The author focuses specifically on information-technology manufacturing that appears to be the core of the new technologically advanced industries. Information-technology industries comprise semiconductors, computers, communications equipment, electronic automated machines and genetic engineering.

204. Christy, Craig V., and R. C. Ironside. 1988. "Performance of High-Technology Firms in a Peripheral Resource-Based Economy: Alberta, Canada." *Growth and Change* 19(4):88-100.

Focuses on the performance of high technology firms in Alberta, measured by financial growth, R&D activity, employment creation, and marketing. Data were drawn from a 100 percent survey of all identifiable high-tech firms in the province. A response rate of 34 percent (116 responses) was obtained. Results indicate that Alberta's high technology sector is composed mainly of small independent firms in the early stages of growth. Widely divergent revenue and profit trends were found among all firms while 41 percent of the respondents received government assistance to fund R&D programs. Of the respondent firms, 74 percent had recorded a net increase in full-time jobs in the preceding five years, or 27 jobs per firm. Markets within the province were most important to these firms (49 percent), followed by Canadian markets outside Alberta (35 percent) and foreign markets (16 percent). Overall, the systematic policies of support by the Alberta government were found to assist the growth of the high-tech industry.

205. Clair, Robert T. 1986. "The Labor-Intensive Nature of Manufacturing High-Technology Capital Goods." *Economic Review* (Federal Reserve Bank of Dallas) (1986):11-19.

Analyzes the production process for manufacturing high-technology equipment in an effort to determine whether the production characteristics of the industry are consistent with state objectives to encourage the expansion of labor-intensive industries. The author uses the U.S. Department of Commerce definition of high-technology equipment, which consists of office, computing, and accounting equipment, communications equipment, and instruments. The results show that an expansion in high-technology equipment manufacturing will create more jobs than expansion in manufacturing of other types of producers' durable goods but that high-technology manufacturing utilizes low-skilled workers and that the average wage in this industry is relatively low.

206. Cooper, Arnold C. 1986. "Entrepreneurship and High Technology," pp. 153-180 in *The Art and Sciences of Entrepreneurship*, D. L. Sexton and R. W. Smilor, eds. Cambridge, MA: Lexington Books.

Points out reasons why particular attention has been focused on new, high-technology firms. These are (1) high-tech firms offer possibilities for great growth (e.g., Apple Computer, Compaq Computer), (2) these firms are attractive from the standpoint of regional economic development as they produce little pollution and employ highly paid engineers and technicians, (3) small high-tech firms appear to account for a disproportionately high percentage of major technological innovations, (4) for potential entrepreneurs, the relatively high success rate of new high technology firms appears to offer attractive risk/return relationships, and (5) they add to the vitality and flexibility of the economy.

207.   Denison, Daniel R., and Stuart L. Hart. 1987. *Revival in the Rust Belt: Tracking the Evolution of an Urban Industrial Region.* Ann Arbor, MI: The University of Michigan, Graduate School of Business Administration and Institute for Social Research, 214 pp.

Argues that understanding the evolution of regional economies and the growth and decline of organizations is an important step in the formulation of state and local economic development policies, and also to the progress of academic research on organizations and the creation of new business. The authors describe a program of research on the evolution and development of an urban region, based on a detailed knowledge of the firms within it. The project focuses on Oakland County in southeastern Michigan, an area of the country which over the past few years has been better known for decline than for growth and development. It focuses in particular on the growing collection of technology-based firms that have gathered in this area in the northern Detroit suburbs. The area, "Automation Alley," is one of the fastest-growing high-technology corridors in the nation.

208.   Flynn, Patricia M. 1986. "Technological Change, the "Training Cycle," and Economic Development," pp. 282-308 in *Technology, Regions, and Policy*, J. Rees, ed. Totowa, NJ: Rowman and Littlefield.

Deals with industrial change and its implications for education and training, with emphasis on recent developments in high technology. The first section presents an overview of the effects of production life cycles on jobs and skill requirements. A "training cycle" in occupational preparation is delineated that evolves as the locus of training shifts from the workplace to the schools over the course of industrial development. A case study of the Lowell (Massachusetts) Labor Market Area (LMA) illustrates the usefulness of this approach in designing education and training policies to facilitate structural change and foster economic growth. The author then describes the changes that took place in the Lowell area during its transformation from a depressed, stagnating economy to a booming center of high-technology employment. The third section of the chapter summarizes the response of the educational institutions in the Lowell area to these labor market changes. The author concludes with a discussion of policy implications concerning training for industrial change and economic development.

209. Galbraith, Craig, and Alex F. DeNoble. 1988. "Location Decisions by High Technology Firms: A Comparison of Firm Size, Industry Type, and Institutional Form." *Entrepreneurship Theory and Practice* 13(2):31-47.

Reports results of a survey of 226 high technology firms regarding location decisions. Differences in location behavior between smaller and larger companies were examined as were differences based on industry type and institutional form. Results suggested that high technology firms are "footloose" in geographical location decisions, emphasizing factors such as ambience and availability of labor and property. Results also suggested smaller firms place more emphasis on ambience, while larger ones emphasize business-related factors. For site-specific decisions, firms (smaller companies in particular) were influenced by cost and access factors. These findings are relevant for municipalities and other ancillary services interested in high technology development.

210. Giaoutzi, Maria, and Peter Nijkamp, eds. 1988. *Informatics and Regional Development.* Aldershot, Hants, England: Gower Publishing Company, Ltd., 344 pp.

Defines informatics as the set of all modern high-tech activities involved in the design, use, and management of information systems, including hardware, software, and orgware. The authors argue that informatics may affect the "dictatorship of distance friction," while it also has an impact on the locational profile of entrepreneurs and households. The volume is based on papers presented at a conference in Delphi, Greece in 1986. The authors point out that the introduction of informatics will have urban and regional consequences, which are as yet hard to foresee, but which need to be given careful consideration.

211. Glasmeier, Amy K. 1986. "High-Tech Industries and the Regional Division of Labor." *Industrial Relations* 25(2):197-211.

Examines the possibility that high-tech industry is creating a spatial division of labor in which firms segment the more technical aspects of manufacturing from those of production and assembly, and seek out labor markets where the type of skill and labor relations needed to support different elements of production are found. The author presents the results of a two-stage analysis of the occupational structure and spatial location of high-tech industries and employment. After a brief review of theoretical and empirical work on the spatial division of labor, a model of the division of labor in high-tech industries is presented and then tested using industry occupational data for states for the years 1977 and 1980. Factors that may have encouraged the clustering of the more technical aspects of the high-tech industries in a few states, largely outside the traditional manufacturing belt, are proposed. The paper concludes with remarks about the impact of high-tech industries on the regional division of labor.

212. Glasmeier, Amy. 1990. "High-Tech Policy, High-Tech Realities: The Spatial Distribution of High-Tech Industry in America," pp. 67-96 in *Growth Policy in the Age of High Technology*, J. Schmandt and R. Wilson, eds. Winchester, MA: Unwin Hyman, Inc.

Examines the spatial distribution of high-tech industrial development during the 1970s and early 1980s (a period of rapid high-technology growth). Policy concerns are addressed through a systematic analysis of high-tech employment and industrial location behavior. The author begins by providing a broad overview of manufacturing location in the U.S. since the 1950s and discusses recent literature on high-tech industry location. Analysis of the distribution of high-tech jobs over the 1972-1982 period reveals that manufacturing states are still important centers for high-tech industry.

213. Glasmeier, Amy K. 1991. *The High-Tech Potential: Economic Development in Rural America*. New Brunswick, NJ: Rutgers University, Center for Urban Policy Research, 225 pp.

Examines the potential for rural America to participate in the development of high-technology industries and advanced services. The author examines the spatial evolution of high-tech industry across America's urban-rural continuum. Her analysis focuses on two distinct periods in the development of high-tech industry: premicroelectronics and postmicroelectronics. The author blends industry and place analysis to examine high-tech industries across the urban-rural continuum of counties in the United States. This analysis sets the stage for studying the spatial location of high-tech industries in rural counties within the four broad census regions. The author then examines the most glamorous and sought-after high-tech industries--computers, electronics, communications, and defense-dependent sectors--and evaluates the roles of various factors in influencing their location in rural regions. In subsequent chapters, the author examines the role of high-tech industries in rural counties of individual states. The role of state development policies in influencing location patterns is a special focus. The final section analyzes factors associated with nonmetropolitan high-tech plants and employment and changes over the 1972-82 period and discusses policy implications.

214. Glasmeier, Amy K. 1993. "High-Tech Manufacturing: Problems and Prospects," pp. 165-184 in *Economic Adaptation: Alternatives for Nonmetropolitan Areas*, D. L. Barkley, ed. Boulder, CO: Westview Press.

Argues that explanations of rural industrialization, based on models of cost-driven industry decentralization, have been superseded by production imperatives that emphasize workplace skills over strict differences in labor cost. In the past, rural areas could compete for low-skilled, branch plant employment. But today, skill requirements of high-tech industry are limiting industrial movement toward rural areas, and those relatively few high-tech employers locating in rural communities are only modestly changing the skill composition of rural labor markets. Nonmetro communities may benefit to a greater extent from future high-tech development; however, state and federal policy must be cognizant of the unintended urban bias of most technology-based industrial programs.

215. Goldstein, Harvey, and Emil E. Malizia. 1985. "Microelectronics and Economic Development in North Carolina," pp. 225-255 in *High Hopes for High Tech: Microelectronics Policy in North Carolina*, D. Whittington, ed. Chapel Hill, NC: University of North Carolina Press.

Discusses a number of issues: (1) likely trade impacts of forward and backward linkages between microelectronics and other industries in North Carolina, (2) the likely impacts on local labor markets, (3) the likely impacts on patterns of public expenditures and revenue generation, and (4) the potential for formation of new companies through spin-offs from microelectronic enterprises.

216. Gripaios, Peter, Paul Bishop, Rose Gripaios, and Claire Herbert. 1989. "High Technology Industry in a Peripheral Area: The Case of Plymouth." *Regional Studies* 23(2):151-157.

Presents a profile of high technology industry in Plymouth based upon the results of a postal survey and a series of interviews. The results suggest that, despite recent growth, Plymouth has not yet created an interlinked high technology sector. The firms in the sample operate in diverse areas, purchase little from the local economy, and are concerned about the lack of local suppliers. However, the attractive local environment and the availability of relatively cheap labor are important locational advantages. Finally, the authors discuss the results within the context of similar studies of other areas.

217. Hagey, M. J., and E. J. Malecki. 1986. "Linkages in High Technology Industries: A Florida Case Study." *Environment and Planning A* 18:1477-1498.

Uses survey and interview data from four high technology industrial sectors in northern Florida to examine the effect of several establishment and organizational characteristics on the strength of intrastate linkages, both for sophisticated and for routine inputs. The empirical findings show that local linkages of Florida's high technology industries are generally weak. Local linkages are strongest among small, locally owned research and development-intensive establishments.

218. Jarboe, Kenan Patrick. 1986. "Location Decisions of High-Technology Firms: A Case Study." *Technovation* 4:117-129.

Reports on a survey to determine factors affecting location decisions of 46 firms in the Ann Arbor, Michigan area. The firms spanned the range of "high-technology," including biomedical, computers, integrated manufacturing, optics, remote sensing, and others. The firms were generally small, rapidly growing, new companies with a large percentage of their personnel devoted to research and development activities. The majority of the firms were founded in the area, rather than attracted from the outside; most did not consider sites outside the Ann Arbor area when choosing their current site. According to the survey, the perceived strengths of the Ann Arbor area are its universities, quality of life, transportation networks, and work force. On the negative side, state and local taxes are seen as the area's greatest weaknesses. The area's lack of venture capital, certain local government regulations, and the perceived unavailability of certain support services and facilities are also troublesome.

219. Johnson, Merrill L. 1989. "Industrial Transition and the Location of High-Technology Branch Plants in the Nonmetropolitan Southeast." *Economic Geography* 65(1):33-47.

Examines the broad issue of industrial restructuring in the South, focusing on the role of industrial experience as a locational influence on selected high-technology industrial sectors. All counties in North Carolina, South Carolina, and Georgia were initially included in an examination using published data sources. A subsequent, more detailed analysis covers only high-technology branch plants in nonmetropolitan counties, using questionnaires as the primary source of information. The author concludes that no clear labor-oriented industrial transition process is identifiable in these states and that the introduction of high-technology branch plants to the nonmetropolitan South should not necessarily be interpreted as a meaningful departure from post industrial trends.

220. Joseph, R. A. 1989. "Technology Parks and Their Contribution to the Development of Technology-Oriented Complexes in Australia." *Environment and Planning C* 7:173-192.

Reports that one of the features that Australia has in common with other countries has been the encouragement of clusters of high-technology firms or technology-oriented complexes (TOCs). In Australia, the primary mechanism, for promoting TOCs has been technology parks. In this paper, technology park developments in Australia are reviewed from a perspective which emphasizes some key conceptual features of the literature in this area: agglomeration economies of high-technology firms and firm-university interaction; the creation of new high-technology complexes; and locational factors which make technology parks attractive to high-technology companies. Three Australian case studies, based on interviews with high-technology firms, are reported. One of the key findings from the research is that if Australian technology parks are aiming to establish TOCs that exhibit a high level of interaction between the park and a host university, then the present situation in Australia is far removed from this goal.

221. Keeble, D. E. 1989. "High-Technology Industry and Regional Development in Britain: The Case of the Cambridge Phenomenon." *Environment and Planning C* 7:153-172.

Discusses the nature and definition of high-technology industry and presents original evidence on the regional and local evolution of high-technology industry during 1981-1984 in Britain. The case of the Cambridge Phenomenon is reviewed in detail, drawing upon a range of recent research to document the scale, nature, and impacts of rapid high-technology growth in the Cambridge region, especially in the 1980s. The volume of such growth in the period 1981-1984 was greater in

Cambridgeshire than in any other county of Britain. The reasons for Cambridge's exceptional performance are discussed, and the article concludes with a brief consideration of policy issues arising from the region's experience, including the role of universities and science parks, of government defense and procurement policies, of local small-firm assistance structures, and of selective help to "threshold" firms.

222. Lugar, Michael I. 1984. "Does North Carolina's High-Tech Development Program Work?" *Journal of the American Planning Association* 50(3):280-289.

Evaluates high-tech economic development programs used in North Carolina in terms of their cost-effectiveness and their likely contribution to higher wages, more jobs, greater employment stability, and regionally balanced development. The author concludes that although North Carolina's high-tech economic development strategy is often cited as exemplary, it is not likely to achieve its development goals, mainly because it overemphasizes recruitment of industries. The author recommends a more even approach to economic development that emphasizes programs that are cost-effective and are aimed at existing traditional and emerging new businesses.

223. Malecki, Edward J. 1984. "High Technology and Local Economic Development." *Journal of the American Planning Association* 50(3):262-269.

Points out that structural changes in the American economy have prompted a shift in state and local economic growth policies toward attracting and generating high-technology industry. High technology is best defined as nonroutine economic activities directed toward developing new products and processes and toward small-volume production of innovative products and services. High technology relies most heavily on the availability of professional personnel and the diverse cultural, educational, and labor market attributes that attract those personnel. Two patterns are evident in the location of nonroutine high technology activity: continued agglomeration in established urban centers of high-technology, and dispersal to some new, smaller cities that have a set of attractive amenities. Public investment in education, research, and infrastructure will improve regions' capability to accommodate and benefit from future economic and technological change.

224. Malecki, Edward J. 1986. "Research and Development and the Geography of High-Technology Complexes," pp. 51-74 in

Technology, Regions, and Policy, J. Rees, ed. Totowa, NJ: Rowman and Littlefield.

Addresses the process of regional "high-tech" growth. The first section reviews the experience of four U.S. regions that may be labeled "high-tech": Boston and Route 128, Silicon Valley (California), Research Triangle (North Carolina), and Austin, Texas. The next section contrasts R&D and high-tech as different types of economic activity with substantially different regional development implications. Location decisions by high-technology firms illustrate the distinction and its significance for regional growth. The chapter concludes with some thoughts on the role of R&D in regional economic development.

225. Malecki, Edward J. 1989. "What About People in High Technology? Some Research and Policy Considerations." *Growth and Change* 20(1):67-79.

Suggests that an orientation towards people relates more accurately to the underlying processes of regional development and change, particularly those that focus on flows of people and information. The author undertakes a re-examination of several elements of regional research and policy in the high-tech context, including technical workers, entrepreneurship, the effect of new technology in the workplace, and the potential of public policies to address people related issues. The author concludes that a long-term perspective is necessary for public policies that address regional competitiveness.

226. Markusen, Ann. 1986. "High-Tech Plants and Jobs: What Really Lures Them?" *Economic Development Commentary* 10(3):3-7.

Reports on a study of 100 selected, four-digit (S.I.C.) industries that examines the geographical preferences and mobility of high-tech firms. The author concludes that amenities such as mild climate and a superior set of educational options are important to high-tech firms, but that high tech is not primarily concentrated in small firms, is not closely associated with university research efforts, and tends to draw highly skilled labor in its wake, rather than flock to it. Defense spending emerges as a major locational factor for this industry.

227. Miller, Roger, and Marcel Cote. 1987. *Growing the Next Silicon Valley: A Guide for Successful Regional Planning.* Lexington, MA: D.C. Heath and Co., 158 pp.

Deals with promoting economic development through high technology. The book is divided into four parts and nine chapters. The first part provides an introduction and examines the geography of high technology in the United States. The authors point out that while clusters may form in areas where leading-edge research is conducted, entrepreneurs will seize opportunities and rapidly diffuse the technology. The second part outlines a conceptual framework, first describing the key characteristics of a high-technology cluster and then explaining the processes of "incubation," "role modeling," and "sponsorship." The institutional infrastructures that fuel the agglomeration and entrepreneurial processes are analyzed, and then two case histories are presented. These are a detailed history of the growth of high technology in the Twin Cities (Minneapolis-St. Paul) and an account of the resurgence of high technology in Philadelphia, a city hard hit by the loss of manufacturing jobs. The book concludes with a discussion of action programs designed by public-private partnerships to accelerate the growth of high technology in a region.

228. Oakey, Ray. 1984. *High Technology Small Firms: Regional Development in Britain and the United States.* New York, NY: St. Martin's Press, 179 pp.

Examines the innovation process in small independent high technology firms. Within this wider investigation, detailed consideration is given to the manner in which innovation in these small firms is affected by diverse local industrial environments in Britain and the United States. Specific topics addressed include (1) effects of industrial structure on regional small firm growth, (2) agglomeration, innovation, and high technology industrial production, (3) linkages and innovation, (4) research and development and innovation, (5) labor and innovation, and (6) finance and innovation.

229. Premus, Robert. 1982. *Location of High Technology Firms and Regional Economic Development.* A staff study for the subcommittee on Monetary and Fiscal Policy of the Joint Economics Committee, Congress of the United States. Washington, D.C.: U.S. Government Printing Office, 70 pp.

Points out that more and more state and local governments are turning to local development programs to accelerate local economic growth and boost revenues. These development programs often center around such high growth and high technology industries as semiconductors, telecommunications, medical instruments, and related products. The author expresses that the enhanced competitive atmosphere that is emerging among states and localities has great potential to stimulate industrial innovation and technical change and thus enhance the Nation's competitive position and long-term economic progress. The study examines the growth of high technology sector jobs in the U.S. economy and concludes that these industries accounted for 75 percent of the net increase in manufacturing jobs between 1955 and 1979. The results of a survey of 691 high technology manufacturers are presented. The respondents reported on their plant expansion plans, the factors that influenced their choice of a region in which to locate, and factors that influenced choice of location within the region.

230. Rees, John, and Tim Lewington. 1990. "An Assessment of State Technology Development Programs," pp. 195-209 in *Growth Policy in the Age of High Technology*, J. Schmandt and R. Wilson, eds. Winchester, MA: Unwin Hyman, Inc.

Deals with the evolution of state, technology-based economic development programs and presents preliminary results of a national survey of companies aimed at assessing their experience with these new state initiatives. A taxonomy of state technology development programs is presented. The programs are classified into three main groups: (1) university-industry relationships, (2) encouraging new business startups, and (3) technology upgrading. Assessment of the impact of state technology development centers was focused on centers involved in microelectronics and computer-aided manufacturing. A survey of state officials in 1987 identified 38 of these centers in 20 states.

231. Rees, John and Howard A. Stafford. 1986. "Theories of Regional Growth and Industrial Location: Their Relevance for Understanding High-Technology Complexes," pp. 23-50 in *Technology, Regions, and Policy*, J. Rees, ed. Totowa, NJ: Rowman and Littlefield.

Begins with a review of the various partial theories of regional economic growth, each dealing with technological change in either an explicit or implicit fashion. From this review, the most appropriate elements of regional growth theory that help explain the development of high-technology complexes are identified. The authors point out that in order to appreciate the geographical orientation of high-technology industry, it is necessary to examine industrial location theory and how location factors implicit in that theory relate to high-technology industry. This is the focus of the second part of the chapter. The increasing involvement of states and cities in the competition for high-technology jobs has made it imperative that communities be aware of the location factors perceived to be important by decision makers before they develop strategies to lure high-technology companies.

232. Sampson, Gregory B. 1985. "Employment and Earnings in the Semiconductor Electronics Industry: Implications for North Carolina," pp. 256-295 in *High Hopes for High Tech: Microelectronics Policy in North Carolina*, D. Whittington, ed. Chapel Hill, NC: The University of North Carolina Press.

Examines employment and earnings in the semiconductor electronics industry and their implications for the recent efforts in North Carolina to make the state a new center for the microelectronics industry.

233. Sanderson, Susan W., and Brian J. L. Berry. 1986. "Robotics and Regional Development," pp. 171-186 in *Technology, Regions, and Policy*, J. Rees, ed. Totowa, NJ: Rowman and Littlefield.

Addresses two questions that arise in considering the role of robotics in regional development. These are (1) Is it likely that the emerging U.S. robotics industry will become localized in one or more regions of the country that will repeat Silicon Valley's experience as an industrial seedbed? and (2) What will be the impacts of robotics on the organization and location of user industries? Autonomous manufacturing systems, which apply sophisticated technology to improve the quality and efficiency of production, substitute capital for certain types of labor. Is it possible that these capital-labor substitutions will lead to new locational choice by user industries and cut short the development of low-wage regions, both domestically and overseas?

234. Sanderson, Susan Walsh, Gregory Williams, Timothy Ballenger, and Brian J. L. Berry. 1987. "Impacts of Computer-Aided Manufacturing on Offshore Assembly and Future Manufacturing Locations." *Regional Studies* 21(2):131-142.

Points out that multinational firms are rethinking their strategies for manufacturing in the face of increased international competition and global markets. New technologies, such as computer-aided manufacturing and robotics, have the potential for altering location decisions, in particular co-production activities between developed and developing countries. This paper develops unit cost models for comparing manual offshore assembly in Mexico and Singapore with automated manufacturing in the United States. Results show that for the range of generally less-sophisticated products currently assembled there, Mexico retains its cost advantage for all volumes considered. However, for volumes exceeding 310,000 units per year, U.S. flexible assembly begins to show lower unit costs than manual assembly in Singapore.

235. Smith, Stephen M., and David L. Barkley. 1989. "Contributions of High-Tech Manufacturing to Rural Economies." *Rural Development Perspectives* 5(3):6-11.

Reports results of a survey of 927 high- and low-tech nonmetropolitan manufacturing establishments in 11 western states. The high-tech facilities that were either headquarters or single-unit plants had a substantially higher percentage of their employees in the highest skill occupations (professional/technical and skilled production workers) than their low-tech counterparts. Among branch plants, however, there was no significant difference between high-tech and low-tech firms. The high-tech facilities also employed a slightly higher percentage of women (31 versus 28 percent). High-tech plants purchased a smaller percentage of their nonlabor inputs within the local area, 33 versus 42 percent.

236. Smith, Stephen M., and David L. Barkley. 1991. "Local Input Linkages of Rural High-Technology Manufacturers." *Land Economics* 67(4):472-483.

Identifies the determinants of the level of local backward linkages (input purchases) for high- and low-tech manufacturers located in nonmetropolitan counties in the western United States. The authors first discuss data definitions and sources and then describe the general characteristics of the establishments surveyed and the analytical model. Next, an econometric analysis of manufacturers' market linkages is undertaken to determine if the backward linkages of high- and low-tech establishments differ significantly after controlling for plant and community characteristics. Finally, the implications of the results are discussed.

237. Whittington, Dale, ed. 1985. *High Hopes for High Tech: Microelectronics Policy in North Carolina.* Chapel Hill: The University of North Carolina Press, 341 pp.

Reports that the microelectronics industry has become not only a focus of national economic policy, but also a target of numerous state and local economic development efforts. Strategies to attract microelectronics firms to specific locales have thus far taken two general forms: (1) the familiar industrial promotion policies that advertise the desirability of a state's "business climate," local quality of life, availability of industrial land and raw materials, and low interest loans, and (2) economic development strategies specifically directed at the microelectronics industry. The papers collected in this volume examine some of the planning and policy issues raised by North Carolina's effort to attract the microelectronics industry to the state. Although North Carolina's effort is representative of state polices adopted elsewhere, it has two distinguishing features that especially justify closer scrutiny. First, North Carolina is seeking to achieve excellence in microelectronics education within universities where that branch of technology has been relatively neglected. Second, it hopes to establish an industrial base in microelectronics in a region that lacks substantial existing investment in microelectronics.

AGE/TENURE

238. Buss, Terry F., and Xiannuan Lin. 1990. "Business Survival in Rural America: A Three-State Study." *Growth and Change* 21(3):1-8.

Uses employment insurance tax records (ES202) for Arkansas, Maine, and North Dakota to calculate and analyze new firm survival rates. Results show that new business survival rates are as high in rural areas as they are in urban areas. Further, survival rates in different industrial sectors are comparable, even when level of urbanization is taken into account.

239. Buss, Terry F., and Mark G. Popovich. 1988. *Growth From Within: New Businesses and Rural Economic Development in North Dakota.* Washington, D.C.: Council of State Planning Agencies, 105 pp.

Reports results of a study to examine the role and impact of new businesses on North Dakota. Some of the findings were (1) new businesses created during 1980-87 accounted for about 23 percent of all jobs (covered by unemployment insurance) in 1987, (2) most new rural businesses were started by long-term local residents, (3) the rate of job creation by new businesses was about the same in rural and urban areas, (4) most of the new businesses were in the trade and services sectors, (5) most rural new businesses required less than $25,000 to start and just over half were able to secure bank financing, (6) only 18 percent of the new rural businesses had used business assistance programs but, when these programs were used, they were highly rated, and (7) one-third of the new rural businesses intended to expand operations or add employees in the future.

240. Delaney, Edward J. 1993. "Technology Search and Firm Bounds in Biotechnology: New Firms as Agents of Change." *Growth and Change* 24(2):206-228.

Seeks to articulate the nature of change in relationships between firms in science-based industries and the technological infrastructure accessed to support innovation, as such industries mature out of the birth phase. Innovation is treated as decision making, identifying the firms as innovator and agent of change. Survey research suggests that a shift in the sourcing of information, and an associated shift in the character of the information accessed, occurred with maturation in the study industry, comprised of biotechnology firms in the U.S. "Early" and "later" forming firms show somewhat different technology sourcing patterns. Interviews were conducted to help interpret these findings. Implications for industry development are suggested.

241. Dillman, Buddy L., and Gordon L. Carriker. 1989. *New Business Starts in a South Carolina Piedmont County*. Bulletin 668. Clemson: South Carolina Agricultural Experiment Station, 29 pp.

Reports on research designed to enhance understanding of the present state of new business policy and practice. The first objective was to evaluate the availability and usefulness of the whole spectrum of business services as perceived by a variety of new business owners/operators, as contrasted with the perceptions of public- and private-sector service providers. A second objective was to ascertain whether there were any differences in the services provided in rural and urban areas.

242. Duche, Genevieve, and Suzane Savey. 1987. "The Rising Importance of Small and Medium-Sized Firms: Towards a New Industrial System," pp. 1-12 in *Industrial Change in Advanced Economies*, F. E. Ian Hamilton, ed. Beckenham, Kent, U.K.: Croom Helm Ltd.

Examines why the small firm is now the major element in the new organization of production. The authors use the French classification that defines small firms as those with less than 50 employees and medium sized enterprises as those with 50-499 workers. Three main reasons are seen as explaining the role of small-and medium-scale firms in reshaping the capitalist mode of production. First is their ability to accept some tasks or segments of the production process which have been externalized by large corporations. Second is their structural vocation to develop and to impose a new way of managing the workforce. Third is their ability to contribute to the stability of a minimum social consensus linked with the creation of jobs and the stabilization of the unemployment rate.

243.   Gould, Andrew, and David Keeble.   1985.   "New Firms and Rural
       Industrialization in East Anglia," pp. 43-71 in *Small Firms in
       Regional Economic Development: Britain, Ireland, and the United
       States*, D. J. Storey, ed. Cambridge, England: Cambridge University
       Press.

Examines the nature and extent of new manufacturing firm formation in
the predominately rural region of East Anglia between 1971-81. Since
the 1960s, East Anglia has been the fastest growing industrial region in
the U.K. with manufacturing employment increasing by 23 percent from
1965 to 1974. The findings indicate that East Anglia appears to be an
exceptionally conducive environment for new enterprise creation.   In
addition, the authors investigate the temporal pattern of new firm
formation, the nature of and reasons for marked spatial variations and
rural bias in formation rates, and the distinctive nature and locational
clustering of new "high technology" firms. The findings indicate that
small firm policies are not likely to be a major force in national industrial
regeneration, at least in the short run, because new firms (created between
1971 and 1981) provided only 4.7 percent of the region's total
manufacturing employment in 1981, although they comprised 18 percent
of the population of firms.

244.   Gruidl, John S. 1991. *New Businesses in Downstate Illinois.* Macomb,
       IL: Western Illinois University, Illinois Institute for Rural Affairs,
       60 pp.

Reports results of a 1990 survey of 731 entrepreneurs in downstate
Illinois.   The study area included all Illinois counties except for the
Chicago MSA. Key findings from the study were (1) entrepreneurs rarely
relocate to start a business, (2) they generally have long experience in a
source organization in the same industry as the new firm, (3) many have
experience starting other companies, (4) they generally commit large
amounts of personal funds to the enterprise, (5) bank financing for new
ventures is more readily available than is commonly perceived, (6) the
problems frequently mentioned by new business founders relate to
recruiting qualified employees, inadequate cash flow, and government
regulations, (7) the new business operators rely primarily on informal
networks of family, friends, and business associates for assistance, and (8)
employment growth of beginning businesses in rural areas lags behind
that of urban (metro) firms.

245.   Keeble, David, and Egbert Wever, eds. 1986. *New Firms and Regional
       Development in Europe.* Dover, NH: Croom Helm, 322 pp.

Focuses on new firms and research by economic geographers and regional economists on their spatial distribution in the countries of the European Community. New firms are defined as those which did not exist before and which are set up by their founders as independent businesses. Following an introductory section that establishes the framework for the volume, 13 chapters explore issues related to the formation and location of new firms in Belgium, Denmark, France, Germany, Greece, Ireland, Italy, The Netherlands, and the United Kingdom. In addition, one chapter addresses small and medium sized establishments in western Europe (i.e., the EEC-member states). The authors find that there is clear evidence of a substantial resurgence in the numbers of new, independent small businesses in most European countries since the 1960s, after decades of decline. With respect to the geography of new firm formation, they find that (1) Europe's largest diversified cities and their surrounding metropolitan regions tend to exhibit high rates, and large volumes, of new firm formation in both manufacturing and service industries, (2) high rates were also characteristic of a number of previously unindustrialized rural regions, including southern France (the Midi), several regions of Britain (the South West, East Anglia, West Midlands and Central Wales, and the Scottish Highlands), north-central Ireland, Denmark's Jutland, and Adriatic Central Italy, and (3) the lowest rates of new manufacturing firm formation are now found in Europe's old specialized urban-industrial regions.

246. Kirchhoff, Bruce A., and Bruce D. Phillips. 1988. "The Effect of Firm Formation and Growth on Job Creation in the United States." *Journal of Business Venturing* 3:261-272.

Demonstrates the importance of new firm formation to economic growth. It begins by providing data that describe the United States as having had greater employment growth then most developed nations of the world over the last 25 years, and focuses upon why job growth in the United States has exceeded that of other nations. The authors examine data on the relative contribution of small and large firms to U.S. job growth and conclude that small (less than 100 employees) firms are the major source of net new job creation. They also find that firm entry rates vary considerably from period to period (range: 10.4 percent to 12.5 percent) whereas exit rates remain relatively stable from period to period (range: 9.6 percent to 10.4 percent). Thus, variation in entrepreneurial activity (the formation of new firms) is the major cause of net increases in the number of firms. In both the U.S. and the U.K., net firm increases are positively related to overall economic activity. Data for 1976 through 1984 are analyzed, and the results show that new entries account for 74.0

percent of the 50.8 million new jobs created in the U.S. Expansions of existing firms accounted for 26.0 percent. Small firms (less than 500 employees) produced 54.6 percent of the entry jobs and 56.8 percent of the expansion jobs. Job losses total 33.8 million, 79.0 percent due to exits and 21.0 percent to contractions. Small firms accounted for 53.6 percent of the jobs lost from exits and 47.8 percent of those lost from contractions. Overall, small firms accounted for 60.5 percent of the 17.0 million net new jobs.

247.   Leistritz, F. Larry. 1991. "New or Expanding Basic Sector Firms in the Upper Great Plains: Implications for Community Development Practitioners." *Journal of the Community Development Society* 22(1):56-82.

Identifies new or growing basic sector businesses in the Upper Midwest and estimates both their contribution to local economies and factors critical to their location decisions. Manufacturing firms made up more than 78 percent of the 314 respondents. Total annual sales per firm averaged about $8.5 million, with close to 65 percent to out-of-state markets. The average firm reported annual expenditures within the state of $3.8 million, or 55 percent of average total outlays. The percentage of nonlabor expenditures made within the state, however, was quite variable among firms. The surveyed firms created an average of 39 jobs per firm over the previous 10 years. The ratings of different factors related to making location decisions were generally similar among all types of firms. Work attitudes and labor productivity were generally rated more highly than were wage levels. State incentives and regulatory climate were also important to many firms.

248.   Leistritz, F. Larry. 1992. "Economic Impacts of New and Expanding Firms in the Upper Great Plains." *Review of Agricultural Economics* 14(1):81-91.

Reports on a study that identified new or growing basic sector businesses in Nebraska, North Dakota, and South Dakota and determined their contribution to the state economy, as measured by their employment creation and expenditures to suppliers within the state. Data from 314 firms were used in the analysis. The average firm reported annual expenditures within the state of $3.8 million or 55 percent of total outlays, but the percentages of nonlabor expenditures made within the state were quite variable. Expansion of existing firms accounted for 45 percent of all new jobs created by the group, while relocating firms were responsible for 33 percent and new firms were credited with almost 23 percent.

249. Lin, Xiannuan, Terry F. Buss, and Mark Popovich. 1990. "Entrepreneurship Is Alive and Well in Rural America: A Four State Study." *Economic Development Quarterly* 4(3):254-259.

Finds that rural new businesses contribute substantially to job creation, that rural areas are as competitive as urban areas in developing new businesses, and that rural new businesses are as diversified as urban businesses. Based on analysis of employment insurance (ES202) data for Arkansas, Iowa, Maine, and North Dakota, the authors conclude that rural economies are not as disadvantageous to entrepreneurship as conventional wisdom would have us believe.

250. Malecki, Edward J. 1988. "New Firm Startups: Key to Rural Growth." *Rural Development Perspectives* 4(2):18-23.

Indicates that new startup firms may be more important to economic development than either branch plants or expansion of existing businesses. The author discusses factors influencing new firm formation, rural-urban differences in these factors, and strategies that rural areas might pursue to encourage entrepreneurship.

251. Miller, James P. 1989. *Survival and Growth of Independent Firms and Corporate Affiliates in Metro and Nonmetro America.* Rural Development Research Report No. 74. Washington, D.C.: USDA, Economic Research Service, ARED.

Analysis of new firm survival and growth during 1980-1986 reveals that local, independent firms survived better and grew faster than corporate affiliates in nonmetro areas. Independent firms quickly reached their optimum size after beginning operation. The rate of employment expansion for nonmetro independent firms was about half that of metro independent firms. Corporate affiliates in traditional nonmetro industries dependent on natural resources and low-wage labor continued to locate mostly in nonmetro areas. In developing future strategies for industrial development, the strengths and weaknesses of corporate ownership and control should be balanced against those of local ownership.

252. Miller, James P. 1990. "Business Expansion and Retention in the Great Lakes States, 1976-1980," pp. 17-31 in *The Retention and Expansion of Existing Businesses*, George W. Morse, ed. Ames, IA: Iowa State University Press.

Investigates the importance of existing businesses in the job generation process in the East North Central census division (i.e., Wisconsin, Illinois,

Michigan, Indiana, and Ohio) from 1976 to 1980. The author uses the phrase, job generation process, to refer to the relative contribution of business startups, closings, and expansions to total employment growth. The analysis was based on the U.S. Establishment and Enterprise Microdata (USEEM), created by the Brookings Institution for the U.S. Small Business Administration and derived from the Dun and Bradstreet files. Results indicate that expansions of existing businesses created new jobs at a faster rate than startups in every sector except trade.

253. Miller, James P. 1991. "New Rural Businesses Show Good Survival and Growth Rates." *Rural Development Perspectives* 7(3):25-29.

Reports that local independent businesses foster self-identity in rural communities much more than do corporate affiliates, and data from 1980-86 show that they may also weather recession better. As sales fall, parent companies often close down rural branches to streamline operations. "Homegrown" rural firms benefit from low startup (land and labor) costs, but once established, their employment grows more slowly than metro businesses.

254. O'Farrell, P. N., and R. Crouchley. 1985. "An Industrial and Spatial Analysis of New Firm Formation in Ireland," pp. 101-134 in *Small Firms in Regional Economic Development: Britain, Ireland, and the United States*, D. J. Storey, ed. Cambridge, England: Cambridge University Press.

Focuses upon the indigenous new firm formation process and presents evidence on temporal trends in formation rates, spatial variations at regional and county level, and inter-industry differences. The authors also analyze new firm formation rates both sectorally and spatially within a multivariate framework in order to identify some of the factors underlying variations in entry. Finally, policy implications of the results are discussed. The results indicate that the entry rate of new firms in Ireland is similar to those observed in Norway, Canada, and the U.S. (although for different periods), but perhaps 40 percent higher than the rate for the U.K.

255. Popovich, Mark G., and Terry F. Buss. 1987. *Rural Enterprise Development: An Iowa Case Study*. Washington, D.C.: Council of State Policy and Planning Agencies. 83 pp.

Summarizes results of a study that sought to (1) determine the characteristics of new enterprises and their owners in rural areas, (2) identify the barriers and problems encountered in the formation and operation of new enterprises, and (3) analyze implications of the data for development and implementation of public policy. Telephone interviews with businesses in four Iowa counties constituted the primary data base for the study. Almost two-thirds of the new enterprises were retail trade or service firms. Most new firms served local markets; 84 percent sold all their goods and services within 50 miles of their business location.

256. Popovich, Mark G., and Terry F. Buss. 1989. "Entrepreneurs Find Niche Even in Rural Communities." *Rural Development Perspectives* 5(3):11-14.

Reports that new businesses, begun since 1980, employed 23 percent of North Dakota's workers in 1987. The percentage of employment accounted for by new firms in agriculturally dependent counties was 24 percent. Service and retail firms accounted for over half of the new businesses and almost two-thirds of the total new business employment. About two-thirds of the entrepreneurs had strong local ties; only about one-fifth changed their county residence to start their business, and 57 percent started their business in the county in which they were born.

257. Reynolds, Paul, and Brenda Miller. 1988. *1987 Minnesota New Firms Study: An Exploration of New Firms and Their Economic Contributions.* Minneapolis, MN: University of Minnesota, Center for Urban and Regional Affairs, 142 pp.

Indicates that new firms contributed between 6 and 14 percent of new jobs and 5 to 12 percent of personal income in Minnesota in 1986. Presence of young adults was the leading explanatory variable. Firms' growth records were analyzed, and characteristics of high growth firms were identified.

258. Schmenner, Roger W., Joel C. Huber, and Randall L. Cook. 1987. "Geographic Differences and the Location of New Manufacturing Facilities." *Journal of Urban Economics* 21:83-104.

Introduces two innovations to the empirical study of plant location: (1) division of the decision into stages and (2) use of plant-specific characteristics to either magnify or temper factors defined at the state level. The plant-specific characteristics derive from a study of Fortune 500 plants that were opened in the 1970s. A number of relationships are derived from considerations of expected profitability that relate site selection to state and firm characteristics. These are tested through a series of multinomial logit models. The results confirm that the plant location decision can be usefully approached as a staged process and that geographically defined differences are not sufficient, by themselves, to explain why some states do better than others in attracting new plants. When plant-specific characteristics are used to modify the state-based factors, the explanation becomes richer and more powerful.

259. Shaffer, Ron E., and Glen C. Pulver. 1985. "Regional Variations in Capital Structure of New Small Businesses: The Wisconsin Case," pp. 101-134 in *Small Firms in Regional Economic Development: Britain, Ireland, and the United States*, D. J. Storey, ed. Cambridge, England: Cambridge University Press.

Examines the functioning of the capital market for new small firms in a thinly populated region compared to a heavily populated region and in urban and rural locations in Wisconsin. The functioning of the capital market is examined through similarities and differences in the financial structure, credit denial experiences, and perceptions of capital availability among firms in the different regions. The thinly populated portion of northern Wisconsin and the more densely populated southern section of the state are the regions used in the analysis. Data was collected in 1979-80 through personal interviews with owners of new small businesses. The businesses employed less than 150 people and had not existed under current ownership prior to 1976. Information from 134 firms constituted the data base for the analysis. The authors conclude that capital markets in Wisconsin appear to be functioning relatively well for small businesses, but they caution that (1) the data came from firms that had successfully started and continued for up to four years, (2) the decision making guidelines and capacity of lending institutions appear to be highly variable, (3) a composite capital stress index indicated that 44 percent of the firms did not believe capital markets were functioning adequately, and (4) capital stress appears to be greater in rural areas.

260. Storey, D. J. 1985. "The Problems Facing New Firms." *Journal of Management Studies* 22(3):327-345.

Investigates problems reportedly encountered by firms new to the county of Cleveland (U.K.) between 1972 and 1979 (i.e., before many of the currently available initiatives designed to assist small firms were implemented). The surveyed firms include both wholly new businesses and those which previously existed outside the county. The purpose of the study was to provide insights into the problems of such firms with a view toward tailoring public policies to more effectively serve their needs.

The study area (the county of Cleveland) is an area which in 1983 had the highest rate of unemployment of any county in mainland Britain. The author compares the problems facing wholly new firms and those of all other firms new to Cleveland (i.e., branch plants and relocating firms).

261. Wilhelm, Phyllis. 1987. *New Business Startups in Rural Northwest Wisconsin.* Madison, WI: University of Wisconsin, Department of Rural Sociology, 88 pp.

Presents the preliminary findings of a study of 300 business owners in Northwest Wisconsin, based on a 1987 survey. The primary purpose of the research was to identify conditions facilitating new business startups in rural regions. The research was designed to focus on four basic issues: (1) structure of new businesses, (2) characteristics of new business owners, (3) major constraints on new business formation, and (4) major facilitators in the creation of new businesses. The survey included 101 new manufacturing firms (a total census) and 199 new nonmanufacturing businesses. The results indicate that new nonmanufacturing businesses generally employ fewer workers and are less likely to offer a benefit package. In addition, nonmanufacturers are more likely to hire part-time workers, rather than full-time employees.

TELECOMMUNICATIONS

262. Arnheim, Louise. 1988. *Telecommunications Infrastructure and Economic Development in the Northeast-Midwest Region.* Washington, D.C.: Northeast-Midwest Institute, 22 pp.

Examines pertinent economic and technological trends, and how telecommunications infrastructure plays a role in various businesses and industries in the 18 states which comprise the Northeast-Midwest region. The author also examines what state and federal policy makers can do to ensure the continued development and vitality of that infrastructure in the future.

263. Arthur D. Little Inc. 1992. *Study of the Role of the Telecommunications Industry in Iowa's Economic Development.* Des Moines, IA: Iowa Utilities Board and Department of Economic Development, 164 pp.

Provides a comprehensive analysis of Iowa's telecommunications resources and needs and offers recommendations on the best ways to ensure deployment of new communications technology for the state's maximum economic advantage. The authors find that Iowa has a strong and advanced telecommunications infrastructure, particularly relative to other rural states. However, Iowa depends too greatly on analog switches and lines, does not have sufficient SS7 capabilities, has too many multiparty lines, does not have universally available cellular or CATV coverage, and has many areas of the state where quality of service and costs of service are inadequate or cause for complaint. Gaps in the telecommunications infrastructure exist and must be addressed. The finance, insurance, and service sectors, as well as network manufacturing and agribusiness sectors in Iowa all require advanced telecommunications technologies and capabilities to stay competitive. The health care and education sectors are particularly exposed without advanced telecommunications infrastructure. The authors also find that improved telecommunications infrastructure is more important to the business climate and quality of life for rural Iowa than for urban Iowa. The authors recommend a development strategy that involves speeding up the time frame for electromechanical switch conversion, conversion of interexchange trunks to fiber, SS7 deployment, cellular coverage, selective fiber deployment to the curb, and the elimination of multiparty lines.

264. Bakis, Henri. 1987. "Telecommunications and the Global Firm," pp. 130-160 in *Industrial Change in Advanced Economies*, F. E. Ian Hamilton, ed. Beckenham, Kent, U.K.: Croom Helm Ltd.

Points out that, although research into local and regional impacts of telecommunications has been undertaken for some time, especially with reference to metropolitan decentralization of nonmanufacturing functions, the international framework into which local and subnational linkages and effects are tied has attracted limited attention. Analysis of the internal telecommunications of a multinational company (International Business Machines [IBM]) is used as a case study to provide insights into information flows between units of a firm as well as into the hierarchy of regional subnational, regional subcontinental, and world patterns of spatial interaction comprising, and dependent upon, those information flows.

265. Blazar, William A. 1985. "Telecommunications: Harnessing It for Development." *Economic Development Commentary* 9(3):8-11.

Points out that the nation's economy, particularly in urban areas, now depends heavily on businesses dealing in information, finance and services rather than goods. As a group these businesses are commonly referred to as the service sector. The author points out that communications systems are to service businesses what railroads, canals, and highways are to heavy manufacturing--they are the principal means for service sector businesses to get their product to market. The author then examines whether a city or region can affect development by improving its telecommunications infrastructure.

266. Bradshaw, Ted K. 1990. *Rural Development and Telecommunications Potential and Policy.* Working Paper 524. Berkeley, CA: University of California, Institute of Urban and Regional Development, 72 pp.

Examines the role of telecommunications in rural economic development and suggests the policy directions that will best utilize the potential of telecommunications in rural areas. The report concludes that telecommunications, like virtually all other technological developments, is one of many factors which are important for rural development and that telecommunications capacity *alone* has virtually no impact on rural development. Consequently, for telecommunications to be a positive benefit for rural communities, it must be part of an integrated local development effort that links telecommunications to economic development through a strategy that includes strengthening community organizations and upgrading human resources.

267. Center for Rural Pennsylvania. 1992. *Telelinked Business: A New Horizon for Rural Pennsylvania.* Technical Paper No. 12. Harrisburg, PA: Center for Rural Pennsylvania, 19 pp.

Explores the potential of telelinked business to bring renewed economic vitality to rural Pennsylvania. The report provides examples of successful telelinked businesses and the advantages for employers, workers, and communities. Special attention is given to the role of state government in promoting private initiatives in the development of rural telelinked businesses.

268. Estabrooks, Maurice F., and Rodolphe H. Lamarche, eds. 1987. *Telecommunications: A Strategic Perspective on Regional, Economic, and Business Development.* Moncton, New Brunswick: The Canadian Institute for Research on Regional Development, 225 pp.

Is based on papers presented at a conference on telecommunications and economic development. The papers address four major themes: (1) historical, technological, and sociocultural perspectives on telecommunications, (2) telecommunications and urban and regional development, (3) telecommunications and international development, and (4) telecommunications and business development.

269. Fulton, William. 1989. "Getting the Wire to the Sticks." *Governing* 2(11):34-43.

Reports on successes of telecommunication-intensive businesses in nonmetropolitan areas and the role of advances in telecommunications technology in fostering those successes. The focus is on the town of Kearney, Nebraska, and on several businesses that are dependent on advanced telecommunications technology. These are (1) Cabela's, a large mail-order sporting goods catalogue house, (2) Electronics Marketing Resource Group, a firm that provides software, consulting, and data processing services for college financial aid offices, and (3) WATS Marketing, a telemarketing firm. The author discusses the need for nonmetropolitan communities to have access to modern telecommunications technology in order to be economically competitive and examines the potential role of the states in ensuring that access. Recent trends toward state deregulation of telecommunications services are discussed, but the author concludes that there is no assurance that rural businesses will benefit from deregulation.

270. Gillespie, A., and H. Williams. 1988. "Telecommunications and the Reconstruction of Regional Comparative Advantage." *Environment and Planning A* 20:1311-1321.

Illustrates the ways in which telecommunications--seen within an information economy perspective--is coming to assume a central status both in the process of economic development and in the redefinition of spatial relationships. This increasing centrality poses major challenges for the regulatory environments within which telecommunications-based innovations are being shaped. Further, a number of questions are raised by these developments concerning the changing nature of regional comparative advantage in an increasingly internationalized information economy.

271. Goddard, J. B., and R. Pye. 1977. "Telecommunications and Office Location." *Regional Studies* 11:19-30.

Reviews the role of communications in office location decisions and the possible effects of relocation on business contacts. These effects are elaborated by reference to surveys of office communications patterns in different locational situations. A simple model is introduced in which the communications costs of possible decentralized locations are compared to potential savings, particularly office rents and clerical wages. The possible impact of telecommunications on the interaction between locations and communications is also considered in the model. A discussion of public policies concerning advanced telecommunications systems concludes the paper.

272.   Hansen, Suella, David Cleevely, Simon Wadsworth, Hilary Bailey, and Oliver Bakewell. 1990. "Telecommunications in Rural Europe: Economic Implications." *Telecommunications Policy* 14:207-222.

Outlines a study undertaken on behalf of the Commission of the European Communities by Analysys Ltd. using advanced econometric modeling techniques. The main findings are that substantial aggregate employment gains are likely to result from investment in telecommunications and information technology in Europe's rural communities. The cost of creating this new employment compares very favorably with other means. However, telecommunications operators may suffer considerable net cash outflows in the initial years of investment, so that it may be necessary to deploy some form of public assistance to get the investment off the ground.

273.   Hudson, Heather E. 1987. "Ending the Tyranny of Distance: The Impact of New Communications Technologies in Rural North America," pp. 91-105 in *Competing Visions, Complex Realities: Social Aspects of the Information Society*, J. R. Schement and L. A. Lieurouw, eds. Norwood, NJ: Ablex Publishing Corporation.

Reviews findings on the role of telecommunications in rural social and economic development, and recent applications of telecommunications and information technologies in agriculture, rural education, and social service delivery. It then examines possible future impacts of these technologies, and the issues that may influence the nature and extent of their effects.

274.   Hudson, Heather E., and Edwin B. Parker. 1990. "Information Gaps in Rural America." *Telecommunications Policy* 14:193-205.

Discusses the challenges facing the U.S. telecommunications industry in the context of rapid changes affecting the rural economy. The structural shift in the national economy towards services and information-based activities has generally worked to the disadvantage of rural areas. Improving the provision of telecommunications services could help overcome their handicaps and improve the efficiency and productivity of rural businesses, but it will be necessary to extend access to telecommunication services and improve switching systems and transmission quality. The article concludes with a set of policy goals and recommendations addressed to federal and state government institutions.

275. Kutay, Aydan. 1986. "Effects of Telecommunications Technology on Office Location." *Urban Geography* 7:243-257.

Investigates the likely impacts of telecommunications technology on the clustering of office activities in central business districts. A survey of the 50 largest companies headquartered in downtown Pittsburgh provided information for a model of office decentralization. One of the major survey findings is that downtown offices are prompted to relocate by the diseconomies of downtown, and telecommunications enable the firm to select a location where it can overcome these downtown diseconomies. High space costs, lack of space for expansion, and high taxes were stated as unfavorable aspects of a downtown location. The authors conclude that modern telecommunications and computer technologies will accelerate the deconcentration of office activities. Some of the office employment displaced from downtown locations may become concentrated around major airports as national and international contacts are gaining more weight than those within the central business district.

276. Leistritz, F. Larry. 1993. "Telecommunications Spur North Dakota's Rural Economy." *Rural Development Perspectives* 8(2):7-11.

Reports that in the past few years, several telecommunications-based firms expanded to rural areas, bringing employment opportunities and boosting rural economies. But what kinds of jobs do they actually offer? In North Dakota, new telecommunication jobs seem to offer employee wages and fringe benefits comparable with those of new manufacturing jobs.

277. Lesser, Barry, and Pamela Hall. 1987. *Telecommunications Services and Regional Development: The Case of Atlantic Canada.* Halifax, Nova Scotia: The Institute for Research on Public Policy, 185 pp.

Points out that the advent of the information age is propelling the Canadian economy and society towards major structural, transformative change. The authors then address the question of how the benefits of this change will be shared among Canada's regions. They point out that in considering the regional impact of the information economy in Canada, the telecommunications sector occupies a central position. For less developed regions, telecommunications could provide a means of compensating for disadvantages of location otherwise posed by distance. However, telecommunications advances may promote either a centralization or a decentralization of economic activity on a regional basis. A modern, up-to-date telecommunications infrastructure is a necessary but not sufficient condition for periphery regions to gain both absolutely and relative to center regions in terms of economic development. Government policy initiatives which could benefit Canada's less advantaged regions are discussed.

278. Mesa Consulting. 1990. *Telecommunications and Rural Economic Development.* Washington, D.C.: United States Telephone Association.

Provides examples of how advanced telecommunications facilities and services can assist in the economic recovery and future development of rural areas in the United States. The study's scope is twofold: (1) to focus on the role that the independent telephone companies, and to a lesser extent the regional Bell operating companies, are playing in the deployment of advanced facilities and services to rural areas, and (2) to examine how a modern network serves as a platform for economic growth and social progress. The report consists primarily of case studies, which fall into four major groups: (1) modern telecommunications networks (five examples of networks serving rural areas), (2) telecommunications and social progress (with examples drawn from education and telemedicine), (3) telecommunications and business development (with examples from telemarketing, agribusiness, and finance), and (4) international overview.

279. Metzger, Robert O., and Mary Ann Von Glinow. 1988. "Off-Site Workers: At Home and Abroad." *California Management Review* 30(3):101-111.

Explores the issues raised by employing off-site workers (i.e., the potential tradeoffs in utilizing the off-site telecommuter) and reflects on the fundamental economic issues raised by these very new telecommunications-based off-site/off-shore jobs. The authors report that there are two distinct types of off-site data processing jobs: (1) the data-processing professional, telemarketer, or administrator, usually based in the home and linked to the employer or customers by computer and telephone line and (2) the off-shore data input clerk processing routine transactions from low wage base countries in the Caribbean and in Asia.

280. National Council for Urban Economic Development. 1992.
      *Telecommunications and Rural Economic Development: Improving
      Local Competitiveness.* Washington, D.C.: National Council for
      Urban Economic Development, U.S. Economic Development
      Administration, and GTE Telephone Operations, 66 pp.

      Presents the discussion of telecommunications and economic development
      in a format that exposes state and local policy makers to the issues while
      offering practitioners ideas of how to implement strategies designed to
      take advantage of their respective localities' changing economic base.
      The report is developed from presentations made at a Policy Forum held
      on September 19, 1991, in Dallas, Texas, combined with additional case
      studies and editorial commentaries developed since that meeting. The
      primary purpose is to begin bridging the gap between telecommunications
      policy, which is being developed at the federal and state level, and the
      rural economic development policy that is being developed in localities
      throughout the country.

281. Parker, Edwin B. 1990. "Communications Investment to Promote
      Economic Development," pp. 43-67 in *Infrastructure Investment and
      Economic Development.* Washington, D.C.: USDA, Economic
      Research Service.

      Points out that investing in telecommunications services for rural areas
      will not ensure economic development in those areas. However, the
      availability of basic telephone service is necessary for the success of
      almost any business or economic development activity. The author
      reports that many rural areas are still served by telephone systems that do
      not offer the basic services needed by businesses (i.e., single-party touch
      tone telephone service that provides quality sufficient for facsimile [fax]
      or data transmission).

282. Parker, Edwin B., and Heather E. Hudson with Don A. Dillman, Sharon
      Strover, and Frederick Williams. 1992. *Electronic Byways: State
      Policies for Rural Development Through Telecommunications.*
      Boulder, CO: Westview Press, 306 pp.

      Argues that, given the dynamics of today's global and national
      economies, a modern telecommunications infrastructure holds one
      promising answer for rural economic development. Advanced
      telecommunications is a versatile enabling tool that, in combination with
      strategic community development planning, can open up a wealth of new
      opportunities--to "grow" businesses, improve government and social

services, enhance public education, and build new bonds of local and regional community. The authors explain how these goals can be achieved through state government policies designed to exploit telecommunications potentials for rural development.

283. Qvortrup, Lars. 1989. "The Nordic Telecottages: Community Teleservice Centres for Rural Regions." *Telecommunications Policy* 13(1):59-68.

Discusses the telecottages (or Community Teleservice Centers, as they are officially called) that have become operative in Denmark, Finland, Norway, and Sweden in recent years. The main function of the centers is to provide isolated villages with access to telecommunications and information services. The background and origins of the telecottages are examined and their structure and functions described. An evaluation of their contribution to local communities is made as well as an assessment of their future potential and development, particularly in the context of a developing country.

284. Rowley, Thomas D., and Shirley L. Porterfield. 1993. "Can Telecommunications Help Rural Areas Overcome Obstacles to Development?" *Rural Development Perspectives* 8(2):2-6.

Reports that telecommunications can help to reduce rural isolation, improve access to services, and increase business efficiency. However, metro and international competition may limit the benefits of telecommunications for rural areas and possibly widen the development gap. Still, telecommunications are essential for full nonmetro participation in the national and international economies and are an essential part of an overall rural development strategy.

285. Rowley, Thomas D., and Shirley L. Porterfield. 1993. "Removing Rural Development Barriers Through Telecommunications: Illusion or Reality?" pp. 247-264 in *Economic Adaption: Alternatives for Nonmetropolitan Areas*, D. L. Barkley, ed. Boulder, CO: Westview Press.

Examines the relationship between rural development and telecommunications by assessing the potential for enhanced telecommunications to overcome barriers to the development of rural economies. While a common perspective for analyzing the role of telecommunication innovations in rural economic development is an accounting of the various ways these innovations may be put to use in rural areas, the authors examine the extent to which telecommunications can alleviate the economic problems of rural areas (low incomes, slow job growth, high unemployment, and population outmigration). First, the authors examine the historical stance of the federal government regarding telecommunications. Next, they turn to the recent flurry of activities promoting telecommunications as a rural development tool. Finally, the principal barriers to nonmetropolitan economic development are summarized, and the role of telecommunications in eliminating these barriers is proposed.

286. Schmandt, Jurgen, Frederick Williams, and Robert H. Wilson, eds. 1989. *Telecommunications Policy and Economic Development: The New State Role.* New York, NY: Praeger Publishers, 299 pp.

Reports that the telecommunications industry has seen tremendous change in the recent years. The forces for change include technological innovation, a move away from strict monopoly regulation, and the continuing transition of the U.S. economy from a traditional manufacturing base to a service base. Telecommunications has been an integral, although often unrecognized, factor in economic development. As the AT&T divestiture and associated decisions have moved a significant part of the telecommunications policy debate from the federal to the state level, many of the arguments to modify state policies have been couched in the language of economic development. The authors examine the link between telecommunications and economic development from two perspectives: (1) that of state programs to retain, attract, or promote formation of businesses within a state and (2) that of efforts to enhance the productive capacity of the economy. The study focuses on nine states: California, Florida, Illinois, Nebraska, New York, Texas, Vermont, Virginia, and Washington. The authors focus on four principal areas: (1) states as telecommunications policymakers, (2) the link between telecommunications and economic development, (3) universal service, and (4) states as users of telecommunications.

287. Schmandt, Jurgen, Frederick Williams, Robert H. Wilson, and Sharon Strover, eds. 1990. *The New Urban Infrastructure: Cities and Telecommunications.* New York, NY: Praeger Publishers, 327 pp.

Explores the state of the telecommunications environment in 12 North American cities and analyzes numerous issues affecting the relationship between cities and telecommunications. The cities studied are Atlanta, Boston, El Paso-Ciudad Jaurez, Houston, Los Angeles, Miami, Minneapolis, New York City, Phoenix, Pittsburgh, Seattle, and Toronto.

The study is organized around four primary topics: (1) the relationship between the cities' characteristics and their level of telecommunications development; (2) the nature of interactions among the various stakeholders in the telecommunications arena and the manner in which the interaction patterns affect telecommunications development; (3) city governments' roles as telecommunications planners and users; and (4) the relationship between telecommunications and urban economic development.

288. Schmandt, Jurgen, Frederick Williams, Robert H. Wilson, and Sharon Strover, eds. 1991. *Telecommunications and Rural Development: A Study of Private and Public Sector Innovation.* New York, NY: Praeger Publishers, 262 pp.

Results from growing interest in how changes in telecommunications and innovation in telecommunications technology can influence rural revitalization. The researchers address three major questions. First, what sorts of innovative telecommunications applications occur in rural areas? The authors attempt to determine the origins of each application and the key players responsible for the innovation (e.g., grassroots organizations, local businesses, telephone companies, and policymakers). Second, what role does telecommunications play in innovation and economic development in rural areas? The authors examine whether and how telecommunications may be a catalyst for rural economic development. Finally, what are the policy and development implications of innovative telecommunications?

289. Steinle, Wolfgang. 1988. "Telematics and Regional Development in Europe: Theoretical Considerations and Empirical Evidence," pp. 72-89 in *Informatics and Regional Development*, M. Giaoutzi and P. Nijkamp, eds. Aldershot, Hants, England: Gower Publishing Company, Ltd.

Defines telematics as the combined use of internal or external telecommunications and data or word processing equipment. The author argues that telematics will have a profound impact on work organization, skills requirements, and task structures. From a regional perspective, the potential for decentralized forms of work are of special interest. The author concentrates on empirical findings and their implications. Infrastructural aspects (telecommunications networks), market-related factors, attitudinal and structural characteristics of the labor force, and diffusion dynamics are discussed.

290. Terrovitis, Theophilos E. 1988. "Telecommunications and Regional Development: The Case of Greece," pp. 249-256 in *Informatics and Regional Development*, M. Giaoutzi and P. Nijkamp, eds. Aldershot, Hants, England: Gower Publishing Company, Ltd.

Argues that the use of telecommunications services is a must for the modernization of economies of peripheral regions, despite their relatively low information requirements. In planning the provision of these services in Greece at national and regional levels, the basic aim is to provide these services in time and according to the information requirements caused by the structure of the socioeconomic environment of each of these regions. It is also clear that for the less developed regions the provision of telecommunication services should have priority.

291. Tweeten, Luther. 1987. "No Great Impact on Rural Areas Expected from Computers and Telecommunications." *Rural Development Perspectives* 3(3):7-10.

Discusses the likely effects of high technology, exemplified by microprocessors, computers, and telecommunications, on rural areas and their residents. The author argues that computer technology and telecommunications will have less impact on rural areas than such past innovations as the tractor, fertilizer, television, and automobile. In general, computers seem to confer no decisive economic advantages to rural areas or to large farms.

292. U.S. Congress, Office of Technology Assessment. 1991. *Rural America at the Crossroads: Networking for the Future*. OTA-TCT-471. Washington, D.C.: U.S. Government Printing Office, 190 pp. S/N 052-003-01228-6.

Reports that rural America is at the proverbial crossroads. Many rural communities show signs that raise concern for their economic future, including loss of economic vitality and exodus of talent. Advances in communication and information technologies, however, hold promise for rural America, by reducing the barriers of distance and space that have disadvantaged rural areas. Rural businesses can now link to other businesses or access major markets, even in other countries, just as readily as those in urban areas. This study explores the role that communications technologies can play in securing rural America's future. It develops several policy strategies and options to encourage such development.

293.   Wilson, Robert H. 1992. "Rural Telecommunications: A Strategy for Community Development." *Policy Studies Journal* 20(2):289-300.

Focuses on identifying types of telecommunications innovations in rural areas and determining origins of the innovation and the policy and development implications of the innovation. The cases studied involve a multitude of actors--local exchange companies, long-distance companies, local firms, branch plants, community development organizations, governmental agencies, and others--and the potential held by telecommunications innovation varies among them. Two dimensions are of particular concern: (1) whether telecommunications can facilitate the community development process in rural areas, and (2) the means by which telecommunications innovations are incorporated in the development process.

294.   Wilson, Robert H., and Paul E. Teske. 1990. "Telecommunications and Economic Development: The State and Local Role." *Economic Development Quarterly* 4(2):158-174.

Has three goals: (1) to identify the forces of change in telecommunications policy, (2) to describe the linkages between telecommunications and economic development, and (3) to examine the policy-making environment and public policy issues faced by state and local governments. The authors point out that the telecommunications infrastructure of the U.S. is becoming an increasingly important part of the economy. In many industries, fast and efficient telecommunications is essential for survival in a competitive environment. However, the relation between telecommunications and economic development is not well understood, particularly in terms of the effect of public policy on this relationship, and federal deregulation has placed greater policy responsibility on state and local governments. A better understanding of the telecommunications industry is important as state and local governments attempt to use telecommunications policy as a tool for economic development.

SIZE

295.   Amin, Ash, and John Goddard, eds. 1986. *Technological Change, Industrial Restructuring, and Regional Development.* London: Allen and Unwin, 287 pp.

Examines issues related to the internationalization of production, technological change, the role of small firms, and how these are related to regional economic development in the United Kingdom. Eleven chapters address specific aspects of these issues, including chapters on (1) internationalization and deindustrialization, (2) the role of technical change in national economic development, (3) the economics of smaller businesses, (4) small firm industrial relations, and (5) high technology small firms.

296. Barron, John M., Dan A. Black, and Mark A. Loewenstein. 1987. "Employer Size: The Implications for Search, Training, Capital Investment, Starting Wages, and Wage Growth." *Journal of Labor Economics* 5(1):76-89.

Examines the effects of employer size on hiring and training decisions, such as choices regarding procedures for screening job applicants, rate of hire, training programs for new employees, the criterion for the retention of new employees after observing their on-the-job performance, a compensation package, and a rate of capital investment so as to minimize production costs over time. A unique data set is employed to estimate the empirical relation among employer size and employer search, training, capital investment, and wages. The data set comes from a 1982 employer survey sponsored by the National Institute of Education and the National Center for Research in Vocational Education.

297. Bartik, Timothy J. 1989. "Small Business Start-Ups in the United States: Estimates of the Effects of Characteristics of States." *Southern Economic Journal* 55(4):1004-1018.

Estimates how the characteristics of American states affect small business startups. Unlike most of the business location literature, this paper relies on microdata. The data came from the U.S. Establishment and Longitudinal Microdata (USELM) file of the Small Business Administration data base, which was developed from Dun and Bradstreet files with information for 1976, 1978, 1980 and 1982. The author finds that small business starts in a state primarily depend on entrepreneurial opportunities offered by high market demand relative to industry supply. State tax cuts have a positive but modestly sized effect on small business starts. If the tax cut requires a reduction in business-related public services, small business starts will be reduced. Finally, small business starts are encouraged by greater competitiveness of state financial markets.

298. Bates, Timothy. 1991. "Commercial Bank Financing of White-and-Black-Owned Small Business Start-ups." *Quarterly Review of Economics and Business* 31(1):64-80.

Analyzes commercial bank financing of small businesses owned by blacks and whites, focusing particularly on the issue of whether discrimination might be responsible for the smaller loans received by black-owned firms. Relative to white-owned firms, black-owned firms were observed to be undercapitalized, and they were more likely to have discontinued business operations by the end of the study period. Black-owned firms received smaller loan amounts than white-owned firms possessing identical measured characteristics, and, while black-owned firms had higher failure rates, they had similar predicted failure rates if they did not receive smaller loans. The analysis utilized nationwide samples of over 7,000 white-and-black-owned businesses whose owners entered self-employment from 1976 to 1982.

299. Birch, David L. 1987. *Job Creation in America: How Our Smallest Companies Put the Most People to Work*. New York, NY: The Free Press.

Reports on extensive analysis of Dun and Bradstreet data. The author concludes that during the period 1981-85 small companies (less than 20 employees) were responsible for 88 percent of all net job creation in the U.S. economy. He also concludes that the rate of job loss (through layoffs and firm failures) is relatively constant between growing and declining areas--the key difference among areas is the rate at which jobs are replaced.

300. Brown, Charles, James Hamilton, and James Medoff. 1990. *Employers Large and Small*. Cambridge, MA: Harvard University Press, 109 pp.

Examines the role of large and small employers in the U.S. economy. The authors find that small employers (those with less than 500 employees) do not create a particularly impressive share of jobs in the economy, especially when the focus is on jobs that are not short-lived. The proportion of workers employed by small firms in 1986 was not very different from (and if anything smaller than) the proportion in 1958. Large employers offers much higher wages than smaller employers, even when differences in employees' education and experiences and the nature of the industry are considered. Large employers also offer better benefits, and the authors conclude that working conditions are at least as favorable in large firms as small firms. Further, the jobs generated by large employers provide greater security than those generated by small firms.

301. Cortright, Joseph. 1988. *Small is Bountiful: Manufacturing, Small Business, and Oregon's Economy*. Staff Report to the Joint

Legislative Committee on Trade and Economic Development. Salem: Oregon State Legislature.

Reports that small businesses were the dominant source of new manufacturing jobs in Oregon during the period 1985-86. Manufacturers with fewer than 20 employees added 4,100 workers while firms with more than 20 employees lost 5,400 jobs. The authors conclude that expansions and layoffs are frequent events within the Oregon manufacturing sector and that public subsidies of firms that are creating new jobs should be carefully targeted in order to avoid wasting resources.

302. Fischer, Manfred M. 1988. "Business Formation and Regional Development: Some Major Issues," pp. 85-103 in *Small and Medium Size Enterprises and Regional Development*, M. Giaoutzi, P. Nijkamp, and D. Storey, eds. London: Routledge.

Reviews research in business formation, the role of new small businesses in regional development, and the role of public policy in stimulating the creation of new small firms. The final section includes suggestions for future research.

303. Fischer, Manfred M., and Peter Nijkamp. 1988. "The Role of Small Firms for Regional Revitalization." *The Annals of Regional Science* 22:28-42.

Discusses the regional development potential offered by the small firm sector. The authors first discuss the role of small and medium-sized enterprises (SMEs) in the economy, with emphasis on their employment and development potential. They then discuss the innovative role of SMEs, arguing that the innovation potential of SMEs is co-determined by the regional incubator profile at hand. Some empirical evidence from The Netherlands is presented to support this position. The authors then outline the principles of a multidimensional locational profile analysis for SMEs and describe the results of a case study in which a regional incubator profile is related to the specific regional importance of a set of SME branches. This approach is tested empirically for 18 regions of the European Common Market.

304. Flora, Jan L., and Thomas G. Johnson. 1991. "Small Businesses," pp. 47-59 in *Rural Policies for the 1990s*, C. Flora and J. Christenson, eds. Boulder, CO: Westview Press.

Examines the role of small businesses in contributing to the vitality of rural communities. Among the questions addressed are the following: (1)

Should states have a small business policy, a rural development policy, simply an economic development policy, or some combination of these? (2) What role should small business retention, growth, and recruitment play in local policy in rural areas? (3) What small business and economic development policies at federal, state, and local levels are detrimental to the well-being of rural people and communities? Should they be changed, and, if so, how? Small businesses are defined by these authors as firms with 20 or fewer employees.

305.   Gallagher, C. C., and H. Stewart. 1986. "Jobs and the Business Life-cycle in the U.K." *Applied Economics* 18:875-900.

Analyzes job generation performance in Britain between 1971 and 1981 using data from Dun and Bradstreet (U.K.). Computer software was developed to enable the authors to analyze the file, which contained records for 180,000 establishments in 1971 and 200,000 in 1981. The file represents about 75 percent of private sector employment. The results indicated that small firms performed very well, providing 36 percent of new jobs over the 1971-1981 period while consisting of only 12 percent of all employment in the sample in 1971. Firms employing 20-99 people also performed well, producing more jobs than their proportion of employment. Over 50 percent of all new jobs were created in firms employing less than 100 people, but all firm size groups made a positive contribution to job creation.

306.   Garsombke, Thomas W., and Diane J. Garsombke. 1989. "Strategic Implications Facing Small Manufacturers: The Linkage Between Robotization, Computerization, Automation, and Performance." *Journal of Small Business Management* 27:34-44.

Examines the linkage between the use of technologies in manufacturing operations and positive performance in small business firms. In addition, the authors analyze the relationship between technology use and the inhibitors to implementing new technologies in small manufacturing firms. A group of 144 firms listed in the *1987 Maine Directory of Small and Medium-sized Manufacturers* provided data for the study. More than one-third of the sample firms had adopted or developed highly automated, robotized, or computerized manufacturing processes. Firms which had adopted little or no high technology saw very few barriers to technology uses. These respondents seemed content with the present status of their firms, yet they had experienced few positive changes in performance. Firms which had adopted the new technologies more extensively perceived many barriers to technology and had experienced many indicators of successful performance.

307. Hansen, Niles. 1990. "Innovative Regional Milieux, Small Firms, and Regional Development: Evidence from Mediterranean France." *The Annals of Regional Science* 24:107-123.

Examines key factors that have been involved in the remarkable economic turnaround of Mediterranean France, which until recently was always considered to be a peripheral zone within the national economy. Particular attention is given to the role of noneconomic factors that condition the location choices of households and firms and to the role of technological innovation, service activities, and small and medium-size enterprises (SMEs) in the regional development process. With increasing vertical disintegration, Mediterranean France has been realizing external economies from the expansion of the entire system of production. SMEs, which are especially prevalent in the region--and which have behavior patterns that follow a logic that is more spatial than sectoral in nature-- have contributed significantly to endogenous regional development through their growth as an ensemble. The new regional organizational paradigm transcends older forms of industrialization.

308. Hoke, Linda. 1990. *Creating an Entrepreneurial Culture: Microenterprises in the Southern Economy.* SGPB Alert, Analysis of Emerging Issues, No. 32. Research Triangle Park, North Carolina: Southern Growth Policies Board, 29 pp.

Examines the role of microenterprises (employing fewer than five persons) in the South. The author finds that over half the business enterprises in the South have fewer than five employees. These small firms accounted for 7 percent of all jobs in the region in 1987. In addition, nonfarm, unincorporated self-employment has increased dramatically in the U.S.--by more than 63 percent between 1970 and 1988, compared with a 48 percent increase in company jobs. Self-employment and microenterprise activities are seen as particularly important to areas where there are few formal job opportunities--such as many rural areas and inner-city urban areas--and to groups of people who have few job options due to lack of formal education or training. Publicly supported financial assistance to such enterprises may be warranted.

309. Horvitz, Paul M., and R. Richardson Pettit. 1984. *Small Business Financing: Sources of Financing for Small Business.* Greenwich, CT: JAI Press, Inc., 351 pp.

Provides a broad overview of problems and issues associated with financing small businesses in the United States. Major chapters address such topics as the role of small business in the U.S. economy, the demand for small business loans, and sources of financing for small businesses. Special attention is focused on whether small businesses are treated fairly in capital markets. Specific topics in this regard include the impact of usury laws, implications of bank regulation, effects of tax policy, and small firms' access to public equity financing.

310. Hull, C. J. 1985. "Job Generation Among Independent West German Manufacturing Firms, 1974-1980--Evidence From Four Regions." *Environment and Planning C* 3:215-234.

Provides a West German contribution, with the use of firm-level data, to the emergent international "job generation" literature. The basic question is about the relationship between firm size and employment change, the central hypothesis being that smaller firms generate more new jobs than larger firms do. The findings are limited in their interpretation by data base and methodological constraints. Within these constraints, they tend to confirm the higher job generation performance of smaller firms. Further analysis, however, shows that it is not so much the size of a firm as its age that explains the growth of smaller firms. The paper also shows that there are substantial differences in job generation behavior between the four localities under study, differences which are not explained by the three factors of age, size, and sectoral affiliations of firms.

311. Imrie, R. F. 1986. "Work Decentralization From Large to Small Firms: A Preliminary Analysis of Subcontracting." *Environment and Planning A* 18:949-965.

Provides a preliminary review of small firm subcontracting. The author argues that increasingly subcontracting and other forms of small firm activities are becoming a central part of the operations of large firms. As a result, small firms have to be viewed as central elements in the economy. In this paper, three issues are reviewed as a prerequisite to empirical research. First, an outline of theoretical proposals on interfirm linkages is presented. Second, the nature of subcontracting is outlined. The paper concludes with a categorization of different ways in which subcontracting relations are formed.

312. Kraybill, David S., and Jayachandran N. Variyam. 1993. *The Effects of Employer Size and Human Capital on Rural Wages and Employee Benefits.* SRDC Series No. 170. Mississippi State, MS: Southern Rural Development Center, 23 pp.

Analyzes the effects of employer size on wages and employee benefits to aid in the evaluation of the small business approach to rural development. The authors first discuss recent rural trends and the emergence of small business development programs as a policy response to these trends. Then, they present an overview of the policy debate concerning employer size and its effects. Data for the study came from (1) telephone interviews with 98 actively employed heads of households in Putnam County, Georgia and (2) a survey of 1,252 small businesses in 25 rural counties in Georgia. The authors use regression analysis to evaluate the effects of employer size on wages and benefits. Policy implications are then discussed.

313. Kraybill, David S., Michael J. Yoder, and Kevin T. McNamara. 1991. "Employer Size, Human Capital, and Rural Wages: Implications for Southern Rural Development." *Southern Journal of Agricultural Economics* 23(2):85-94.

Explores the potential consequences of rural development policies that emphasize small business development in place of industrial recruitment, which could be expected to lead to a growing proportion of small firms in local economies. An empirical wage rate model incorporating employer size was developed, and parameters were estimated using household data from rural Putnam County, Georgia. The estimates indicated that large employers offered higher wages than small employers and that the wage premium they offered was greater for blacks than for whites. Other factors associated with higher wages included level of education, previous labor force experience, and employment in certain occupations and industries.

314. Loscocco, Karyn A., Joyce Robinson, Richard H. Hall, and John K. Allen. 1991. "Gender and Small Business Success: An Inquiry into Women's Relative Disadvantage." *Social Forces* 70(1):65-85.

Reports that even among a successful group of small business owners, women generate lower sales volumes and derive less income than their male counterparts. The authors systematically evaluate alternative explanations of women's relative disadvantages. The characteristics of the owner and the small business that differ between genders explain the discrepancy in financial success, with the smaller size of women's businesses emerging as the major explanatory factor. Women's lack of experience and their concentration in the least profitable industries contribute strongly to the gender discrepancy as well.

315. O'Farrell, P. N., and D. M. W. N. Hitchens. 1989. "The Relative Competitiveness and Performance of Small Manufacturing Firms in Scotland and Mid-West of Ireland: An Analysis of Matched Pairs." *Regional Studies* 22(5):399-416.

Presents a comparative analysis of the competitiveness and performance of matched pairs of small manufacturing firms in Scotland and the Mid-West of Ireland. Several dimensions of performance are investigated, and evaluations of the price and quality competitiveness of product samples are made. Based on these results, the paper draws a number of policy conclusions, most notably that the shift in state aid away from fixed to soft assets--especially towards training and quality control--should be intensified.

316. Pratten, Cliff. 1991. *The Competitiveness of Small Firms.* Cambridge, Great Britain: Cambridge University Press, 262 pp.

Analyzes the practical sources of competitiveness of more than one hundred small firms in the computer, machinery, building, electrical and electronics, instruments, chemicals, and food industries. The competition faced by the small firms, the sources of their competitiveness, the handicaps they encounter when competing with larger firms, and the effects on their costs of increasing their output are described. The book provides proprietors of existing small firms and those planning to set up small firms in manufacturing industry with detailed information about the competitiveness of small firms including firms operating in hi-tech industries. Completion of the internal EEC market is seen as a way of increasing the competitiveness of European firms in competition with American and Japanese firms. Yet small firms are taking an increasing share of output in many industries. The book explains the coexistence of large economies of scale and the resurgence of small firms.

317. Rosenfeld, Stuart A. 1990. "Regional Development, European Style." *Issues in Science and Technology* 6(2):63-70.

Discusses advances in such European countries as Italy, West Germany, and Denmark in fostering competitiveness of small and medium-sized enterprises (SME). Common elements in the programs of the three countries include (1) an extensive mechanism for disseminating information about technological advances, (2) applied research and development reflecting the needs of the SMEs, (3) development of industrial networks and consortia, (4) technical education that alternates between the classroom and the workplace, (5) interdependent development of technology and markets, and (6) international cooperation that fortifies regional technology programs. The author concludes that in the U.S., state programs might be more productive if directed toward supporting SMEs.

318. Saren, M. A. J. 1985. "Bridging the Gap: The Marketing Problems Facing Technology-Based Industrial Firms Operating in Science Parks," pp. 261-267 in *Science Parks and Innovation Centres: Their Economic and Social Impact*, J. M. Gibb, ed. Amsterdam, The Netherlands: Elsevier Science Publishers B.V.

Reports that many of the firms locating in science parks or innovation centers are small, comparatively new enterprises. Marketing can be particularly difficult for such firms which may lack visibility, finance for promotion, and well-established communication channels with their customer or client base. Also, they are often faced with the problems of developing a new market based on a technologically innovative product or service. The author reviews what is known about the pattern of development of a new market for a technological innovation and from this sets out the main strategic marketing objective for firms operating in these conditions in terms of the acceleration of the diffusion process. In order to achieve this, the "activating mechanisms" of user influence must be identified from the total population of potential customers in the market. This requires a clear definition and analysis of the total market so that the various categories of users--and their specific requirements--can be accurately assessed. An example of this type of market research procedure is shown.

319. Shutt, John, and Richard Whittington. 1987. "Fragmentation Strategies and the Rise of Small Units: Cases from the North West." *Regional Studies* 21(1):13-23.

Relates the recent growth of small firms in the U.K. to the simultaneous growth of small plants and stabilization of large firms in the late 1970s and early 1980s. It argues that the growth in small firms and small plants can be partly understood as the result of large firm fragmentation strategies in response to increasing demand and innovation risk and to crisis over control of the labor process. Consequently, much small firm growth should be regarded as employment transfer, often entailing job losses. The paper goes on to examine the recent fragmentation strategies of three large manufacturing companies in the North West. In conclusion, the authors argue that regions dominated by large manufacturing firms, such as the North West, are likely to suffer most from the fragmentation process.

320. Sommers, Paul. 1989. *Forging Sectoral Linkages: Strategies for Increasing the Vitality of the Wood Products, Food Products, and Metal Manufacturing Industries in Washington.* Seattle, WA: University of Washington, Northwest Policy Center, 158 pp.

Characterizes competitive conditions in the wood products, food products, and metal-machining sectors of Washington's economy and assesses public policy options for improving the competitiveness of these industries by increasing collaboration among firms and through other strategies. The long-term vitality of the smaller firms in these sectors is the central focus. The report was commissioned by the Business Assistance Center of the Washington Department of Trade and Economic Development. Project staff interviewed over 100 company officials and representatives of trade associations.

321. Storey, D. J. 1982. *Entrepreneurship and the Firm.* London: Croom Helm, 233 pp.

Reviews the resurrection of the small firm, partly by a multidisciplined examination of the existing literature on small and new firms and partly by reporting the results of a study of firms new to the county of Cleveland, in northeast England. The author combines theory and practice, with the emphasis on obtaining a broad view on trends and policies.

322. Storey, D. J., ed. 1985. *Smaller Firms in Regional Economic Development: Britain, Ireland, and the United States.* Cambridge, England: Cambridge University Press, 234 pp.

Reports that over the last 20 years or so major changes have taken place in the attitude of governments toward small firms. Several European governments have initiated programs of assistance to small businesses, while the United States which has a much longer history of encouraging small businesses is giving increased emphasis to this sector in its development efforts. Several groups have, however, challenged this new orthodoxy, and in this collection of papers the contribution of small businesses to economic development is assessed in a number of diverse localities. The findings indicate that the major contribution to economic development in a locality is made by a handful of firms, which in turn suggests that since public policy cannot assist all small firms, it should be directed towards those firms whose improvement in performance has maximum benefits for the economy as a whole.

323. Storey, D. J. 1986. "The Economics of Smaller Business: Some Implications for Regional Economic Development," pp. 215-232 in *Technological Change, Industrial Restructuring, and Regional Development*, A. Amin and J. Goddard, eds. London: Allen and Unwin.

Discusses factors affecting the establishment and performance of the small firm sector, defined in manufacturing as firms with fewer than 200 employees. The author points out that research has generally been directed toward larger firms but that public policy is now increasingly being directed toward firms with 2 to 50 employees. The second half of the chapter is devoted to the role of small firms in leading economic development at local or regional levels. Review of past research indicates that new and small firms have made only a modest contribution to the creation of new employment in the United Kingdom over the past decade and that it is in the more prosperous areas that the contribution has been greatest.

324. Storey, D. J., and S. Johnson. 1987. *Job Generation and Labour Market Change*. London: The Macmillan Press Ltd., 262 pp.

Provides a review of research on job generation that is being undertaken around the world. The authors explore the implications for the labor market of changes in the world economy since the early 1970s. In particular, they investigate the causes and implications of the relative shift in employment from large to small firms. It is not a change that has necessarily occurred in all countries or at the same rates. The authors find that the shift has taken place most rapidly in the United States, the United Kingdom, and Germany, whereas in several smaller developed countries such trends are less clear. The purpose of the book is twofold (1) to provide a statement on the nature and scale of the change in the size structure of employment units and (2) to provide a more complete explanation of why these changes have occurred.

325. Sweeney, G. P. 1987. *Innovation, Entrepreneurs, and Regional Development*. New York, NY: St. Martin's Press, 271 pp.

Focuses on the major determinants of regional economic growth and prosperity which are seen in the entrepreneurial vitality of a region, the regional innovation potential, and the quality and intensiveness of information flow between firms. Major emphasis is placed on the role of small firms and their interaction with large ones and on the role of technological knowledge as a source for regional innovation potentials.

326.   White, Sammis B., and Jeffrey D. Osterman. 1991. "Is Employment
        Growth Really Coming from Small Establishments?" *Economic
        Development Quarterly* 5(3):241-257.

Re-examines the issue of the contribution of various size business
establishments to job growth using a better dataset, a modified definition
of a "small business," and an ability to track the job-generating
contributions of various size establishments across segments of the
business cycle, across industry sectors, and specific industries, and across
differing geographic locations. In addition, the authors examine the role
of using gross versus net job generation contribution.   The article
concludes that the role of establishment size varies by definition, time
period, industry, and location.

327.   Young, Ruth C., and Joe D. Francis.   1989.   "Who Helps Small
        Manufacturing Firms Get Started?" *Rural Development Perspectives*
        6(1):21-25.

Reports results of a survey of 123 small manufacturers in 10 mostly rural
counties in New York state. About 38 percent of the firms were 5 years
old or less, 62 percent were 10 years old or less, and 81 percent were less
than 20 years old. The authors found that over half of the firms had
received support from Federal, State, or local government, generally in
regard to financing.   They also found that nearly all the new
manufacturing firms had roots in another company and that many
continue to survive as part of a network of companies. These small firms
(84 percent had 50 or fewer employees) primarily fill special market
niches. Sixty percent did custom work, and 48 percent produced short
batches with minor modifications. Despite support from public agencies
and other firms, the founders of these companies were required to make
a major investment of personal funds, foregone salary, and time in
launching their firms.

328.   Young, Ruth C., and Joe D. Francis. 1991. *The Role of Self Help,
        Private Help, and Community Assistance for Small Manufacturing
        Firms*.   Bulletin No. 160.   Ithaca, NY: Cornell University,
        Department of Rural Sociology, 16 pp.

Reports on a study of small manufacturing firms in Monroe County, New
York, that examined what firms do for themselves, what assistance they
secure from private sources, and what help they get from public programs
and agencies. Chief executive officers of 117 firms provided information
for the study.   Of the sample firms, 52 percent had 20 or fewer

employees, 19 percent had 21 to 50, 15 percent had 51 to 100, and only 14 percent had 101 or more workers. About 36 percent of the firms were 10 years old or less. Over half of these small manufacturing firms were contacted by community organizations offering various kinds of help, and about one-fourth actually received financial aid. Future plans of the firms also contemplate much self-help and some public help.

329. Zipp, John F. 1991. "The Quality of Jobs in Small Business." *Economic Development Quarterly* 5(1):9-22.

Assesses the quality of jobs in small, medium and large establishments. The principal data source was the 1977 Quality of Employment Survey done by the University of Michigan. The survey was nationwide with a weighted sample size of 2,291. The author finds that, in general, small businesses provide jobs with lower wages, benefits, and stability, but with more creativity, interesting work, autonomy, and overall job satisfaction. The implications of this for economic development are discussed.

ENTREPRENEURS/ENTREPRENEURIAL ACTIVITY

330. Bastow-Shoop, Holly, Brenda L. Ekstrom, and F. Larry Leistritz. 1990. *Business Development in Rural Areas: A Selected Annotated Bibliography.* Ag. Econ. Misc. Rpt. No. 126. Fargo, ND: North Dakota State University, Department of Agricultural Economics, 77 pp.

Provides a guide to the rapidly burgeoning literature dealing with business development in rural areas which is intended to be useful both to economic development practitioners and to researchers and teachers in the area. The 252 entries are drawn primarily from the period since 1980 and are grouped into 6 major topic areas. These are (1) entrepreneurship, (2) business planning, including financial planning and market analysis, (3) productivity, (4) management, (5) outshopping, and (6) other issues affecting small businesses in rural areas.

331. Begley, Thomas M., and David P. Boyd. 1987. "A Comparison of Entrepreneurs and Managers of Small Business Firms." *Journal of Management* 13(1):99-108.

Explores the relationship between entrepreneurship and small business management. Business founders are classified as entrepreneurs and nonfounding chief executives are classified as small business managers.

Findings indicate that (1) on personal and firm characteristics, eight variables differentiate the groups; (2) on financial performance indicators, entrepreneurial firms show higher growth rates; and (3) hard-driving competitiveness consistently associates with financial performance for small business managers but not for entrepreneurs.

332. Bryant, Christopher. 1989. "Entrepreneurs in the Rural Environment." *Journal of Rural Studies* 5(4):337-348.

Presents a framework to place entrepreneurs and entrepreneurial activity into the context first, of decision-taking generally in the rural environment, and second, of the broader "enabling" environment. The author argues that constraints originating in the broader environment are often necessary, but they may have unforeseen side-effects in discouraging innovation. Changes in such constraints or in the manner in which they are implemented may be a necessary ingredient to maintain rural vitality through encouraging entrepreneurial activity.

333. Council of State Policy and Planning Agencies. 1990. *101 Ideas for Stimulating Rural Entrepreneurship and New Business Development.* Washington, D.C.: Council of State Policy and Planning Agencies, 23 pp.

Lists ways that states can stimulate business development by nurturing and rewarding entrepreneurial activity. The ideas in this listing are not prescriptive. Rather they are intended to suggest the array of approaches that could be considered in constructing a rural development strategy focused on entrepreneurship or new business development. Some of the policies have already proven effective. Others are considered promising ideas that merit consideration. Also, a number of publications are listed that provide more detailed descriptions of the policies outlined.

334. Curran, James, John Stanworth, and David Watkins, eds. 1986. *The Survival of the Small Firm: Vol. 1, The Economics of Survival and Entrepreneurship.* Aldershot, Hants, England: Gower Publishing Co., Ltd., 248 pp.

Contains 13 papers that analyze and discuss various kinds of small enterprises and facets of their operations. The contributions are organized into three sections which deal with (1) the economics of survival, (2) the survival of entrepreneurship, and (3) contemporary varieties of small enterprise.

335. Frederick, Martha, and Celeste A. Long. 1989. *Entrepreneurship Theories and Their Use in Rural Development: An Annotated Bibliography*. Bibliographies and Literature of Agriculture No. 74. Washington, D.C.: USDA, Economic Research Service, 82 pp.

Reports that research on entrepreneurship has changed over the 250 years since the concept was born in economic theory. The focus changed from the characteristics of an individual entrepreneur to the current emphasis on the contributions of entrepreneurship to economic development. This bibliography (with 360 entries) is a guide to theoretical material and to more recent empirical work on entrepreneurs in different economic climates. By using background references and the literature specifically on rural entrepreneurs cited here, rural development strategists can build a foundation of knowledge for use in their efforts to promote local independent business development.

336. Freier, S. 1985. "Parks of Science-Based Industries in Israel," pp. 107-110 in *Science Parks and Innovation Centres: Their Economic and Social Impact*, J. M. Gibb, ed. Amsterdam, The Netherlands: Elsevier Science Publishers B.V.

Reports that Universities and Research Institutes can become the center of science-based industries, without altering their character. In Israel, it was the Weizmann Institute of Science which first posed the question squarely, of how it could best contribute to the rapid development of science-based industry, without any industrial expertise. The Institute realized that it could give substantial aid during the initial high risk phase of an enterprise. It put at the disposal of such entrepreneurs 300 sq. meters each for 3 years, as well as scientific advice and all its facilities and amenities, for a nominal fee. It also established simple criteria in order to assess a candidate's prospects and admissibility under this program. The risks for the investors were thereby greatly reduced, and this caused an influx of entrepreneurs. Land was set aside next to the Institute and developed to accommodate fledgling industries which had successfully passed the incubatory period at the Institute, had shown promise and found investors to sustain their prospect. This became the first park for science-based industries in Israel, with 30 firms employing 3,000 people at the end of 15 years. The example was successfully copied by the major universities in Israel.

337. Gladwin, C. H., B. F. Long, E. M. Babb, L. J. Beaulieu, A. Moseley, D. Mulkey, and D. J. Zimet. 1989. "Rural Entrepreneurship: One Key to Rural Revitalization." *American Journal of Agricultural Economics* 71(5):1305-1314.

Seeks to (1) provide a brief critique of theoretical concepts, methods of analysis, and research findings on entrepreneurship from various disciplines, and (2) summarize research in progress on rural entrepreneurs in north Florida and their impact on the local economy. Specific questions addressed include (1) What distinguishes founders and non-founders of firms? (2) What are the differences between rural and urban entrepreneurs and businesses? (3) What types of businesses survive and prosper in different rural settings? (4) How are businesses started or taken over? (5) What do rural businesses contribute to the local economy and (6) How well are rural businesses performing?

338. Hjalager, Anne-Mette. 1989. "Why No Entrepreneurs? Lifemodes, Everyday Life, and Unemployment Strategies in an Underdeveloped Region." *Entrepreneurship and Regional Development* 1:85-97.

Reports that the Lolland region in southern Denmark has a high rate of unemployment resulting from plant closures and relocation. In a pilot project based on a qualitative life-mode methodology, five families were interviewed to explore the reasons why Lolland was not creating its own economic activities, in contrast with other parts of Denmark. The attitudes, skills, and networks of self-employed, wage workers, and professionals demonstrate why the region has a dependency rather than entrepreneurial culture.

339. Jarillo, J. Carlos. 1989. "Entrepreneurship and Growth: The Strategic Use of External Resources." *Journal of Business Venturing* 4:133-147.

Proposes a view whereby the essence of entrepreneurship is seen precisely in the ability and willingness to use external resources. A statistical validation of the main hypothesis (i.e., that entrepreneurial, fast-growing firms do use more external resources than their competitors) is then attempted. The results, based on data for almost 2000 companies over the period 1972-82, strongly support the hypothesis. It is found that the fastest-growing firms in a very large sample of public companies are much less integrated (make more use of external resources) than their competitors; in addition, those firms that are at the forefront of using external resources grow, on average, much faster (more than 10 percent every year) than their competitors over a long period of time (ten years). The study's implications for managers seem clear. The findings constitute yet another piece of evidence in favor of the efficiency of networking arrangements. Being flexible enough to use external resources allows the entrepreneurial firm to break through the limits of sustainable growth and, at the same time, lowers its risk, for it taps into someone else's experience and know-how. Entrepreneurs and entrepreneurial managers must not be deterred by lack of resources in pursuit of opportunities.

340. Johnson, Thomas G. 1989. "Entrepreneurship and Development Finance: Keys to Rural Revitalization, Discussion." *American Journal of Agricultural Economics* 71(5):1324-1328.

Discusses papers by Gladwin et al. and by Drabenstott and Morris (see items 337 and 610).

341. MacKenzie, Lynn Ryan. 1992. "Fostering Entrepreneurship as a Rural Development Strategy." *Economic Development Review* 10(4):38-44.

Focuses on the fostering of entrepreneurship as part of an integrated approach to economic development. Rural economies are examined in the context of current shifts in the world economy and modes of production. A review of the literature is undertaken regarding rural assets and liabilities, characteristics of entrepreneurial environments, the role of history, place, and social context, and liabilities of entrepreneurship as a model for addressing rural poverty. Primary strategies for stimulating and supporting entrepreneurial enterprise are summarized.

342. O'Farrell, P. N. 1986. "Entrepreneurship and Regional Development: Some Conceptual Issues." *Regional Studies* 20(6):565-574.

Attempts to clarify and improve understanding of the concept of entrepreneurship in national and regional development. The nature of entrepreneurship is discussed, and it is shown that the entrepreneur and the capitalist are conceptually distinct; that it is useful to differentiate between the entrepreneurial and managerial functions; and that the essence of the concept is the initiation of entrepreneurial acts when the individual is behaving in an innovative way under uncertainty. The distinction between entrepreneurship and arbitrage is briefly clarified, and the relationship between entrepreneurship and large organizations is discussed. Our understanding of spatial variations in entrepreneurial behavior is currently insufficient for the purpose of explanation and policy prescription.

343. Sexton, Donald L., and Raymond W. Smilor, eds. 1986. *The Art and Science of Entrepreneurship*. Cambridge, MA: Ballinger Publishing Company, 422 pp.

Contains 12 major chapters dealing with various aspects of entrepreneurship. The work is based on a conference on State-of-the-Art in Entrepreneurship Research sponsored by the RGK Foundation, the IC^2 Institute at the University of Texas at Austin and the Center for Entrepreneurship at Baylor University. Several conclusions about the current state-of-the-art are readily apparent. First, entrepreneurship is in the early stages of a rapid growth cycle in both industry and academia. Second, not all areas have progressed at the same rate. Third, there is an unfulfilled obligation to develop convergent theories that provide an overall understanding of the entire entrepreneurial process rather than specific narrow areas and to convey this perspective to a broader audience. Finally, the study of entrepreneurship has a much more important function than the satisfaction of intellectual curiosity. Basic research must lead to applications in industry and in the public as well as private sector.

344. Sokolow, Alvin D., and Julie Spezia. 1990. *Political Leaders as Entrepreneurs? Economic Development in Small Communities.* Rural Dev. Res. Rpt. No. 77. Washington, D.C.: USDA, Economic Research Service, 33 pp.

Reports that, while local government officials are heavily involved in the implementation of rural economic development efforts in rural and other small communities, they are much less represented among the initiators of such projects. A major reason is that elected political leaders generally lack the skills, motivations, and priorities demanded of economic development entrepreneurship. A review of 17 successful cases of small town development, which compares project initiators and their actions, suggests several critical differences between local political leadership and entrepreneurship. Elected officials in small towns generally are adverse to risk-taking, easily become preoccupied with routine matters, lack the driving force of political ambition, and accept the pre-eminence of business people and other leaders in the economic development arena.

345. Wortman, Max S., Jr. 1990. "A Unified Approach for Developing Rural Entrepreneurship in the U.S." *Agribusiness* 6(3):221-236.

Points out that rural entrepreneurship is one of the foundations of rural economic development but that rural entrepreneurship has only recently been defined and few major research studies have been attempted. This article analyzes current research on rural entrepreneurship, examines current strategies and programs in the area, proposes a unified public-private approach to rural entrepreneurship, and suggests an integrated program to support rural entrepreneurship in the United States. Such a program would, the author believes, strengthen the competitive opportunities for rural areas in the United States.

346. Wortman, Max S., Jr. 1990. "Rural Entrepreneurship Research: An Integration into the Entrepreneurship Field." *Agribusiness* 6(4):329-344.

Points out that rural entrepreneurship is one of the newest areas of research in the entrepreneurship field. It has become one of the significant supportive factors for rural economic development and agribusiness. This article defines rural entrepreneurship, integrates the current rural entrepreneurship research into an entrepreneurship typology, critiques current rural entrepreneurship research, analyzes data sources and research methods being used, and proposes future research questions in rural entrepreneurship.

CONTEXTUAL FACTORS

STRUCTURE

Business Climate

347. Atash, Farhad. 1991. "Fiscal Impacts of Economic Changes on the Revenues and Expenditures of Rural Local Governments and Communities," pp. 29-49 in *Economic Productivity and Adaptability*. University Park, PA: Northeast Regional Center for Rural Development.

Reports that national and international economic changes have had impacts on the budgetary condition of rural local governments and on residents and businesses in rural communities in both growing and declining areas. This study reviews past literature on the impacts that economic changes have had on revenues and expenditures in rural local governments and communities, and identifies specific objectives for future research and extension programs for the Northeast region.

348. Barkley, David L., Kevin T. McNamara, and Charles T. Hancock. 1990. "Foreign Direct Investment in the United States and South Carolina." *Issues in Community and Economic Development* 1(2):1-6.

Examines patterns of foreign direct investment (FDI) in the U.S. and South Carolina. FDI is defined (by the U.S. Department of Commerce) as ownership or control by a foreign entity of 10 percent or more of a corporation's voting securities, or an equivalent ownership interest in a nonincorporated enterprise. In 1988, South Carolina had more FDI employment per capita than any other state and ranked behind only Louisiana in dollars of foreign investment per capita. Most of the state's

FDI was in manufacturing, and most of these facilities were located in metropolitan areas in the Piedmont region. Facilities affiliated with West German and French manufacturers accounted for 50 percent of FDI manufacturing employment. Employment of the FDI manufacturers was heavily concentrated in the chemicals, plastics, and rubber (35.4 percent) and machinery, electronics, and transportation equipment (26.5 percent) industries.

349. Bartik, Timothy J. 1985. "Business Location Decisions in the United States: Estimates of the Effects of Unionization, Taxes, and Other Characteristics of States." *Journal of Business and Economic Statistics* 3(1):14-22.

Examines how corporate decisions about the location for a new manufacturing plant in the U.S. are influenced by unionization, taxes, and other characteristics of states. The conditional logit model is used with some modifications to make the model more applicable to the business location decision. The most important finding is that the union sympathies of states have a major effect on business location. The results also indicate that state taxes affect business location, contradicting the conventional wisdom in the economic literature, although the tax effect is of modest magnitude. In addition, there is some evidence that improved public services (e.g., roads) can attract business.

350. Bartik, Timothy J. 1988. "Tennessee: The Emergence of an Industrial State Economy," pp. 141-164 in *The New Economic Role of American States*, R. Scott Fosler, ed. New York, NY: Oxford University Press.

Points out that Tennessee has made great economic progress in the past forty years. Per capita income has grown much more rapidly than the U.S. average. The state has increasingly become a center of sophisticated manufacturing as well as of traditional low-wage industries, and the state's capital, Nashville, is one of the true boom towns of the South. The author finds that Tennessee's success is based largely on strong economic fundamentals. Central location, good transportation, low wages and unionization, and a traditional work ethic are powerful economic forces that attract firms to the state. However, state officials also have engaged in a vigorous industrial recruitment effort, and the author concludes that this recruitment activity has positively affected the state's economy, although its effect is secondary to that of more fundamental economic forces.

351. Bartik, Timothy J. 1988. "The Effects of Environmental Regulation on Business Location in the United States." *Growth and Change* 19(3):22-44.

Empirically examines whether variations in state environmental regulations have affected the location of manufacturing branch plants by the Fortune 500 companies. Using several measures of environmental regulation, no statistically significant effects of environmental regulation on business location were found. For most manufacturing industries, the estimates are precise enough to rule out the possibility of large effects of environmental regulation on business location. For highly polluting industries, however, the variance in the estimates is quite large. The possibility that the effects of environmental regulation on the location of highly polluting industries are large enough to be important to policy makers cannot be ruled out.

352. Bergeron, Tom. 1990. "Corporate Executives Rate Site Selection Factors." *Area Development* 25(12):22-24,28,30,35,39.

Reports results of a readership survey in which respondents were asked to rate 23 site selection factors and nine quality of life factors. The most highly rated site selection factors (based on the percentage rating them "very important" or "important") were: (1) highway accessibility, (2) labor costs, (3) state and local incentives, (4) occupancy or construction costs, and (5) energy availability and costs. The most highly rated quality-of-life factors were (1) low crime rate, (2) rating of public schools, (3) health facilities, (4) housing availability, and (5) housing costs. When asked "What factors do you consider most critical facing U.S. manufacturing today?", the highest percentages named (1) availability of skilled labor (17.5%), (2) availability of semi-skilled or unskilled labor (13.4%), and (3) environmental considerations (13.1%).

353. Bierman, Wallace W. 1984. "The Validity of Business Climate Rankings: A Test." *Industrial Development* 153(2):17-25.

Discusses the history of attempts to rank state business climates. The specific studies discussed are those conducted by the Fantus Co. (1975), the California Department of Finance (1977), the Alexander Grant Co. (1979, 1980, 1981, 1982), and Inc. Magazine (1982, 1983). The author concludes that states' business climate rankings, from the Alexander Grant reports, did little to explain their economic performance, measured by growth in manufacturing employment from 1975 to 1979.

354.   Bryant, Christopher. 1992. "Community Development and Changing Rural Employment in Canada," pp. 265-278 in *Contemporary Rural Systems in Transition: Volume 2, Economy and Society*, I. R. Bowler, C. Bryant, and M. Nellis, eds. Wallingford, Oxon, U.K.: CAB International.

Reports that Canada has experienced substantial sectoral shifts in employment since the mid-20th century. Other structural changes have involved the reorganization of economic activities in terms of enterprise size, labor-management relationships, and the role of capital. The author addresses several questions related to these changes. How have these changes affected rural areas? Has the response of rural areas been reactionary or proactive? What are the prospects for the last decade of the 20th century?

355.   Calzonetti, F. J., and Robert T. Walker. 1991. "Factors Affecting Industrial Location Decisions: A Survey Approach," pp. 221-240 in *Industry Location and Public Policy*, H. Herzog and A. Schlottmann, eds. Knoxville, TN: The University of Tennessee Press.

Provides an overview of factors that influence industrial location decisions in the U.S., considers the approaches used in identifying these factors and their role in the location decision, and presents the results of a recent national study rating factors that influence industrial location decisions. The authors also suggest how this knowledge can be helpful to policy makers involved in stimulating regional growth and development. The authors address studies that involve collection of data from individual firms through questionnaires and interviews, as contrasted with studies that use aggregated data available at state, regional, or national levels. Based on a nationwide survey conducted in 1988 of manufacturers that had started operating new plants since 1978, the authors found that there is considerable variation in the rated significance of industrial location factors across regions, plant type, and level of location search. In the regional search (to select the region to locate a facility), access to markets appears to be the most important factor, followed by labor. In the local search (to choose a specific site), markets is also the highest-rated factor when all responses are aggregated, but there is much more variation in the factor ratings when the responses are disaggregated by plant type and region.

356.   Corporation for Enterprise Development. 1989. *The 1989 Development Report Card for the States*. Washington, D.C.: The Corporation for Enterprise Development, 170 pp.

Examines the business climate of the states and presents rankings in four categories: 1) business vitality, 2) capacity, 3) policy, and 4) performance. The authors contend that the businesses that are the engines of growth are market-driven, technology-intensive, highly flexible, quality-based manufacturing and service firms. For such firms, what matters is not the absence of business costs, but the responsiveness to business needs. The authors believe that four major lessons can be drawn from their study: 1) rural America is in trouble, 2) investing in a better economic climate pays, 3) the disparity between rich and poor is increasing in virtually every state, and 4) leading the U.S. economy is not enough (i.e., American producers are facing challenges from abroad).

357.   Cullen, Kathryn Sutton, and Barbara M. Sullivan. 1986. "The Rising Sun Over Moses Lake." *Pacific Northwest Executive* 2(3):17-21.

Discusses investment by Japanese firms in the town of Moses Lake, Washington, the factors that have influenced these investment decisions, and whether the Moses Lake model can be applied to other communities. Economic factors that encouraged investment in Moses Lake included low electrical rates, plentiful, low-priced industrial sites, and an available labor force due to high unemployment rates. These generally could be duplicated by other communities. The Moses Lake experience in the sociocultural area would be more difficult to duplicate. Key to the Moses Lake advantage in this area are a long-established Japanese agricultural training program and a training center established by Japanese Airlines in 1968.

358.   Findeis, Jill L. 1993. "Utilization of Rural Labor Resources," pp. 49-68 in *Economic Adaptation: Alternatives for Nonmetropolitan Areas*, D. L. Barkley, ed. Boulder, CO: Westview Press.

Assesses the use of labor resources in the nonmetro United States and examines the implications of alternative industries and labor market structures for generating (adequate) employment and improving economic well-being. The author draws on literature from economics, sociology, and regional science, first examining studies of underemployment and focusing on differences in labor market outcomes between demographic groups and the relationships between these and specific industries. Next, labor market research analyzing rural or nonmetro labor markets is assessed. Finally, the implications of employment generation strategies for labor utilization are summarized.

359.   Friedman, Julia Mason. 1988. *Credit Rationing in Non-Metropolitan Markets for Small Business Loans*. State and Regional Research

Center Working Paper 88-02. St. Paul: University of Minnesota, 33 pp.

Examines capital market obstacles that could prevent small businesses in nonmetropolitan areas from obtaining loans under the terms available to comparable projects. The author points out that such obstacles can arise from costs of loan transactions, from the structure of the lending market, and from benefits generated by the project for which the business will not receive payments. She indicates that some of these barriers can potentially be more severe in nonmetropolitan areas, and particularly in areas with declining economies. She then outlines questions for further research.

360.   Glaser, Mark A., and Joe P. Pisciotte. 1991. "Listening to Business Executives: Labor Concerns for Job Conservation and Business Investment." *Economic Development Quarterly* 5(2):168-174.

Uses input from over 800 business leaders in Wichita, Kansas, to define the relative value of selected labor issues. In general, business leaders' first concern was meeting the short-run skill requirements of their businesses. Productivity was a predictable concern, but leaders clearly recognized that U.S. business ability to compete in world markets is being challenged. Surprisingly, few businesses defined high school preparation as an important labor issue. A portion of this devaluation of the role of high schools as a labor issue is related to quality control. Business leaders no longer feel that the high school diploma is a useful indicator of basic skills. Business leaders did not define issues related to labor unions as being an important labor concern.

361.   Glickman, Norman J., and Douglas P. Woodward. 1989. *The New Competitors: How Foreign Investors are Changing the U.S. Economy.* New York, NY: Basic Books, Inc., 374 pp.

Provides a detailed examination of direct foreign investment in the U.S. economy. Foreign direct investment takes place when a foreign entity purchases controlling interest in an American company or real estate. The authors examine such issues as (1) which nations are the leading investors, (2) how they invest (e.g., through acquisitions and mergers), (3) what types of assets they have been acquiring (with emphasis on investments in manufacturing), (4) the motivations for investing, (5) the domestic consequences of foreign investment, and (6) policies toward foreign investment. The domestic consequences of foreign investment that the authors examine include job creation and labor relations.

Community development implications are also addressed, and the regional patterns of foreign investment are examined.

362. Grant Thornton. 1990. *Eleventh Annual Grant Thornton Manufacturing Climates Study*. Chicago, IL: Grant Thornton, 162 pp.

Presents rankings of states based on 16 factors that affect the cost of manufacturing. States are ranked in relation to all other states and also in comparison to other states with similar levels of manufacturing intensity. The 29 states classed as high-intensity manufacturing states met one or both of the following criteria: (1) the state's manufacturing sector contributed more than 2.0 percent of the total value of manufacturing shipments in the United States and (2) more than 16.5 percent of the state's workforce was employed in manufacturing. Factors used to compare the states are (1) average hourly wage, (2) education, (3) worker's compensation insurance levels, (4) statutory average workers' compensation cost per case, (5) percentage of manufacturing workers unionized, (6) expenditure growth vs. personal income growth, (7) value added, (8) fuel and electric energy costs, (9) tax effort, (10) change in average hourly wage, (11) unemployment compensation trust fund net worth, (12) average unemployment compensation benefits, (13) change in tax effort, (14) change in unionization, (15) debt growth vs. personal income growth, and (16) manhours lost to work stoppages.

363. Great Plains Agricultural Council. 1987. *The Rural Great Plains of the Future*. Great Plains Agricultural Council Pub. No. 125. Lincoln, NE: Great Plains Agricultural Council, 254 pp.

Contains 14 papers addressing different aspects of changes occurring in the Great Plains Region. Major sections address (1) the structure, competitive position, and longer term prospects of the agricultural sector, (2) forces for change in the agricultural economy, (3) challenges of the future for rural communities, and (4) institutional impacts, including those affecting the land grant system, states, and local governments.

364. Gunderson, Ralph O., and J. Scott McDonald. 1990. *1989 Survey of Foreign Investors in Wisconsin: Information Sources and Location Factors*. Oshkosh, WI: University of Wisconsin-Oshkosh, Department of Public Affairs, 33 pp.

Uses data from a 1989 survey of 41 foreign firms to determine the relative importance of different information sources and location factors. The most common nationality of the foreign firms was Japanese (10 of

41), followed by German (9), United Kingdom (8), French (4), Canadian (3), and other (7). The most important information sources affecting the siting decision were the owner's experience, followed by company staff, consultants, other firms, and local agencies. Among the general factors affecting siting, labor was the most important, followed closely by existing facilities (buildings), transportation, community attributes, and personal preference.

365. Gustafson, Cole R., and Shaun C. Beauclair. 1990. *Community Development and Commercial Bank Performance: A Mutually-Dependent Relationship.* Ag. Econ. Rpt. No. 254. Fargo, ND: North Dakota State University, Department of Agricultural Economics, 20 pp.

Quantifies the interaction between commercial bank lending practices and local community development. Historically, rural communities have relied heavily on local commercial banks for investment capital and financial services. Commercial bank lending policies are therefore likely to be an important determinant of economic development. However, local economic development also affects the prosperity of local financial institutions. Results of the study show that economic activity at the retail, wholesale, and farm level is strongly influenced by commercial bank lending policies. Increased credit at each level heightens economic activity. On the other side, increases in community economic activity lead to greater loan demand and bank profitability. Thus, local communities and commercial banks are mutually dependent on each other.

366. Hack, George D. 1984. "The Plant Location Decision Making Process." *Industrial Development* (Sept./Oct.):31-33.

Discusses the decision-making process used to locate a new plant, which the author feels is usually not clearly understood. The decision to locate, he contends, is based on intensive research and analysis which includes in-office study and field reconnaissance of a community. Major factors considered in this process include operating costs, operating conditions, and the living environment of the community. The author believes that more companies are now directing greater attention to social and cultural factors.

367. Hagstrom, Jerry, and Robert Guskind. 1984. "Playing the State Ranking Game--A New National Pastime Catches On." *National Journal* (6-30-84):1268-1274.

Discusses the rankings of state business climates prepared by Alexander Grant and Co. and by Inc. Magazine. A number of other state ranking systems also are published, including the annual number of business failures, average hourly manufacturing wage, jobless rate, and a stress index.

368. Hamilton, F. E. Ian, ed. 1987. *Industrial Change in Advanced Economies.* Beckenham, Kent, U.K.: Croom Helm Ltd., 308 pp.

Contains 17 chapters that examine various aspects of industrial change from the perspectives of (1) industrialized European and North American countries, (2) centrally managed economies, and (3) Japan. The chapters are contributed by both younger and established researchers from more than a dozen countries. The chapters represent papers originally presented at, or submitted for, the International Geophysical Union Commission on Industrial Systems' symposium held in France in 1984. The book is organized into five major sections which examine (1) the explanations for, and the nature of, industrial reorganization in both East and West and the effects of reorganization on work and labor, decisions, and society, (2) recent trends in the character and location of selected industries, (3) the nature of multinational enterprise, (4) organizational changes, and (5) technological issues and business services.

369. Hanson, Russell L. 1993. "Bidding for Business: A Second War Between the States?" *Economic Development Quarterly* 7(2):183-198.

Reports that states compete for investment by offering a variety of incentives to businesses. Because these incentives play only a small role in corporate deliberations, some observers worry that public resources may be allocated inefficiently and inequitably as a result of bidding wars between the states. An empirical analysis of the effects of competition suggests these fears are exaggerated; interstate rivalries have only a limited impact on development policy choices. Consequently, proposals to end the war between the states will not eliminate the inefficiency and inequity often attributed to development policy. More effective reforms must await a political explanation of who gets what, when, and how in state politics.

370. Hanson, Russell L., and Michael B. Berkman. 1991. "Gauging the Rainmakers: Toward a Meteorology of State Legislative Climates." *Economic Development Quarterly* 5(3):213-228.

Points out that the notion of a "business climate" has been poorly conceptualized and crudely measured. The authors propose a multidimensional measure derived from a weakly confirmatory factor analysis and shows how this measure illuminates substantive differences among economic development policies--differences that are obscured by conventional measures of policy activity. The validity of the measure is illustrated by tracking its movement in relation to the evolution of development strategy in Indiana. The authors then demonstrate the utility of the measure in quantitative analysis of the determinants of development policies and their impact on state economies.

371. Harding, Charles F. 1984. "New Plant Location Strategies." *Dun's Business Month Focus* 121:111-126.

Draws on experience of the Fantus Company in site selection studies and defines five facility location strategies that can be used effectively by firms facing the economic conditions of the 1980s. These are (1) identifying communities that have pockets of low cost labor, (2) choosing a site in a less developed country, (3) locate plants close to regional markets, (4) use upgraded technology to reduce plant operating costs, and (5) use a solar/planetary strategy, which involves locating several facilities near each other to facilitate sharing managerial and engineering overhead and ensuring just-in-time delivery.

372. Helms, L. Jay. 1985. "The Effect of State and Local Taxes on Economic Growth: A Time-Series, Cross-Sectional Approach." *The Review of Economics and Statistics* 67(4):574-582.

Presents results based on pooled time series and cross section data, which indicate that state and local tax increases significantly retard economic growth when the revenues are used to fund transfer payments. However, when the revenue is used instead to finance improved public services (such as education, highways, and public health and safety), the favorable impact on location and production decisions provided by the enhanced services may more than counterbalance the disincentive effects of the associated taxes. These findings underscore the importance of considering the incentives provided by a state's expenditures as well as by its taxes.

373. Henry, Mark S. 1993. "The Rural Economic Gap: Fact or Fiction?" pp. 9-28 in *Economic Adaptation: Alternatives for Nonmetropolitan Areas*, D. L. Barkley, ed. Boulder, CO: Westview Press.

Addresses the widening of the urban-rural economic gap that occurred in
the United States during the 1980s and assesses whether convergence of
urban and rural incomes can be expected in the longer run. The author
first presents evidence that suggests the existence of a metro-nonmetro
gap in earnings and employment, as well as income. Next, the conceptual
issues in the convergence-divergence process are reviewed with a focus
on implications for growth in rural America. An outlook for how areas
might adapt to the dynamic economic forces that have been observed in
recent years is provided in the conclusion.

374. Hiemstra, Stephen W. 1990. *Prospective Rural Effects of Bank
      Deregulation.* Rural Development Research Report No. 76.
      Washington, D.C.: USDA, Economic Research Service, Agriculture
      and Rural Economy Division, 56 pp.

Examines legislation, under consideration by Congress since 1978, that
would repeal provisions of the National Bank Act of 1933, known
collectively as the Glass-Steagall Act. The proposed legislation would
expand the powers of commercial banks to underwrite securities both in
the bank and through a bank holding company affiliate. These powers
may generally encourage greater bank operating efficiency and reduce
portfolio risk through diversification. Rural bank participation is expected
to be low, however, because most rural banks are small, and they have
relatively little experience with securities markets. Little net increase in
rural growth is expected because efficiency gains are likely to be small.
Few benefits of new bank powers are likely to accrue to rural banks to
offset insolvency risks and increased competition from innovative urban
banks.

375. Hill, Stephen, and Max Munday. 1992. "The U.K. Regional Distribution
      of Foreign Direct Investment: Analysis and Determinants." *Regional
      Studies* 26(6):535-544.

Analyses the regional distribution of foreign direct investment (FDI)
within the U.K. Following an examination of those regions that have
been successful in winning new inward investment, the paper goes on to
consider hypotheses that can be used to explain relative regional success
in attracting new FDI projects and jobs. Empirical testing of these
hypotheses suggests that both financial incentives and access to markets
are important determinants of the regional distribution of new FDI
projects and jobs.

376. Hoare, A. G. 1985. "Industrial Linkage Studies," pp. 40-81 in *Progress
      in Industrial Geography*, M. Pacione, ed. London: Croom Helm.

Discusses analyses of industrial linkages undertaken historically by geographers to arrive at a definition of these linkages. The author then turns to discussion of the practical importance of industrial linkages, including analysis of linkages as a factor in location and relocation of industry. Studies of linkages undertaken both in Europe and North America are extensively reviewed.

377. Jackson, Randall W. 1989. "Conjoining Interindustry Linkages and Ownership Data: An Empirical Application." *Growth and Change* 20(1):34-54.

Uses an interindustry accounting framework conjoined with Dun and Bradstreet corporate ownership data to provide a perspective on the effects of external corporate ownership. The aggregate level measurement method is applied to fifteen multicounty regions in the state of Illinois, and reveals considerable variation in the measures generated. High regional dependence measures were directly related to employment stability and inversely related to employment growth.

378. Lee, Raymond M., ed. 1987. *Redundancy, Layoffs, and Plant Closures: Their Character, Causes, and Consequences.* Wolfeboro, NH: Croom Helm Ltd., 335 pp.

Contains 12 chapters dealing with various dimensions of layoffs and plant closings including differential effects of such actions on older workers and women, effects on the community and labor market, the effect on ethnic minorities, the role of unions, and political consequences. Most examples are drawn from the United Kingdom, but some comparisons to experiences in the U.S. and France also are provided.

379. Lenzi, Raymond C. 1992. "Rural Development Finance Gaps: Bank CDCs as an Alternative." *Journal of the Community Development Society* 23(2):22-38.

Reports that rural areas have seen significantly slower economic growth in the past decade and that a major factor in this slow growth has been the relative lack of finance, including both traditional loans as well as less traditional forms of finance such as subordinated loans, convertible debentures, and equity investment. Rural counties typically have bank loan-to-deposit ratios 30 percent below metropolitan counties. Rural areas need banks and other economic financing institutions that are more willing to participate in economic development financing. Also needed is organizational assistance with "capacity building" to access capital--

completion of business plans, financials, and loan applications. The Bank Community Development Corporation (CDC) is becoming a popular economic development initiative in the effort to stimulate investment in rural areas. Community developers can provide educational programs and technical assistance to rural areas to stimulate both supply and demand for financial capital through establishment of Bank CDCs and other innovations.

380. Lenzi, Raymond C., and Kenneth Pigg. 1989. *Taney County Targeted Industry Study and Economic Development Plan.* Columbia, MO: University of Missouri, 70 pp.

Addresses key issues related to economic and industrial growth in Taney County, Missouri, including: (1) community economic development, (2) labor force, (3) infrastructure and site development, (4) financing, (5) existing businesses, and (6) targeted industry strategy. Specific recommendations include (1) hiring a full-time executive director for the local development organization, (2) establishing a labor recruitment plan for industries expanding or locating in the county, (3) maintaining a customized labor training program with the state department of economic development and area vo-tech school, (4) development of an industrial park, (5) construction of a speculative shell building in the industrial park, (6) completion of a four-lane highway, (7) maintenance and improvement of air service, and (8) creation of an economic development incentive fund. Seven industries are targeted for recruitment.

381. Lohr, Steve. 1988. "The Growth of the Global Office." *The New York Times* (Oct. 18):D1.

Discusses experiences of U.S. companies in moving "back office" operations, such as data processing and computer programming to locations abroad. Specific examples examined include New York Life, which has moved some of its claims processing activity to Ireland, Travelers Corporation, which has a software development office in Ireland, American Airlines, with data processing in Barbados and the Dominican Republic, and Saztec International, with a data processing operation in Manila. Lower wages was the reason most frequently cited to explain these moves, but high worker turnover in U.S. cities also was mentioned.

382. Markley, Deborah M. 1990. *The Impact of Deregulation on Rural Commercial Credit Availability in Four New England States: Empirical Evidence and Policy Implications.* Washington, D.C.: The Aspen Institute, 182 pp.

Evaluates the impact of financial deregulation on rural commercial credit availability, particularly for small business enterprises. Financial deregulation is defined broadly to include (1) expansion of large banks and bank holding companies (BHCs) across state lines, (2) increased branching and acquisition of existing banks by large banks or BHCs within a state, and (3) expanded commercial lending powers for savings banks. The study area comprised the states of Maine, Massachusetts, New Hampshire, and Vermont. Data were obtained from a survey of small businesses and a survey of banks.

383. Markley, Deborah M., with Katharine McKee. 1992. *Business Finance as a Tool for Development.* Washington, D.C.: The Aspen Institute, 91 pp.

Reviews the state-of-the-art in development finance. The authors briefly trace the evolution of development finance from the early, subsidy-driven programs to the emerging "Third Wave" of today. The book outlines the opportunities and limitations of a number of approaches, paying particular attention to the special capital needs of rural areas. It then presents a very practical series of steps to create (or improve) state development finance programs. To add dimension and illustrate the practical workings of development finance, it also offers several detailed case studies of successful programs in Massachusetts, Michigan, North Carolina, Arkansas, and other states. The key points made in the study are (1) successful, innovative development finance programs use public funds to leverage greater amounts of private capital, (2) capital gaps exist in all regions of the country, but may be especially acute in rural areas, (3) the timing is excellent for innovative state development finance programs to flourish, (4) initiating (or improving) state development finance programs involves a series of careful steps, beginning with analysis of the state's capital market, then moving through the development of objectives and targets, the design of the program, and the creation of systems of monitoring and evaluation, and (5) technical assistance is crucial for both the supply and demand sides of the development finance equation.

384. Marlor, Felice S., and James M. McGlone. 1992. *Federal Nonfarm Business Credit Assistance: An Analysis of Disbursements to Rural Areas.* AGES 9214. Washington, D.C.: USDA, Economic Research Service, 24 pp.

Reports on the extent of support for business development by the Federal Government through credit assistance. Although the government uses both direct and indirect programs to disseminate credit assistance, this study focuses on direct programs over the period 1983-89. Rural counties received 27 percent ($6.3 billion) of the total $23.5 billion given in direct assistance. Rural areas received more funding than urban areas when measured on a per capita or per business basis. Low-income areas received less assistance per capita (but more per business). Persistent poverty counties received below-average amounts by whatever measure is used.

385. Matuszewski, Jean. 1993. "Economic Diversification Opportunities in Remote Rural Areas." *Economic Development Review* 11(1):61-63.

Reports that many rural communities whose economy is based on a single major industry are facing major crises, in that a decline in the traditional industrial base produces a decline in employment, which in turn can lead to a decline in population, then decline in real estate values and consumer services, followed by increased difficulty in attracting new workers and even further decline in employment. In addition to or in place of the traditional approaches to addressing the challenge of such an economy, the economic developer may wish to pay attention to stimulating noncore activities, typically business services along with cottage industries.

386. McDonald, J. Scott. 1989. "Industrial Location in Wisconsin: Regional Variation in Siting and Expansion Decisions." Paper presented at Wisconsin and its Regions Conference; October 27, LaCrosse, Wisconsin. Oshkosh, WI: University of Wisconsin-Oshkosh, 20 pp.

Investigates the specific factors that attracted private sector decision makers to particular sites and communities in Wisconsin. A mail survey was used to obtain information from manufacturing facilities that were sited or expanded between January 1982 and January 1988. A response rate of about 50 percent and 247 useable responses were obtained. The questionnaire obtained information about 15 factors affecting siting, 39 subfactors relating to selected factors, organizational information, and personal information. Most of the firms studied had the company headquarters in the same community as the new or expanded facility. Median employment was 25 workers. Among the most important factors influencing location decisions were personal preferences, existing facility, labor, community, and utilities.

387. Milkman, Raymond H. 1990. "Gauging the Local Business Climate," pp. 128-131 in *Plant Closure and Community Recovery*, J. E. Lynch, ed. Washington, D.C.: National Council for Urban Economic Development.

Points out that a first step in responding to economic dislocations and related problems at the local level is to mount an intensive effort to analyze the area's economic problems and potentials. That analysis should be the basis of an adjustment strategy to overcome area problems by taking advantage of whatever local strengths exist. Since the private sector ultimately holds the key to local recovery, any analysis of area problems and potentials should take into account the local business climate as well as related labor force and business trends. The author describes an approach to such an analysis.

388. Morris, Charles, and Mark Drabenstott. 1989. "Financing Rural Businesses: What Role for Public Policy?" *Economic Review* (Federal Reserve Bank of Kansas City) 74:30-45.

Finds that the decline in bank loan growth in most rural areas during the 1980s was primarily due to a slowdown in rural business conditions rather than to a reduction in the willingness of rural bankers to lend. The authors conclude that, in general, expensive government credit programs should be avoided and public assistance should be channeled to a handful of low-cost programs that overcome a few problems in rural capital markets. Under this policy approach, three areas appear to be most promising: secondary markets, technical assistance, and venture capital markets.

389. Newman, Robert J. 1983. "Industry Migration and Growth in the South." *Review of Economics and Statistics* 65:76-86.

Finds that state corporate income taxes, unionization, and right-to-work laws have been significant factors in explaining growth of industry in the South. Corporate income taxes have more effect on capital-intensive manufacturing sectors while unionization and right-to-work are more influential for more labor intensive ones. The independent variable(s) was the comparative change among states in total employment in each of 13 manufacturing sectors over the period 1957-73.

390. O'Farrell, P. N., and R. Crouchley. 1983. "Industrial Closures in Ireland 1973-1981: Analysis and Implications." *Regional Studies* 17(6):411-427.

Analyzes industrial closures in Ireland over the period 1973-81. Evidence is presented concerning temporal trends in closure, annual closure rates by region, and the closure propensity of new plant openings. Hypothesized relationships between closure probability and age, size, sector, ownership, nationality, female intensity, grant aid, regional and town size location are examined within a logit model. Multinational branches display higher closure rates than Irish establishments, and grant aid reduces the probability of closure.

391. Pagano, Michael A., and Ann O'M. Bowman. 1992. "Attributes of Development Tools: Success and Failure in Local Economic Development." *Economic Development Quarterly* 6(2):173-186.

Examines the attributes of local economic development policy instruments and asks whether these attributes can predict (1) project success as defined in archival data and in interviews of city officials and (2) revenue generation as defined in conventional return on investment terms. Based on analyses of quantitative and qualitative data from 40 city-supported development projects nationwide, the authors conclude that the city's economic condition is an important predictor of the revenue-generating success of a project. Further, the less complicated and more routine or standard the bundle of incentives offered (especially by economically healthy cities), the greater the probability of revenue-generating success. Project success, however, is related to other factors. The more controversial the project, the more likely that it will ultimately be regarded as unsuccessful.

392. Pirsig, Susan M., and Ann M. Peterson. 1989. *Southwest Minnesota Regional Labor Survey, 1988.* Slayton, MN: Southwest Regional Development Commission. 18 pp. plus appendices.

Reports results of a labor force survey conducted in a nine-county area in southwest Minnesota in 1988. Survey questions covered such characteristics as employment status (currently employed or not employed), last occupation for those not employed, present work hours, current salary, acceptable salary, job skills, interest in employment or different employment, distance willing to commute, education, and age. A mailed survey was used in data collection; 558 usable surveys representing 944 labor force members constituted the data base of the study. Factors motivating the study included concerns regarding the adequacy of the unemployment rate as a labor market indicator in rural areas and uncertainty regarding the effects of the high levels of out-migration that had occurred in the area during the 1980s.

393. Porter, Michael E. 1990. "The Competitive Advantage of Nations." *Harvard Business Review* 68(2):73-93.

Reports results of a four-year study of 10 important trading nations. Nations included, in addition to the United States, were Denmark, Germany, Italy, Japan, Korea, Singapore, Sweden, Switzerland, and the United Kingdom. Together these 10 nations accounted for fully 50 percent of total world exports in 1985. In each nation, the study consisted of two parts: (1) identification of all industries in which the nation's companies were internationally successful, and (2) examination of the history of competition in particular industries to understand how comparative advantage was created. The author analyzes the determinants of competitive advantage for individual industries and also briefly examines overall implications for government policy and company strategy.

394.   Prestwich, Roger. 1988. *Community Bankers in Rural Minnesota: Their Awareness of Small Business Technical Assistance and Their Business Start-Up Lending Experience.* Wayzata, MN: Spring Hill Center, 25 pp.

Summarizes results of a 1988 telephone survey of rural Minnesota bankers that dealt with two major issues: (1) bankers' knowledge and opinion of small business technical assistance programs and (2) their experience of dealing with nonagricultural startup business lending. Two banks in each of 40 nonmetropolitan counties were selected for the sample, and 56 interviews were completed. Almost 67 percent of the respondents refer clients to technical assistance (TA) programs, but on average they use only one in three of the programs available in the state. Many bankers said they did not know enough about the programs to be able to rate their usefulness. Almost 90 percent of the bankers viewed lending to startup businesses as important, but over half had made four or fewer such loans in the past year, and 18 percent had made none.

395.   Raitz, Karl. 1988. "Advantages of Place as Perceived by Sunbelt Promoters." *Growth and Change* 19(4):14-29.

Summarizes results of a survey of 104 Chamber of Commerce executives in states and cities in the South and Southwest to evaluate the factors they perceive to be important in recruiting business and industrial migrants from the North. The 81 respondents rated 33 location factors. Results show variation in the perceived importance of factors between Southeast states (Alabama, Florida, Georgia, Mississippi, North Carolina, South Carolina, Tennessee, and Virginia), South Central states (Arkansas, Louisiana, Oklahoma, and Texas), Southwest states (Arizona, California, and New Mexico), and border states (Colorado, Delaware, Kansas,

Kentucky, Maryland, Missouri, Nevada, Utah, and West Virginia). Patterns of perceived competition among cities reveal that border cities view Southern cities as their most important competitors but Southern cities see their major competitors as other rapidly growing Southern cities. Large cities do not see smaller cities as competitors with the exception of the "high tech" research centers such as Raleigh, North Carolina.

396. Rathge, Richard W., Gary A. Goreham, and Dena M. Nundahl. 1990. *Ransom County Marketing Area Labor Force Survey: 1990.* Fargo, ND: North Dakota State University, State Census Data Center, 22 pp.

Summarizes a study conducted for the Ransom County Economic Development Authority. The objectives were to (1) determine the present labor force status of the residents of the marketing area, (2) develop an inventory of the job skills available in the labor force, (3) account for those wanting part-time (versus full-time) employment, (4) determine the distance members of the labor force are willing to commute to work, and (5) find what labor force members consider to be acceptable wage levels. Data were from a telephone survey of 360 randomly selected households.

397. Rathge, Richard W., Gary A. Goreham, and Dena Nundahl. 1992. "The Role of Rural Community Development Corporations in Economic Development." *Journal of the Community Development Society* 23(2):39-52.

Analyzes success among rural community development corporations (CDCs) using limited liability theory and organizational characteristics theory. Data were derived from a survey of 106 CDCs in North Dakota and South Dakota collected in the fall of 1989. Indicators of limited liability included membership, support, and activity variables while organizational indicators included leadership and decision making, organizational structure, and finance variables. Success was measured in terms of net change in business and jobs and achievement of the CDC goals. Stepwise regression was used to determine which set of indicators best predicted success. The results indicate that knowledge of the investment atmosphere which surrounds the CDC more effectively predicts the eventual success of a rural CDC than does knowing its organizational structure. Thus, insight into a community's demographic profile and its environment are key to understanding success of rural CDCs.

398. Redwood, Anthony. 1988. "Job Creation in Nonmetropolitan Communities." *State Government* 61(1):9-15.

Reports that rural cities and towns must adapt to global economic changes in order to create jobs and survive as communities. A flexible, well-educated and skilled work force is a key to rural development. States and communities alike must invest in the future if rural areas are to be economically viable.

399. Reeder, Richard J. 1990. *Targeting Aid to Distressed Rural Areas: Indicators of Fiscal and Community Well-Being.* Staff Rpt. No. AGES 9067. Washington, D.C.: USDA, Economic Research Service, 54 pp.

Reports that improving the targeting of aid programs is a high priority among Federal and state policymakers. Commonly used indicators of fiscal and community well-being, such as unemployment, tax effort, and population size, disproportionately favor urban over rural areas. More care in the selection of targeting indicators would improve program efficiency and equity. Greater attention to program details, such as matching requirements, technical assistance, and the statistical properties of the targeting indicators would also help tailor programs to rural conditions. Use of fiscal capacity indicators, such as per capita income, would keep program costs down by targeting aid to rural areas that cannot afford to help themselves.

400. Roberts, Karen, and Phillip R. Smith. 1992. "The Effect of Labor Cost Differences on the Location of Economic Activity Under the U.S.-Canada Free Trade Agreement." *Economic Development Quarterly* 6(1):52-63.

Compares compensation costs for Canadian and U.S. workers to evaluate how relative compensation costs may affect firm location decisions with the implementation of the Free Trade Agreement. Using 1987 data, the authors find that compensation costs for U.S. labor were consistently higher (among major industry groups) than those for Canadian labor. Also, despite apparent Canadian preferences for social insurance, U.S. nonwage compensation also was higher. Higher U.S. costs persisted after allowing for large shifts in the exchange rate except in retail trade. When differences in labor productivity were incorporated, the Canadian cost advantage disappeared except in wholesale trade. Major conclusions were that cost differences will motivate firms to locate distribution centers on the Canadian side of the border and that socialization of medical costs in Canada will increase pressure for restructuring financing of health insurance in the United States.

401. Schmenner, Roger W. 1991. "Geography and the Character and Performance of Factories," pp. 241-253 in *Industry Location and Public Policy*, H. Herzog and A. Schlottmann, eds. Knoxville, TN: The University of Tennessee Press.

Examines whether there are character and performance differences across factories in different regions of the country. In particular, are there any meaningful distinctions between the traditional manufacturing-rich states and the most rapidly industrializing states, loosely referred to as Sunbelt states? The author addresses these questions by examining factory-level data from two mail surveys, one from the late 1970s and the other from 1985. He finds that regions are less tied than ever before to particular industries for their economic development. However, there are some stereotypes that characterize the type of plant that locates in either the Sunbelt or in the more traditional manufacturing states, with Sunbelt states more likely to be the site chosen for new, high-volume, low-cost "production" plants while traditional manufacturing states are more effective in garnering the more specialized facility often tied to company headquarters operations. Finally, the productivity performance of plants does not appear to be related at all to location within the United States, but instead to factors such as just-in-time manufacturing principles.

402. Schmitt, Neal, Sandra E. Gleason, Bruce Pigozzi, and Philip M. Marcus. 1982. "Business Climate Attitudes and Company Relocation Decisions." *Journal of Applied Psychology* 72(4):622-628.

Summarizes results of a survey in which 438 manufacturing firms reported their business relocation activity, their overall attitude toward the business climate in Michigan, and their assessment of 34 business climate dimensions. Using a lens model paradigm, the authors explore reasons for a lack of relation between actual relocation decisions and overall business climate attitudes. Location decisions were most highly correlated with distance and labor factors, whereas overall business climate was most highly correlated with tax considerations, and secondarily correlated with labor problems.

403. Shaffer, Ron, and Glen C. Pulver. 1990. "Rural Nonfarm Business' Access to Debt and Equity Capital," pp. 39-58 in *Financial Market Intervention as a Rural Development Strategy*. ERS Staff Rpt. No. AGES 9070. Washington, D.C.: USDA, Economic Research Service.

Examines whether inadequate capital markets are hindering rural economic development. Based on extensive research on capital markets in rural Wisconsin and the analyses of other rural areas across the country, the authors conclude that financial markets are performing adequately for a high percentage of rural firms. Most rural nonfarm businesses appear to be well served by their financial institutions. Availability of capital is not a widespread problem, and no one type or stage of business will always have difficulty acquiring capital in all rural capital markets. Small, new firms and very large firms, however, often have problems arranging credit through rural lenders. The firms experiencing the most difficulty in acquiring capital, after proper consideration of risk, are often those on the leading edge of rural development. Inadequate skills in packaging funds and assessing risk represent a substantial portion of rural nonfarm businesses' difficulty in acquiring debt and equity capital.

404. Smith, I. J. 1985. "Foreign Direct Investment and Divestment Trends in Industrialized Counties," pp. 142-173 in *Progress in Industrial Geography*, M. Pacione, ed. London: Croom Helm.

Attempts to fill a gap in the literature of the multinational enterprise by assembling and analyzing the rather limited information on international trends in foreign direct investment (FDI) within the major industrialized countries during the 20-year period beginning in the mid-1960s. Because of problems with published data on FDI flows, the analysis focuses on United Kingdom evidence for the late 1970s in the belief that this provides some insight into what is likely to have been happening elsewhere in the developed world. In the final section, the evidence is synthesized in an attempt to isolate the part played by FDI in growth differences between the major industrialized nations.

405. Thompson, Wilbur R., and Philip R. Thompson. 1987. "National Industries and Local Occupational Strengths: The Cross-Hairs of Targeting." *Urban Studies* 24:547-560.

Addresses three broad perspectives of local development: (1) the industry characteristics that most affect the well-being of its locality, (2) the measurement of the functional strengths (or comparative advantage) of a place, expressed not so much in the traditional industry form but more in terms of the various functions common to every industry, and (3) a revitalized industry location theory that matches local strengths with industry locational requirements for more efficient and effective development planning and strategy. A key point developed in the article is that past emphasis in local economic development has been on the local *industry* mix but that analysts should be placing greater emphasis on the local *occupation* mix.

406. Vedder, Richard K. 1982. "Rich States, Poor States: How High Taxes Inhibit Growth." *Journal of Contemporary Studies* (1982):19-32.

Reports results of an analysis of state taxation levels and economic growth rates for the period 1970-80. Tax burden was measured by total state and local taxes per capita in 1980, and economic growth was measured by changes in per capita income. The author concludes that high levels of tax burden were associated with lower than average rates of economic growth.

407. Wasylenko, Michail, and Therese McGuire. 1985. "Jobs and Taxes: The Effect of Business Climate on States' Employment Growth Rates." *National Tax Journal* 38(4):497-511.

Presents an econometric model for total employment growth and for employment growth in six separate industries in states between 1973 and 1980. Results indicate that higher wages, utility prices, personal income tax rates, and an increase in the overall level of taxation discourage employment growth in several industries. Factors such as higher state and local spending on education and per capita income, however, favorably affect job growth.

408. Wolman, Harold, Cary Lichtman, and Suzie Barnes. 1991. "The Impact of Credentials, Skill Levels, Worker Training, and Motivation on Employment Outcomes: Sorting Out the Implications for Economic Development Policy." *Economic Development Quarterly* 5(2):140-151.

Examines the relative impact of general skill level, job-specific training, credentials, and motivation on employment outcomes for labor market entrants who have recently finished their education. The data for the study were drawn from the 1986 follow-up of the High School and Beyond longitudinal survey sponsored by the U.S. Department of Education. The sample consisted of 1980 high school seniors and sophomores who were interviewed first in 1980 and reinterviewed every two years thereafter to 1986. The research findings are examined for their implications for economic development policy.

Technological

409. Brooks, Harvey. 1985. "Technology as a Factor in U.S. Competitiveness." *U.S. Competitiveness in the World Economy*, B.

R. Scott and G. C. Lodge, eds. Boston: Harvard Business School Press, pp. 328-356.

Uses two approaches in assessing the state of U.S. innovation. The first is to examine various aggregate statistics on R&D performance, patent activity, technical manpower, industrial productivity, origination of major industrial innovations, and export market shares in high technology markets. The author believes that these aggregate measures do not support the extreme alarm being expressed in some quarters over the decline in U.S. technical leadership. The second approach is to examine the situation in specific industries or industry segments. Here the evidence of decline is more alarming.

410. Chapman, Keith, and Graham Humphrys, eds. 1987. *Technical Change and Industrial Policy*. New York, NY: Basil Blackwell, Inc., 264 pp.

Points out that the role of technology is a unifying theme relevant to an understanding of both industrial growth and industrial decline. Thus, obsolescence and innovation represent opposite ends of a spectrum epitomized, at the industry scale, by such epithets as "sunset" and "sunrise." A common objective of policy makers at various levels of government is to encourage and to attract those activities which, by virtue of their technological characteristics, are perceived to offer the prospect of future growth in output and, especially, employment. Such an objective often rests upon a kind of technological determinism fostered by life-cycle models applied to products, industries, and regions. It also betrays a belief in the benefits of "high technology" which is not always justified. This volume explores these and other issues regarding the role of technology in the interpretation of spatial patterns of industrial growth and decline. It includes eleven chapters, in addition to introductory and conclusions sections, divided into three sections. The first is concerned with various aspects of the role of technical change as a phenomenon. The second evaluates its role in the restructuring of "traditional" industries, and the third reviews some of its implications for industrial and regional development policies.

411. Dillman, Don A. 1991. "Telematics and Rural Development," pp. 292-306 in *Rural Policies for the 1990s*, C. Flora and J. Christenson, eds. Boulder, CO: Westview Press.

Indicates that a major policy issue facing rural America is, first, developing a telematics infrastructure that will adequately support job creation and other rural development goals and, second, encouraging use of that infrastructure to improve the economic and social well-being of rural people. The author defines telematics as the joining together of telecommunications, broadcast media, and computer technologies into a single infrastructure for developing, sending, receiving, sorting, and utilizing information.

412. Dillman, Don A., Donald M. Beck, and John C. Allen. 1989. "Rural Barriers to Job Creation Remain, Even in Today's Information Age." *Rural Development Perspectives* 5(2):21-27.

Finds that new information technologies hold a promise of integrating rural businesses and communities more closely with the Nation's urban centers of commerce. While allowing rural businesses to compete better for urban jobs, however, those technologies also allow urban businesses to compete better for rural jobs. To take advantage of new opportunities, rural areas will have to modernize their communications networks, educate their workers, and broaden their outlook.

413. Goddard, John and Andrew Gillespie. 1988. "Advanced Telecommunications and Regional Economic Development," pp. 121-146 in *Informatics and Regional Development*, M. Giaoutzi and P. Nijkamp, eds. Aldershot, Hants, England: Gower Publishing Company, Ltd.

Reports that as more and more economic activities become concerned with the generation, processing, and exchange of information, technical developments which affect this activity are of potentially far-reaching significance. Within the European Community, a series of initiatives have been undertaken, including a research and development program for broadband communication technologies and a special program for telecommunications in the less-favored regions of Europe. The authors outline the analytical basis which underlies this type of telecommunications and regional development initiatives. They begin with a review of the issues surrounding the development of an "information economy," and then summarize the major technical and regulatory changes taking place with respect to the supply of telecommunications services. The paper concludes with a discussion of some specific examples of regional and local policy initiatives designed to exploit the opportunities arising from these developments and to counter the threats they pose for less favored regions.

414. Hake, David A., Donald R. Ploch, and William F. Fox. 1985. *Business Location Determinants in Tennessee.* Knoxville, TN: The University of Tennessee Center for Business and Economic Research, 111 pp.

Reports results of a survey of 325 firms that had expanded or developed new sites in Tennessee within the period 1980-83. Respondents were first asked to rate the importance of 21 different factors in influencing selection of the region in which they chose to locate. A second question asked respondents which of 33 factors were used in selecting a final site.

415. Haug, Peter, and Phillip Ness. 1993. "Industrial Location Decisions of Biotechnology Organizations." *Economic Development Quarterly* 7(4):390-402.

Describes research on biotechnology location decisions and economic development and characteristics of American biotechnology companies and employment. This background provides a foundation for discussing empirical evidence from commercial biotechnology enterprises in the Greater Seattle region, a major American biotechnology concentration. Research findings indicate the importance of university research activities, academic spinoffs, and entrepreneurial behavior in biotechnology firm development. Research and development (R&D) and manufacturing facility location decisions emphasized founder preferences, proximity to either university or company facilities, labor agglomeration economies, and the local infrastructure. Federal and state regulations and taxes, marketing capabilities, and financing sources were leading operational restrictions affecting company growth. These findings suggest increasing university and company R&D funding and expanding existing high-technology complexes to encourage regional biotechnology economic development.

416. Hepworth, Mark. 1986. "The Geography of Technological Change in the Information Economy." *Regional Studies* 20(5):407-424.

Reports that innovations in information technology are transforming urban and regional systems through their impacts on production and distribution processes. Case studies of Canadian multilocational firms are used to examine this spatio-economic transformation in the context of the new information-based service economy. By focussing on computer networks as spatial systems of information technology, it is shown that these innovations can lead to centralized and decentralized patterns of direct production and office activity. New insights are also developed into the telecommunications-transportation trade-off and the key role of telecommunications in regional development.

417. Hepworth, M. E., A. E. Green, and A. E. Gillespie. 1987. "The Spatial Division of Information Labour in Great Britain." *Environment and Planning A* 19:793-806.

Examines the geographic distribution of the information economy in Great Britain. The authors find substantial regional differences in the percentage of employment in information occupations, but also observe that job prospects in all parts of the country are increasingly dependent on information-based services. Innovations in information technology are expected to reinforce the uneven geography of employment opportunities. The authors point out that the emerging information economy will place an even greater emphasis on education, training, and retraining. A major shift in public attitudes towards education will be required if Britain is to develop as an information economy competing in world markets.

418. Howland, Marie. 1991. *Rural Computer Services in an International Economy.* Report to the Ford Foundation. College Park, MD: University of Maryland, Department of Urban Studies and Planning, 59 pp.

Evaluates the present and potential role of the computer services industry in rural economic development. The author finds that the computer services industry has potential as a source of economic growth because of its rapid employment growth, its export potential, and its relatively high proportion of professional, well-paid jobs. However, she also finds that the long-run prospects for employment growth *in rural areas* are not promising. The reasons for this conclusion are (1) there is little evidence that urban computer services firms will decentralize, (2) the capital intensive nature of data processing reduces the advantages of low-cost rural labor forces, (3) advances in scanning technologies and bar coding are reducing the importance of labor availability, reliability, and cost, and (4) rural firms are threatened by offshore data entry operations in countries with lower wage rates and solid educational systems.

419. Kasarda, John D. 1991. "Global Air Cargo-Industrial Complexes as Development Tools." *Economic Development Quarterly* 5(3):187-196.

Points out that a new economic era is being spawned by three interacting forces: (1) the globalization of business transactions, (2) a shift to just-in-time manufacturing and inventory control methods, and (3) the growing need of firms to dispatch smaller, more frequent shipments quickly to distant markets. The ability of any state or locality in the coming decades to maximize commercial growth, expand exports, and attract major investment will depend on understanding the new economy and harnessing the forces creating it. In North Carolina, an examination of how these forces might be leveraged to the state's competitive advantage has led to the formulation of a global air cargo-industrial complex. This proposed complex would integrate (both spatially and operationally) just-in-time manufacturing systems with air freight systems such that the two systems function as a synergistic unit. The underlying concepts may prove attractive to other states.

420. Malecki, Edward J. 1981. "Product Cycles, Innovation Cycles, and Regional Economic Change." *Technological Forecasting and Social Change* 19:291-306.

Addresses the frequently overlooked topic of the effects of technological change below the level of national and sectoral aggregations. The author reviews the regional economic changes that result from technological change at both the firm level and in the individual plant. The related concepts of product cycles and innovation cycles provide a perspective for assessing regional and local effects. Government policies related to innovation are examined in the light of regional economic implications.

421. Malecki, Edward J. 1981. "Science, Technology, and Regional Economic Development: Review and Prospects." *Research Policy* 10:312-334.

Reviews the literature on the location and regional effects of science and technology (S&T) in the context of developed economies. Two processes associated with the creation of new products, agglomeration and spin-off, act to attract further innovative activity in those regions. Other regions, where R&D and related activities do not take place, are unlikely to be the locations of new-product production, and instead will tend to specialize in the production of standardized products. Both corporate and government R&D rely on pools of technical labor for technological and new product activities; these pools of mobile workers are most attracted to large urban areas. In only some of these areas, however, does the spin-off process result in the generation of new technology-based firms. The availability of local venture capital appears to be the principal influence on this variation. Government policy regarding science and technology has impacts on regions by contributing to the agglomeration of R&D. Government policy also often fails to recognize that S&T policy and industrial policy have regional effects that may be long-term in nature and most detrimental to those regions whose economies are least competitive. Finally, some priorities for future research on innovation in a regional setting are identified.

422. Malecki, Edward J. 1983. "Technology and Regional Development: A Survey." *International Regional Science Review* 8(2):89-125.

Reviews the literature on the role of technology and technological change in regional development. Three specific themes are identified. First, traditional approaches to technology include those found in models of regional growth, in analyses of innovation diffusion, and in economic analysis of technological change. Second, recent research on regional development has involved technology from two perspectives--that of regional economic structure and that of innovation in the strategies and management of large corporations. Third, the underdevelopment of Third World countries has been attributed in part to technological dependence. The possibilities are abundant for research that would add to current understanding of regional development in an age of rapid technological change.

423. Malecki, Edward J. 1991. *Technology and Economic Development: The Dynamics of Local, Regional, and National Change.* Burnt Mill, Harlow, England: Longman Scientific and Technical, 495 pp.

Synthesizes the large literature which has grown around the topics of economic development and technology. The book is intended to be a resource for further inquiry into topics covered in its pages, and so there are many references to the large and diverse literature which has contributed to development studies, broadly defined. The author surveys theory and empirical findings from a variety of disciplines, such as economic geography, economics, and planning, as well as from interdisciplinary areas such as entrepreneurship studies, regional science, and science and technology policy. The book brings together existing knowledge about economic development, especially at the scale of regions within nations. The author believes that research at the regional scale is the most useful for addressing the realities of economic development in the 1990s, because the openness and vulnerability of regions and nations to outside influences, so evident from the early research into regional development, are now evident at national scale as well. The author finds that technology is a central ingredient in economic development, permitting entrepreneurs to get an edge on competitors and allowing one region to be more prosperous than another.

424. Oksanen, E. H., and J. R. Williams. 1984. "Industrial Location and Inter-Industry Linkages." *Empirical Economics* 9:139-150.

Provides a tentative explanation of the spatial distribution of economic activity in Canada, with a focus upon the role of interindustry linkages. Location of economic activity for each of 109 three-digit SIC manufacturing industries is explained by use of a "Tobit" model incorporating backward and forward linkage variables. The two sets of linkage variables in each Tobit equation were reduced by extraction of one principal component from each set, using the matrix of cosines of the variables. A set of control variables completes the set of explanatory variables. The overall explanatory power of the equations was remarkably high, and the role of inter-industry linkages is unmistakable.

425. Rees, John, ed. 1986. *Technology, Regions, and Policy.* Totowa, NJ: Rowman and Littlefield, 322 pp.

Examines the links between technological change and regional development and how policy encourages change and is then influenced by change. This collection of 13 chapters addresses the development of high-technology complexes, the spread of new industrial technology, and new technology and policy options at the federal, state, and local levels. The chapters provide the results and interpretations of a diverse group of economists, geographers, and planners who have all been actively involved in original research projects pertaining to the links between technology, policy, and regional change in the United States.

Cultural

426. Behrman, Jack N., and Dennis A. Rondinelli. 1992. "The Cultural Imperatives of Globalization: Urban Economic Growth in the 21st Century." *Economic Development Quarterly* 6(2):115-126.

Reports that the progressive opening of national economies in advanced, developing, and transforming countries is reducing the intervention of national policies on trade and investment. Consequently, the responsibility for attracting foreign direct investment will devolve jointly on national, state, and local governments. Although national governments can enhance the country's attraction to foreign investors, the actual location will depend on the attractiveness of the community or city itself. It will be up to those in charge of urban development to see that the conditions are conducive to foreign management and to location of economic activity. These conditions include not only the old standbys of a "favorable investment climate" but increasingly also cultural characteristics that will make the community attractive to sophisticated management and professional people. The challenge for most cities is to change their culture to make it more competitive and attractive.

427. Clark, Thomas A., and Franklin J. James. 1992. "Women-Owned Businesses: Dimensions and Policy Issues." *Economic Development Quarterly* 6(1):25-40.

Reports that women-owned businesses may have grown 6-fold, and the gross receipts of these businesses 50-fold over the past 2 decades. Most businesses owned by women, however, are small, undercapitalized, situated in retailing and the services, and many enable only part-time work. As a result, few women have achieved high earnings from ownership. This study indicates that the potential earnings for most women are substantially higher in management positions on payrolls than in self-employment. Women with continuing care responsibilities, however, are often constrained to worksites in or near the home, and to work schedules that complement these allied activities. Many such women seek to own their own businesses largely because they have no alternative. This may change as current employers, facing labor shortages and external pressures, move to accommodate the particular needs of women. The authors conclude that there is little economic rationale for intense new public efforts to stimulate or support women-owned businesses, but that the federal government must continue to promote equal opportunity within businesses at large.

428. Cole, Robert E., and Donald R. Deskins, Jr. 1988. "Racial Factors in the Employment Patterns of Japanese Auto Firms in America." *California Management Review* 31(1):9-22.

Reports that the auto industry has traditionally been a major source of jobs and income for blacks. As jobs in U.S. companies decline, the newer Japanese plants, both manufacturers and suppliers, are not hiring blacks to a similar extent. The new American plants typically employ higher percentages of blacks than would be expected from their local labor sheds. This has resulted primarily from UAW contractual obligations to accept displaced workers. By contrast, Japanese manufacturers and suppliers locate in areas with few blacks and hire fewer blacks than would be expected from the racial composition of their local labor sheds.

429. Doeringer, Peter B., and David G. Terkla. 1990. "How Intangible Factors Contribute to Economic Development: Lessons From a Mature Local Economy." *World Development* 18(9):1295-1308.

Provides new evidence on the importance of nontraditional cost factors in determining regional growth, building on a case study of a mature manufacturing region in Massachusetts. Specialized mature manufacturing firms that have broken the product cycle are identified. The authors then discuss development strategies for using "intangible" factors to promote such firms.

430. Galgon, Randy. 1993. "The Application of the Terrarium Concept to the Creation of a Business Park." *Economic Development Review* 11(2):35-37.

Reports that environmental opposition is a feature of most economic development projects today. While a number of techniques are available to respond to the environmental challenge, this paper introduces a procedure whereby everything that an industry does must be contained within the company's building. In effect, the community puts performance standards on the building, making it a terrarium.

431. Greenwood, Michael J. 1988. "Changing Patterns of Migration and Regional Economic Growth in the U.S.: A Demographic Perspective." *Growth and Change* 19(4):68-87.

Reports that during the 1970s and early 1980s, the South and West Census regions accounted for over 90 percent of incremental national population, which was easily the highest percentage accounted for by these regions in the nation's history. This paper stresses the importance of powerful demographic forces that contributed to the regional shift, but it does not ignore important economic factors. A major theme of the paper is that because the baby boom has now largely matured out of the most mobile age classes, population and employment growth differentials that strongly favored the South and West will moderate in the future.

432. MacManus, Susan A. 1993. "Minority Contractors' Views of Government Purchasing and Procurement Practices." *Economic Development Quarterly* 7(1):30-49.

Compares and contrasts the reasons American Indian, Asian-, black-, and Hispanic-owned firms sell to government, the problems they encounter, and their assessments of the overall quality of the purchasing practices of the federal, state, county, city, and school district governments. It also focuses on the governments they regard as undesirable customers. It is based on the responses of 325 minority-owned businesses responding to a mail survey. The overwhelming majority of minority (and nonminority) owned firms do not believe the current system is competitive, fair, or efficient. However, minority contractors differ on their specific likes and dislikes, often because they tend to be clustered in different economic sectors.

Infrastructure

433. Ambrose, David M., and Louis G. Pol. 1988. "The Importance of Interstate Highways to Economic Development in Nebraska," pp. 131-154 in *Nebraska Policy Choices*, R. L. Smith, ed. Omaha, NE: University of Nebraska at Omaha, Center for Applied Urban Research.

Focuses on the post-construction impact of interstate highways on income and sales expansion. Using data for all Nebraska and Iowa counties, interstate highways are found to have the most positive economic impact on areas with larger populations; small areas are not likely to experience more than short-term gains.

434. Bamberger, Rita J., William A. Blazar, and George E. Peterson. 1985. *Infrastructure Support for Economic Development.* Chicago: American Planning Association, 38 pp.

Examines the role of infrastructure in economic development. The authors address the following questions (1) What are the consequences for economic growth when existing infrastructure facilities deteriorate? (2) Is an infrastructure network as critical to the new generation of business investment, with its emphasis on service industries and information functions, as it was to the old generation of manufacturing investment? and (3) How can cities plan intelligently for a capital plant that supports their economic development objectives? One chapter addresses telecommunications infrastructure--a topic of great concern for many communities in the 1980s.

435. Campbell, Candace, David Berge, James Janus, and Kevin Olsen. 1987. *Change Agents in the New Economy: Business Incubators and Economic Development.* Minneapolis, MN: University of Minnesota, Hubert H. Humphrey Institute of Public Affairs.

Describes the dynamics of new enterprise formation and growth in incubator facilities and evaluates the incubator's contribution to job creation and economic development. The findings were developed through a series of in-depth case studies that tracked firms as they moved through or within incubator facilities, primarily those with three or more years of operating history. Findings include quantitative measures of effectiveness such as rates of business survival, expansion, and job creation as well as qualitative measures such as the effect of the incubator on the performance of tenant companies, on area redevelopment, on women and minority entrepreneurship and employment, and on local economic development. A review of business incubators in Western Europe is included.

436. Chicoine, David L., and Norman Walzer, eds. 1986. *Financing Local Infrastructure in Nonmetropolitan Areas.* New York, NY: Praeger Publishers, 253 pp.

Reports on the state of transportation infrastructure in the rural areas of the United States and the problems encountered in financing infrastructure improvements. The book is intended to offer a broad background for policy discussions and to be of interest to three main groups: (1) state and federal policymakers facing decisions about infrastructure support, (2) local officials requiring a broad perspective on rural infrastructure, and (3) local public finance experts. The eleven chapters, developed from papers presented at a conference on financing rural infrastructure, are divided into five broad sections ranging from background information on population trends and implications for rural road demands to innovative methods for financing existing transportation systems.

437. Cordes, Sam M. 1989. "The Changing Rural Environment and the Relationship Between Health Services and Rural Development." *Health Services Research* 23:757-784.

Focuses on the relationship between the larger rural environment and the delivery of health services in rural areas. The author first considers definitions of "rural" and explains two taxonomies that go beyond the official definitions. Second, some basic characteristics of rural America are noted, including selected changes in the structure of rural America and reasons for these changes. The third section provides a framework for rural development and illustrates the role of health services within this framework. Finally, the salient features of today's rural America are summarized and related to the challenge faced by researchers and policymakers.

438. Deller, Steven C. 1991. "Economic and Social Outcomes of Public and Private Investments in Physical Infrastructure for Growth and

Stability of Rural Economies," pp. 50-73 in *Economic Productivity and Adaptability*. University Park, PA: Northeast Regional Center for Rural Development.

Serves as an overview of current thoughts about and understanding of the role of infrastructure in rural economic development. Attention is paid to how investments in infrastructure may or may not promote higher rates of economic growth and development. A brief review of studies that examine the link between investment in economic and social overhead capital and economic development and growth is also provided. Suggestions for both research agendas and extension programming are offered.

439. Eberts, Randall W. 1991. "Some Empirical Evidence on the Linkage Between Public Infrastructure and Local Economic Development," pp. 83-96 in *Industry Location and Public Policy*, H. Herzog and A. Schlottmann, eds. Knoxville, TN: The University of Tennessee Press.

Explores the possible linkages between local public infrastructure and economic development. The questions of whether or not public infrastructure affects economic growth goes beyond the direct economic impact of jobs and payrolls generated from public works construction projects. Rather, the question encompasses a broad range of infrastructure effects on economic growth. The author looks at three possible effects and provides empirical evidence in support of these linkages: (1) the use of infrastructure as an input into the production of goods and services, (2) its effect on the growth rate of private capital and labor, and (3) its ability to augment the productivity of other privately provided inputs. The author focuses primarily on the public works component of public infrastructure.

440. Economic Research Service. 1990. *Infrastructure Investment and Economic Development: Rural Strategies for the 1990's*. Staff Rpt. No. AGES 9069. Washington, D.C.: USDA, Economic Research Service, Agriculture and Rural Economy Division, 81 pp.

Examines the effects of investment in transportation, telecommunications, and water and wastewater infrastructure on improving the economies of rural America. The authors are not optimistic about the possibility of the direct stimulation of economic development across the spectrum of rural communities through just any infrastructure investments. On the other hand, they agree that certain carefully selected infrastructure investments may often have good economic development payoffs, when the investments are made in places with the other prerequisites for development.

441. Everitt, John, and Robert Annis. 1992. "The Sustainability of Prairie Rural Communities," pp. 213-222 in *Contemporary Rural Systems in Transition: Volume 2, Economy and Society*, I. R. Bowler, C. Bryant, and M. Nellis, eds. Wallingford, Oxon, U.K.: CAB International.

Is primarily concerned with the sustainability of small communities on the Prairies of Canada, and particularly with those in Manitoba. However, the authors believe that the issues have a wider significance; they can be generalized, in many instances, to other parts of Canada where established lifestyles have also been eroded. The authors advance seven major reasons why more attention should be paid to the maintenance and enhancement of these lifestyles.

442. Fitzgerald, Joan, and Allan McGregor. 1993. "Labor-Community Initiatives in Worker Training in the United States and the United Kingdom." *Economic Development Quarterly* 7(2):172-182.

Examines labor organizing around the training issue in the United States and the United Kingdom. The best practice examples presented are the Machine Action Project in Springfield, Massachusetts and the Inverclyde Training Trust in the Glasgow, Scotland region. In both cases, labor built a response to industrial decline around training. Both cases demonstrate that labor and community organizations can play an increased role in local economic development practice. The U.S. case depicts a proactive response, whereas response in the United Kingdom has been largely reactive. The authors conclude that labor in both places should look to other countries for examples of more proactive shaping of training policy in the interests of workers.

443. Forkenbrock, David J., Thomas F. Pogue, Norman S. J. Foster, and David J. Finnegan. 1990. *Road Investment To Foster Local Economic Development*. Iowa City: The University of Iowa, The Public Policy Center, 98 pp.

Addresses the relationship between road investment and local economic development. The authors attempt to incorporate the best available theory on this illusive relationship into a workable approach for those faced with making road investment decisions. A specific state program (Iowa's

RISE program) is used as a case study. RISE (Revitalize Iowa's Sound Economy) was established in 1985 to promote economic development through improvement of roads and streets and is funded by a dedicated gasoline tax of about $33 million.

444. Garwood, Amy. 1992. *Telecommunications and Rural Economic Development.* Minneapolis, MN: University of Minnesota, H. H. Humphrey Institute of Public Affairs, 37 pp. plus appendices.

Reports that, while all communities in rural America must consider their potential telecommunication needs in an environment defined by rapid technological and economic change, rural communities face particularly difficult problems. Because telecommunications services will become increasingly critical for economic opportunity, rural communities will need to promote an entrepreneurial spirit that employs advancing information technologies. Further, because these areas have traditionally been the last served by the public network, rural communities will need to demand the basic structural capacity to compete in a changing global economy. The author addresses several policy questions: (1) What level of advanced telecommunications is necessary for the future development of rural America? (2) Who should pay? (3) What is the most appropriate role for government? (4) How can we foster coordination between economic developers and telecommunications regulators?

445. Hansen, Niles. 1988. "Regional Consequences of Structural Changes in the National and International Division of Labor." *International Regional Science Review* 11(2):121-136.

Argues that for the past two decades, regional scientists have not been successful in anticipating structural changes in the spatial division of labor. A major reason has been the excessive emphasis placed on static analytic constructs based on city sizes and systems of cities. A more instructive approach would analyze the dynamic interrelations among the three functional levels through which changes in the division of labor operate, that is, workplaces, business organization, and spatial systems. The product cycle, the manufacturing process cycle, and a more broadly conceived view of regional production processes are considered in this context.

446. Munnell, Alicia H., with Leah M. Cook. 1990. "How Does Public Infrastructure Affect Regional Economic Performance?" *New England Economic Review* (Sept./Oct):11-33.

Explores the impact of public capital on output, employment growth, and private investment at the state and regional level. The authors (1) explain the construction of measures of public and private capital at the state level, (2) use these data to estimate an aggregate production function to estimate the relationship between output and public capital at the state level, (3) explore the relationship between public investment and private investment, and (4) introduce the public capital data into a firm location model to test whether variations in public capital have any impact on state-by-state employment growth. The authors conclude that those states that have invested more in infrastructure tend to have greater output, more private investment, and more employment growth.

447. Nathan, Richard P. 1992. "Needed: A Marshall Plan for Ourselves." *Economic Development Quarterly* 6(4):347-355.

Points out that the movement of goods, people, and information and the smooth functioning of cities are vital to our nation's economic well-being. This article reviews several studies that document public infrastructure needs. The purpose of the article is to urge a shift in U.S. economic policy to favor state and local infrastructure investment ("a Marshall Plan for ourselves").

448. Paulsen David F., and Burton J. Reed. 1987. "Nebraska's Small Towns and Their Capacity for Economic Development," pp. 43-77 in *Nebraska Policy Choices*, R. L. Smith, ed. Omaha, NE: University of Nebraska at Omaha, Center for Applied Urban Research.

Points out that small Nebraska towns have declined in population and wealth, while facing increasing demands, higher costs, and more problems. For them, economic development may be a way out, but the authors found that participation was related to having governmental capacities and physical facilities in place. In turn, these capacities were related to the size and wealth of the communities. Given limited resources, federal, state, and other agencies should direct their assistance to those small towns with a demonstrated capacity and commitment. Other small towns may need help to build capacities toward a threshold of economic development.

449. Reisdorph, David H. 1991. "Industrial Parks as an Economic Development Asset." *Economic Development Review* 9(4):29-30.

Summarizes findings of a study of 10 rural communities with industrial parks that were underutilized. The author finds that there are two important factors associated with successful industrial parks: (1) economic characteristics conducive to the type of development the industrial park is designed to facilitate and (2) effective marketing of the industrial park. Unfortunately, some industrial parks have been built in the hope that they will offset such negative community characteristics as an unskilled labor force or mediocre transportation access. Also, the community economic development organizations that have sponsored many of the parks have sometimes lacked the resources and continuity necessary to develop, market, and maintain an industrial park over a long period.

450. Rowley, Thomas D., and Peter L. Stenberg. 1993. *A Comparison of Military Base Closures: Metro and Nonmetro Counties, 1961-90.* Staff Report No. AGES 9307. Washington, D.C.: USDA, Economic Research Service, 20 pp.

Describes socioeconomic changes in local economies following closure of a military base. Comparisons are drawn between effects in nonmetro and metro counties, and between counties experiencing a base closing and other counties. Despite extreme variation in economic growth among base closing counties, three intriguing conclusions are found: (1) job losses tended to constitute a higher percentage of total employment in nonmetro counties than in metro counties, (2) of the 83 base-closing counties studied, one-third did not regain as many civilian jobs as were lost, (3) growth rates for employment, income, and population were slower in the average nonmetro base-closing county than in both the average metro base-closing county and the average nonmetro county nationwide.

451. Southern Rural Development Center. 1990. *Case Studies: Examples of Innovative Infrastructure Financing and Delivery Systems.* SRDC No. 128. Mississippi State, MS: Southern Rural Development Center, 120 pp.

Is the result of a detailed national search for innovative infrastructure financing and delivery systems. Types of facilities and services included were fire protection, business incubators, water, sewer, hospitals, social services, roads and bridges, education, emergency medical service, airports, and solid waste. The aim of the report is to provide community leaders with insight into ways of providing better infrastructure at the same or lower costs, thus improving the quality of life and promoting economic growth.

452. Steinnes, Donald N. 1990. "An Analysis of Infrastructure Provision and Local Economic Development Policy." *Journal of the Community Development Society* 21(1):33-53.

Examines the relationship between the provision of infrastructure by state and local government and economic growth during the 1962-1982 time frame by specifying and testing a policy evaluation model for a sample of cities. The cities chosen had populations of 20,000 to 100,000 and were located in the states of Iowa, Minnesota, North Dakota, South Dakota, and Wisconsin. The results suggest that infrastructure does stimulate job growth. The author calls for a more comprehensive analysis of the economic development process so that infrastructure and more direct job creation policies can be compared.

453. Taylor, Leon. 1991. "The Race to Build: Infrastructure Competition Among Communities." *Economic Development Quarterly* 5(1):60-63.

Reports that jurisdictions build infrastructures not only to accommodate recent growth but also to compete for new growth. Infrastructural competition can waste resources, particularly when subsidies make it cheap for localities to undertake such contests. By contrast, the author contends, tax competition wastes few resources. Communities might reduce waste by financing infrastructure through user or impact fees.

454. Thompson, Lyke. 1983. "New Jobs Versus Net Jobs: Measuring the Results of an Economic Development Program." *Policy Studies Journal* 12(2):365-375.

Evaluates the results of an industrial park development project in Battle Creek, Michigan. The author finds that, although approximately 700 new jobs were located at the park, statistical analysis indicates that the facility had no net impact on local employment. The author concludes that a leakage of jobs to other areas (i.e., via commuting) and some substitution of new jobs for old jobs were the most plausible explanation for these results.

455. U.S. General Accounting Office. 1992. *Availability of Credit for Agriculture, Rural Development, and Infrastructure.* GAO/RCED - 93-27. Washington, D.C.: U.S. General Accounting Office, 35 pp.

Addresses (1) the extent to which there is adequate credit available to fund agricultural production; rural development, which for purposes of this report is limited to needs of businesses; and the development of the rural infrastructure (including roads, bridges, and water systems), and (2) the extent to which rural lending institutions are investing in their communities as opposed to areas outside their communities. Information was obtained from interviews with over 300 officials representing federal, state, and local governments; universities; and organizations in the private sector such as economic development agencies and commercial banks. The conclusions were that credit for agricultural production was generally available for credit worthy borrowers, although loan standards were more stringent than in the past. There was less consensus on the availability of credit for rural businesses.

MARKETS

Local (Trade Area)

456.   Albrecht, Don E. 1993. "The Renewal of Population Loss in the Nonmetropolitan Great Plains." *Rural Sociology* 58(2):233-246.

Reports an analysis of population trends in 293 nonmetropolitan Great Plains counties from 1950 to 1990 that reveals that the population turnaround of the 1970s has indeed ended. During the 1980s, 84 percent of these nonmetropolitan counties had population declines, a proportion greater than in any other decade studied. A majority of counties had natural population increase, but such increases were offset by net outmigration as 96 percent of the counties had such losses during the 1980s. The influence of the independent variables on population change shifted from decade to decade. The most important variable in producing positive population trends was the ability of the county to attract retirement migrants.

457.   Anding, Thomas L., John S. Adams, William Casey, Sandra de Montille, and Miriam Goldfein. 1990. *Trade Centers of the Upper Midwest: Changes from 1960 to 1989.* Minneapolis, MN: University of Minnesota, Center for Urban and Regional Affairs, 59 pp.

Analyzes changes in trade centers and their economic activities over a 30-year period in a 7-state region. The states included are Iowa, Minnesota, Montana, Nebraska, North Dakota, South Dakota, and Wisconsin. Dun and Bradstreet data provided information about the number of business establishments at each location as well as other economic measures. The authors define a hierarchy of trade centers consisting of eight levels. These range from metropolitan centers with an average population of 983,869 and an average of 23,836 business establishments to hamlets with an average population of 625 and an average of 10 business establishments. They conclude that the hierarchy has remained quite stable; fewer than 10 percent of the towns and cities have moved up or down within the hierarchy. There were, however, major changes in the mix of business activities, with substantial growth in the number of service establishments, a moderate increase in the number of manufacturing establishments, and a decrease in the number of retail establishments. Retail business activity has tended to consolidate into larger establishments, which were most often located in higher level trade centers.

458.   Bangsund, Dean A., F. Larry Leistritz, Janet K. Wanzek, Dale Zetocha, and Holly E. Bastow-Shoop. 1991. *North Dakota Trade Areas: An Overview.* Ag. Econ. Rpt. No. 265. Fargo, ND: North Dakota State University, Department of Agricultural Economics, 42 pp.

Provides an overview and summary of current trade area information obtained from a statewide survey of retail trade patterns conducted by the Department of Agricultural Economics at North Dakota State University in 1989. Information on the 3 most frequently patronized towns where each of 37 goods and services were purchased, the percentage purchased in each town, the socioeconomic characteristics of the respondents, and their exposure to newspapers and radio stations was obtained by surveying almost 50,000 households across North Dakota. The report summarizes trade area delineation criteria, methods, and procedures used to map trade areas for a large number of North Dakota communities. Maps of the main trade areas for the wholesale-retail centers, complete shopping centers, and partial shopping centers are presented.

459.   Deller, Steven C., and James C. McConnon, Jr. 1991. *A Trade Area Analysis of New England Retail Markets.* Misc. Rpt. 356. Orono, ME: Maine Agricultural Experiment Station, 101 pp.

Points out that development of a town's retail sector should be an integral part of the community development process. A strong business district helps ensure that money earned in the community is spent in the community to achieve the maximum multiplier effect. The authors present an assessment of the status of retail districts in New England in order to provide insights into the individual market's strengths and weaknesses. The report is composed of five sections: (1) a general description of the New England retail market, (2) market performance in each of the six New England states is examined, (3) tools of trade area analysis are presented, (4) an evaluation of the performance of the aggregate market for counties within each New England state is provided, and (5) a summary.

460. Lukermann, Barbara, Miriam Goldfein, and Sandra de Montille. 1991. *Trade Centers of the Upper Midwest: Three Case Studies Examining Changes from 1960 to 1989.* Pub. No. CURA 91-4. Minneapolis, MN: University of Minnesota, Center for Urban and Regional Affairs, 78 pp.

Consists of three case studies that are companion pieces to a 1990 study examining the way trade centers in the Upper Midwest responded to economic trends between 1960 and 1989. The 1990 study, based on Dun and Bradstreet data on the number of business establishments and their Standard Industrial Classification (SIC) code, painted a picture of the Upper Midwest as a region in which large trade centers have expanded their spheres of influence at the expense of smaller communities. The case studies largely corroborate, and in some cases intensify, some of the major trends reported in the regional (1990) study.

International

461. Baltezore, James F., Cole R. Gustafson, and F. Larry Leistritz. 1992. *Financial Barriers to International Trade in North Dakota.* Ag. Econ. Rpt. No. 292. Fargo, ND: North Dakota State University, Department of Agricultural Economics, 41 pp.

Assesses the extent to which financing is a barrier to international trade for North Dakota manufacturers. Data were drawn from a survey of North Dakota manufacturers that served international markets, had attempted to expand into international markets within the past five years, or planned to begin serving international markets within the next five years. Of 152 firms in the sample, 91 provided useable questionnaires. The firms reported that 10 percent of their 1991 sales were international, and North Dakota manufacturers conducted international trade with 19 separate countries. The manufacturers felt that credit availability was the main financial obstacle to international trade. Firms with international trade financing indicated that collateral requirements were excessive, while those without such financing felt short-term capital was not available.

462. Cantlon, John E., and Herman E. Koenig. 1990. "Global Economic Competitiveness and the Land-Grant University." *Economic Development Quarterly* 4(1):40-46.

Presents the basic thesis that, for the United States, the fundamental economic issues of our time have to do with global economic competitiveness that is dependent upon innovation and entrepreneurship, and all that this implies socially, culturally, and technologically. Further, small-and medium-sized firms, both existing and new technology-driven companies are likely to be the key to regional economic development, diversification, and global economic competitiveness. The objective of this article is to review the experiences of a major land-grant university in realigning its programs and priorities consistent with this thesis. The realignment involves four major goals: (1) to facilitate the spin-off of new technology-driven, private-sector commercial ventures with which the university maintains a variety of special arrangements, (2) to develop "bridging structures" and incentives within the university to engage multidisciplinary academic resources of the university in providing customized assistance to existing small-and medium-sized firms, (3) to network the resources of the university with sister institutions and public-sector local and state level economic development initiatives, and (4) to adapt on-campus and lifelong educational programs consistent with contemporary economic competitiveness issues.

463.   Cheney, David W. 1993. "International Competitiveness and Sustainable Development." *Economic Development Review* 11(3):68-70.

Presents three trends that affect international competitiveness and also affect economic development at the state and local level. The increasing and continuing globalization of businesses, markets, and competition is one; the second is the fundamental change in business practices. The third is the importance of environmental issues and their link with competitiveness. As a result of these trends, communities should try to channel their economic development efforts into investments in infrastructure, technology development and diffusion, and education and training.

464.   Copeland, Brian R. 1989. "Of Mice and Elephants: The Canada-U.S. Free Trade Agreement." *Contemporary Policy Issues* 7(3):42-60.

Critically assesses the free trade agreement between Canada and the United States. Reviewing the theoretical literature on the gains from trade and the empirical literature on bilateral trade liberalization reveals that no presumption should exist that bilateral free trade would significantly improve Canada's welfare. Moreover, because of uncertainty over future abrogation or contingent protection actions, much of the predicted rationalization of Canadian industry may not occur. If, on the other hand, firms in Canada make major investments to take advantage of the agreement, Canada's bargaining position with the United States on trade and other issues could be weakened.

465. Easton, Stephen T. 1989. "Free Trade, Nationalism, and the Common Man: The Free Trade Agreement Between Canada and the United States." *Contemporary Policy Issues* 7(3):61-77.

Discusses the forces that have been at play in the debate over the recently concluded Canada-U.S. Free Trade Agreement. Most economists agree that free trade is desirable and that both parties likely will gain from specialization and exchange. But many objections to this agreement have been raised, some of which are very different from those that economists usually consider. A review of the agreement and many of the arguments raised against it reinforces the basic credo that freer exchange between consenting parties leads to improved economic well-being.

466. Featherstone, Kevin. 1991. "1992--The European Challenge for U.S. Business: Issues and Interests." *Economic Development Quarterly* 5(2):104-113.

Points out that the move toward a single market in the European Community (EC) has unleashed a wider impetus for economic and political change in Western Europe. These developments have major implications for U.S. business and public administration, which need to prepare for them. The author outlines the conflicts of trading interest which have arisen between the U.S. and the EC. These conflicts are seen as inevitable given the attraction and the increasing status of the EC market. Both the U.S. and the EC share a common interest in avoiding trade wars: the challenge for the 1990s is for national, state, and local actors to recognize this and to establish a new era of cooperation.

467. Flynn, Michael S. 1991. "International Competition, Automotive Decline, and Regional Economies." *Economic Development Quarterly* 5(1):77-90.

Reviews some recent books on automotive competition that broadly focus on the rise of the Japanese industry and the competitive decline of the traditional North American industry. Each book suggests, if not always explicitly, a likely structure for and distribution of future automotive manufacturing. The implications of these analyses for national and regional automotive production vary substantially. Some scenarios call for further erosion of domestic production in the face of international competition and pressures to move remaining activity to offshore locations. Other scenarios suggest a revitalization of domestic automotive production, although not necessarily within the traditional companies.

468.   Golz, Theresa K., Joel T. Golz, and Won W. Koo. 1992. *Economic Feasibility of an Air Cargo Handling Facility at Fargo, North Dakota.* Ag. Econ. Misc. Rpt. No. 161. Fargo, ND: North Dakota State University, Department of Agricultural Economics, 17 pp.

Evaluates the economic feasibility of Fargo, North Dakota as an air cargo handling facility for products shipped to (from) Taiwan. Exports to Taiwan in 1990 via air freight were approximately $2.9 billion, and imports via air freight to the United States were $3.1 billion. China Airlines operates three air cargo hubs in the United States: New York, Los Angeles, and Dallas. Two static trans-shipment models were used to determine the economic feasibility of an air cargo hub being located at Fargo. Both trans-shipment models minimized trucking costs of cargo from (to) customs districts to (from) air cargo hubs and air cargo costs from (to) hubs to (from) Taiwan for exports and imports.

469.   Jenswold, Joel, and William Parle. 1992. "The Role of the American States in Promoting Trade Relations with Eastern Europe and the Soviet Union." *Economic Development Quarterly* 6(3):320-326.

Examines the responses of the American States to new trade opportunities created by recent political and economic reforms in Eastern Europe and the Soviet Union. Specifically, the research focuses on the level of business interest in these potential new markets and on the type and amount of assistance that states are providing to firms seeking trade opportunities in this region. The analysis suggests that interest on the part of domestic firms is high and that states are responding by providing business firms with a variety of different types and levels of assistance.

470.   Kasoff, Mark J. 1993. "Canada-Ohio Economic Relations." *Economic Development Review* 11(2):46-50.

Describes how the State of Ohio and Bowling Green State University have joined forces to better understand and strengthen economic relations with Canada. The author reviews trade and investment flows between Ohio and Canada, the Buckeye State's most important international relationship.

471.   Maki, Wilbur. 1988. *Minnesota's Place in the Global Economy.* Staff Paper P 88-18. St. Paul, MN: University of Minnesota, Institute of Agriculture, Forestry and Home Economics, 52 pp.

Assesses Minnesota's ties to the new global economy. The author reports that in 1982 Minnesota's total foreign exports amounted to $5.4 billion, or 14 percent of the $39.5 billion in total exports from the state. Foreign exports also accounted for 18 percent of total export-oriented employment.

472. Office of Technology Assessment. 1990. *Workers Training: Competing in the New International Economy (Summary)*. Washington, D.C.: Congress of the United States, Office of Technology Assessment, 31 pp.

Reports that effective use of technology depends as much on people as on the technology itself. This is of particular concern today because the once great technological advantage of American firms has narrowed in many industries. Increasingly, the competitive edge will go to the company or country with flexible, well trained workers who can adjust quickly to rapidly changing demands and who have the skills to fully exploit new technology. Such workers are the key to the creation of more productive, effective enterprises--the kind likely to contribute to raising living standards. For these reasons, employee training, once a minor concern in American industry and largely ignored in public policy, must move toward center stage. This report focuses on the training given to employed workers, both from the standpoint of the competitiveness of U.S. industry and from the standpoint of the individual worker who may need training to advance.

473. Scott, Bruce R., and George C. Lodge, eds. 1985. *U.S. Competitiveness in the World Economy*. Boston, MA: Harvard Business School Press, 543 pp.

Contains 14 chapters that describe and evaluate America's changing position in the world economy. Some of the basic findings are (1) for about 15 years the U.S. has been losing its capacity to compete in the world economy, (2) declining U.S. competitiveness is reflected in a shift from trade surpluses to substantial deficits. Eroding market share in most sectors and declining real, after-tax earnings of American workers also reflect the decline in competitiveness, (3) the principal challenge comes from a new group of competitors in East Asia (Japan, South Korea, Taiwan, Singapore, and Hong Kong), (4) the competitive thrust of the new challengers comes not from favorable endowments of natural resources but from coherent national strategies through which each country mobilizes and shapes its productive capabilities to achieve economic growth and global competitiveness, (5) the U.S. and most of the West European industrial democracies suffer by comparison from increasingly less competitive strategies that emphasize more secure and equitable distribution of current income and encourage current consumption at the expense of investment for long-term benefits, and (6) unless the U.S. modifies its basic economic strategy, it cannot expect to generate the performance necessary to finance its simultaneous commitments.

Marketing Approaches

474.   Haider, Donald.   1992.   "Place Wars: New Realities of the 1990s." *Economic Development Quarterly* 6(2):127-134.

Points out that, in a world economy, every place competes against every other place (city, county, region, state, and nation). The competitive advantages that places pursue change over time and due to circumstances (e.g., jobs, plants, investment, tourists, specific industries, sports teams, and better quality of life). In this competition, marketing is emerging as the driving force in how places position themselves in the marketplace as sellers of products to serve customers' (buyers') needs and wants. As marketing has become the integrative function of modern business, its application to place improvement is only now becoming better appreciated.

475.   Narver, John C., and Stanley F. Slater. 1990. "The Effect of a Market Orientation on Business Profitability." *Journal of Marketing* 54(October):20-35.

Observes that marketing academicians and practitioners have been observing for more than three decades that business performance is affected by market orientation, yet to date, there has been no valid measure of a market orientation and hence no systematic analysis of its effect on a business' performance. The authors report the development of a valid measure of market orientation and analyze its effect on a business' profitability. Using a sample of 140 business units consisting of commodity products businesses and noncommodity businesses, they find a substantial positive effect of a market orientation on the profitability of both types of businesses.

MODERNIZATION

Technology Transfer

476. Abetti, Pier A., and Robert W. Stuart. 1986. "Entrepreneurship and Technology Transfer: Key Factors in the Innovation Process," pp. 181-220 in *The Art and Science of Entrepreneurship*, D. L. Sexton and R. W. Smilor, eds. Cambridge, MA: Ballinger Publishing Company.

Reviews the state-of-the-art knowledge on the process of technological innovation and highlights the key roles of entrepreneurship and technology transfer for ensuring the technical, commercial, financial and social success of an innovation. Two case histories are used to illustrate the main points; these are parallel case histories of successful and unsuccessful technological innovations. The authors show that the probability of success of a technological innovation is enhanced by the presence of an entrepreneur who ensures effective technology transfer with the scientific/technological environment and with the marketplace. They also illustrate the necessity of horizontal technology transfer to augment traditional vertical technology transfer. They conclude that companies must develop a climate conducive to entrepreneurship and technology transfer for their own success and for a reversal of the decline in America's competitive position.

477. Allen, Thomas J., Diane B. Hyman, and David L. Pinckney. 1983. "Transferring Technology to the Small Manufacturing Firm: A Study of Technology Transfer in Three Countries." *Research Policy* 12:199-211.

Analyzes case histories of 100 instances of technological change in 102 manufacturing companies in eight industries in Ireland, Spain, and Mexico. The cases were analyzed for the source of initial ideas and for sources of technology employed in resolving major problems. Technology was found to flow principally through informal channels within industries. Very little information was obtained from the formal mechanisms or institutions normally considered central to the technology transfer process. Foreign subsidiaries obtained the greatest proportion of their technology from their parent firms. However, they were found to have several channels of technology blocked to them, which are more readily available to domestic firms. Thus, domestic firms in many ways have easier access to foreign technology than do the subsidiaries of multinational firms. Process innovations are somewhat more likely to be based on foreign technology; product innovations are more likely to be based on domestic technology.

478.   Anders, Gary C. 1992. "The Changing Role of the Public University in Local Economic Development." *Economic Development Review* 10(4):76-79.

Examines the changing economic development role of public universities in the U.S. with specific examples drawn from a review of literature. It discusses how demands for concrete economic development outcomes and commercially applied research have changed the traditional orientations. The long-term goal of this research is to identify and evaluate both the explicit and implicit impacts of university development approaches on the regional economies where they are located. The conclusion offers suggestions for further research toward an empirical framework for evaluation studies.

479.   Baran, Barbara. 1985. "Office Automation and Women's Work: The Technological Transformation of the Insurance Industry," pp. 143-171 in *High Technology, Space, and Society*, M. Castells, ed. Beverly Hills, CA: Sage Publications.

Contends that, although the "office revolution" has been much heralded but long awaited, the combined forces of heightened competition and technological innovation have sped the process of diffusion in the last few years. In a number of industries, information technologies are beginning to have a major impact on the size of the work force and the nature of work. The author argues that in the insurance industry current and future applications of computer technologies are likely to differ significantly from earlier implementations of office automation equipment (with which most of the literature is concerned). This is because of important changes that are occurring in the competitive environment, in markets, products, and in the technology itself. Finally, the likely effects of the new implementations on manpower requirements, the occupational structure, and women's labor are examined.

480.   Baron, Jonathan. 1992. "A Breakthrough in Technology Transfer." *Economic Development Review* 10(4):60-63.

Reports that the U.S. has an enormous stock of scientific and technical expertise and at the same time has many businesses that could use this information. Fortunately a system is in place to share this knowledge. This new approach to technology transfer was developed originally by

Teltech of Minneapolis, Minnesota. The author believes that the available evidence indicates that the information shared has had a large positive impact on the companies which have used the system. Accelerating the utilization of this system can be beneficial to the firms and the communities in which they are located, as well as the entire country.

481.   Bond, C. P. 1985. "Targeting a Science Park to Its Task and Market," pp. 135-139 in *Science Parks and Innovation Centres: Their Economic and Social Impact*, J. M. Gibb, ed. Amsterdam, The Netherlands: Elsevier Science Publishers B.V.

Reports that the successful development of a science park requires close attention to three elements: its objectives, its resources, and its marketplace. A model is presented for the structured examination of these three elements in the development of such an initiative, with examples taken from an operating science park. Objectives are considered as social, sectional, and personal with respect to the founding institution, and a plea is made for realistic and achievable objectives. Resources are assessed under the headings of the academic institution, real estate, and park management. The match of resources and objectives is addressed to the practical marketplace which is viewed as comprising seven discrete market segments with differing needs and competitive environments.

482.   Cox, R. N. 1985. "Lessons From 30 Years of Science Parks in the U.S.A.," pp. 17-24 in *Science Parks and Innovation Centres: Their Economic and Social Impact*, J. M. Gibb, ed. Amsterdam, The Netherlands: Elsevier Science Publishers B.V.

Reports that science parks in the U.S. evolved from suburban industrial parks and old mill buildings in regions with certain natural advantages. Today science parks range from sectors of communities to restricted developments with specialized support facilities. The job impact of high tech innovation is seen in Massachusetts, which has the lowest unemployment in the U.S.A. at 3.4 percent. The author summarizes some lessons learned from 30 years of participation in science park development and entrepreneurial support, including (1) the ingredients that are essential for success of a science park, (2) the two distinct phases of development, (3) the characteristics of employment growth, (4) the community actions that can influence success, and (5) the support required for entrepreneurial business development. The author concludes that science parks are a service function that can strengthen a trend toward high-tech business development, but they cannot create the trend.

483. Gibb, John Michel. 1985. *Science Parks and Innovation Centres: Their Economic and Social Impact.* Amsterdam, The Netherlands: Elsevier Science Publishers B.V. 477 pp.

Contains the proceedings of a conference held in Berlin in February 1985. More than 40 speakers addressed issues associated with science parks from a variety of perspectives. Major papers specifically address the situation in Europe generally, The Netherlands, Italy, France, the Federal Republic of Germany, Belgium, the United Kingdom, the U.S.A., Israel, and the Far East. The eight major topic areas addressed were (1) science parks and innovation centers as instruments of regional policy, (2) the contribution of universities and research establishments to science parks and innovation centers, (3) organization and management of science/parks and innovation centers, (4) finance for operations of science parks and for the creation of new enterprises, (5) regional impact of science parks and innovation centers, (6) selection of entrepreneurs, training programs and advisory services for entrepreneurs, (7) case studies on development of young technology-based firms in science parks, and (8) solving the marketing problems of young technologically based enterprises.

484. Goldstein, Harvey A., and Michael I. Luger. 1990. "Science/Technology Parks and Regional Development Theory." *Economic Development Quarterly* 4(1):64-78.

Points out that science/technology (or research) parks have become a prominent element in regional development strategies. However, there has been little analysis of the types of regional development outcomes that can be expected from science/technology parks and how and why these outcomes might vary. The authors address these issues by drawing on the regional development theory literature. They review different theories that can be used as ex post rationales for science/technology park development, critically assess each as an explanation of research park development, focus on the particular hypotheses suggested by theory that relate variations in regional development impacts to different input elements of science/technology parks, and place science/technology park development within the broader scope of regional development and technology policy.

485. Haude, G. 1985. "The Role of Polytechnics in the Creation of Enterprises," pp. 103-106 in *Science Parks and Innovation Centres: Their Economic and Social Impact,* J. M. Gibb, ed. Amsterdam, The Netherlands: Elsevier Science Publishers B.V.

Reports that, in sparsely populated regions, economic development is characterized by a large number of deficits, which have to be made up by indigenous resources. Innovation centers and technology parks should serve to develop the incentive and entrepreneurial potential in these regions. However, the problems involved in preparing startup businesses and placing them on a sound footing are greater than in the major urban centers. Competent and suitable partners to cooperate in solving these problems may be found in the regional polytechnics in Germany. Alongside their practical orientation, their tasks include applied R&D, consultancy, and technology transfer. Concentration in the engineering sciences, staff structure, and the availability of industrial equipment enable the polytechnics to engage in information transfer, consultancy, and test, trial, and measurement projects. The formal business requirements of enterprises are largely covered by the facilities offered by the polytechnics.

486. Justice, Craig. 1988. "The Business of Technology Transfer." *Pacific Northwest Executive* 4(1):2-7.

Reports that the major universities of the Northwest region have increased their technology licensing efforts in response to a changing world economy and a 1980 amendment to the nation's patent laws, which allows universities to own and license inventions discovered by faculty working on federally funded projects. One policy issue associated with these activities is whether technologies developed at a state institution should be licensed to the highest up-front bidder or licensed to entities pledged to create jobs within the state. The author reports that the licensing program adopted by Stanford University in 1970 has served as a model for institutions throughout the United States.

487. Lowe, Julian. 1985. "Science Parks as a Vehicle for Technology Transfer," pp. 111-117 in *Science Parks and Innovation Centres: Their Economic and Social Impact*, J. M. Gibb, ed. Amsterdam, The Netherlands: Elsevier Science Publishers B.V.

Reports that early growth of science parks in the U.K. has been haphazard although recently there has been substantial new activity. Although achieving technology transfer is a major goal of most parks, it has only rarely been tackled in a proactive and planned manner. The inadequacy of current science parks' formats in achieving satisfactory technology transfer is in many ways not surprising, since the diffusion of technology is a complex and multifaceted problem which may best be dealt with separately. Some forms of technology transfer require substantial scale of operation to be effective, while other aspects of technology transfer rely on close and sustained liaison between key individuals over long periods of time. Finally, effective technology transfer may also demand substantial financial investments by both buyer and seller. The various alternative and complementary structures to science parks which have taken cognizance of these factors have brought together market intelligence, finance, human capital, and technology to deal with technology transfer in a more effective way than many science parks have so far been able. However, through informal networks, science parks have been able to participate in the creation of a good deal of new industrial activity based on university links.

488. Lugar, Michael I., and Harvey A. Goldstein. 1990. *Technology in the Garden: Research Parks and Regional Economic Development*. Chapel Hill, NC: University of North Carolina, Department of City and Regional Planning, 242 pp.

Has two major objectives (1) to assess the impact of research parks on regional economic development, including job creation, new business formation, and average wage and salary levels, and (2) to assess how the benefits of such parks are distributed among population groups, and particularly among minorities and women. The researchers employed two types of research designs or methods: (1) a multiple case study and (2) a quasi-experimental design employing nonequivalent control groups and multivariate statistical analysis. Case studies were conducted for Research Triangle Park (North Carolina), Stanford Research Park (California), and Salt Lake City (Utah). The quasi-experimental approach involved 116 parks and a number of control areas.

489. Malecki, Edward J. 1990. "Technological Innovation and Paths to Regional Economic Growth," pp. 97-126 in *Growth Policy in the Age of High Technology*, J. Schmandt and R. Wilson, eds. Winchester, MA: Unwin Hyman, Inc.

Reviews the theoretical and empirical work on technological innovation and deals with the major stages of activity within technological change, including research and development, innovation, diffusion of innovations and technology transfer, and new firm formation in regional growth. Although the focus of the chapter is not on policy, it suggests avenues by which public policies can influence the process of technical change. The intention is to emphasize the diverse ways in which technology refashions regional economies and the critical role of entrepreneurship in the passage from innovation to regional economic change.

490. National Council for Urban Economic Development. 1990. *Technology Transfer and Economic Development*. Washington, D.C.: National Council for Urban Economic Development, 60 pp.

Summarizes a forum conducted to inform and familiarize economic development professionals with current initiatives and issues in technology commercialization and to provide technology assistance to small and medium-sized manufacturers. Technology transfer has taken on a critical dimension in the context of the national effort to become more competitive with other nations. Within domestic economic development circles, it is equally critical in the competition among states and metropolitan areas to attract and retain companies. The forum was organized to cover two fundamental uses of technology. The first is the process of bringing new technologies from development to the marketplace. The second is the critical area of applying technology to U.S. manufacturing, particularly small and medium-sized companies, to make them more productive and competitive.

491. National Governors' Association. 1987. *The Role of Science and Technology in Economic Competitiveness*. Washington, D.C.: National Governors' Association, 51 pp.

Focused on three primary topics: (1) the adequacy of U.S. human resources and their relationship to our ability to compete, (2) U.S. investment in research and development, and (3) technology transfer (i.e., the ability to transform research findings into new products and processes). These topics are addressed in the context of the country's competitive position in the global marketplace. It responds to concerns about a pattern over the previous 15 years that included slowing productivity growth combined with growing competition from foreign producers which led to growing trade deficits, a decline in real earnings of American workers, and a stagnant standard of living.

492. Peddle, Michael T. 1993. "Planned Industrial and Commercial Developments in the United States: A Review of the History, Literature, and Empirical Evidence Regarding Industrial Parks and Research Parks." *Economic Development Quarterly* 7(1):107-124.

Traces the evolution of planned industrial and commercial developments in the United States and examines some of the literature relating to planned developments and their role in local and regional economic development, including a look at the evolution of zoning and land use controls as applied to planned developments. The available evidence leads to the conclusion that the most successful of recent planned developments have been mixed use developments that make use of agglomeration economies of several types of industries simultaneously, and diversify the economies and risk portfolios of the host regions.

493. Raafat, Feraidoon (Fred), Massoud M. Sagafi, Robert J. Schlesinger, and Kenichi Kiyota. 1992. "Training and Technology Transfer: Efforts of Japanese, Mexican, and American Maquiladora Companies in Mexico." *Socio-Economic Planning Sciences* 26(3):181-190.

Presents the results of an empirical study comparing the training programs of American, Japanese, and Mexican maquiladora companies in Tijuana, Mexico. The relationship between training and technology transfer is discussed and a model provided for the analysis of the level of technology transfer. The research was carried out in Tijuana where 30 companies in the electronics industry were surveyed. Almost all of the companies were found to provide some type of basic-skills training in the form of 1 week or less formal training and some on-the-job training thereafter. There appeared to be little transfer of advanced technology in product design, process design, or industrial management. The technology that Mexican workers currently absorb is almost exclusively limited to elementary quality control techniques and supervisory skills. Japanese maquiladoras train a large percentage of their Mexican managers and technical workers and provide a greater degree of technology transfer through training than do American or Mexican maquiladoras.

494. Rahm, Dianne, and Thomas F. Luce, Jr. 1992. "Issues in the Design of State Science- and Technology-Based Economic Development Programs: The Case of Pennsylvania's Ben Franklin Partnership." *Economic Development Quarterly* 6(1):41-51.

Points out that Pennsylvania, primarily through the Ben Franklin Partnership Program, has vigorously pursued science and technology (S&T)-based economic development strategies. The authors describe the partnership and highlight the policy choices model when establishing this S&T-based economic development policy. Emphasis is placed on organizational form, the attract or develop question, issues relating to firm size, and targeting by sectors or technologies.

495. Romano, A., and U. Bozzo. 1985. "Technopolis Novus Ortus: The Participation of Southern Italy in the European Technological Challenge," pp. 81-86 in *Science Parks and Innovation Centres: Their Economic and Social Impact*, J. M. Gibb, ed. Amsterdam, The Netherlands: Elsevier Science Publishers B.V.

Describes Technopolis Novus Ortus on the outskirts of Bari (Italy), which is an example of the way in which the projects for the development of the South are being brought into line with the transition towards an information society. Novus Ortus is an environment which favors the modernization of the existing economic structure and which creates the conditions that will generate opportunities in the job sector and in private enterprise. Agreements have already been drawn up along several different lines with multinationals, with research institutions, with leading companies in the new technology market, and with local production firms. Thanks to the involvement of the financial sector and the provision of services for the new initiatives (including creation of an infrastructure for an industrial area, availability of consultation facilities, access to technical services and to documentation, and training and refresher courses for the workforce) the risks involved in setting up business concerns in innovative sectors have been dramatically reduced. Novus Ortus is aimed at the countries of the Mediterranean, with more emphasis being given to developing countries.

496. Segal, N. S., and R. E. Quince. 1985. "The Cambridge Phenomenon and the Role of the Cambridge Science Park," pp. 172-195 in *Science Parks and Innovation Centres: Their Economic and Social Impact,* J. M. Gibb, ed. Amsterdam, The Netherlands: Elsevier Science Publishers B.V.

Reports that the Cambridge Science Park is the best known and most successful science park in Britain and probably also in Europe. Its success derives from many factors, the most important of which is the emergence of Cambridge in recent years as a leading center of high technology industry in Britain. The University and its constituent colleges and scientific and technological departments have exercised a profoundly important influence on these developments in Cambridge, and after a slow start the science park has itself come to play a key role in the further growth of local science-based industry.

497. Shapira, Phillip. 1990. "Modern Times: Learning From State Initiatives in Industrial Extension and Technology Transfer." *Economic Development Quarterly* 4(3):186-202.

Examines five state industrial extension or technology transfer programs, looking at their approaches to technology transfer, services provided, targeting, staffing, field service, user fees, and training. Although the programs use varied delivery mechanisms, they all emphasize the value of one-on-one technology transfer relationships with firms and the importance of focusing on pragmatic, easily customizable technologies. As a growing number of states consider initiating programs to disseminate manufacturing technologies through industrial extension services and related programs, these findings may have widespread application.

498. Shattock, M. L. 1985. "Investment Factors in British Science Park Development," pp. 142-148 in *Science Parks and Innovation Centres: Their Economic and Social Impact*, J. M. Gibb, ed. Amsterdam, The Netherlands: Elsevier Science Publishers B.V.

Argues that too little attention has been paid to the problem of financing science park development in Britain and that a lack of forward investment in management costs, site infrastructure, and buildings may be an inhibiting factor in British science parks' success. This paper draws attention to the location of the various science parks and to the difficulty of attracting investment to areas of high unemployment and industrial decline. It suggests that some positive steps need to be taken to create conditions where science parks can develop.

499. Shove, Christopher. 1991. "Key Site Characteristics of Industrial Research and Development Laboratories." *Economic Development Review* 9(4):56-64.

Attempts to identify and test for statistically significant spatial characteristics of private sector industrial research and development (R&D) activities. The product cycle concept was selected as the theoretical framework for understanding R&D spatial characteristics. The author finds that this concept has significant explanatory power (coefficient of determination of 0.9). Based on the results, the author concludes that the most effective method of encouraging the location of R&D activities in an area is to develop such activities locally rather than trying to recruit them. Furthermore, policies aimed at small firms may have more impact than those directed at large firms.

500. Wyckoff, Andrew W., and Louis G. Tornatzky. 1988. "State-Level Efforts to Transfer Manufacturing Technology: A Survey of Programs and Practices." *Management Science* 34(4):469-481.

Analyzed state-level university-based efforts to increase manufacturing productivity through the transfer of technologies, such as robotics and microcomputers, to manufacturing establishments. A telephone survey of 15 programs that were operating in 1985 provided the data base. Programs fell into three types: (1) active, (2) broker, and (3) passive.

Major issues identified by program personnel included conflicts with the academic context, difficulties in keeping technically up to date, and problems in retaining quality staff.

Assistance/Education

501. American Association of State Colleges and Universities. 1986. *The Higher Education-Economic Development Connection: Emerging Roles for Public Colleges and Universities in a Changing Economy.* Washington, D.C.: U.S. Department of Commerce, Economic Development Administration.

    Examines the roles America's public colleges and universities are playing in local economic development. It highlights the rationale and benefits for college and university involvement in economic development. The report also provides general information on the current state of the art of college and university involvement in economic development by examining the full range of roles that institutions can play and the development of those roles at different institutions. Finally, the report identifies key programmatic, policy, organizational, and strategic issues that need to be addressed as institutions participate more actively in this field.

502. Ayres, Janet, Robert Cole, Clair Hein, Stuart Huntington, Wayne Kobberdahl, Wanda Leonard, and Dale Zetocha. 1990. *Take Charge: Economic Development in Small Communities.* Ames, IA: North Central Regional Center for Rural Development, 227 pp. plus appendix.

    Presents an educational program designed to enable leaders, decision makers, and residents in small communities to analyze the community, think about alternatives, and plan an action strategy for community economic development. Specific emphases of the program are (1) helping communities explore short- and long-term development strategies and gain a vision of their own future, (2) gaining broad community involvement and support, (3) building on existing resources, (4) assisting communities in analyzing their strengths and weaknesses and choosing the most appropriate development opportunities, and (5) implementing an action plan.

503. Bartel, Ann P., and Frank R. Lichtenberg. 1987. "The Comparative Advantage of Educated Workers in Implementing New Technology." *The Review of Economics and Statistics* 69(1):1-11.

Estimates labor demand equations derived from a (restricted variable) cost function in which "experience" on a technology (proxied by the mean age of the capital stock) enters "non-neutrally." The authors' specification of the underlying cost function is based on the hypothesis that highly educated workers have a comparative advantage with respect to the adjustment to and implementation of new technologies. The empirical results are consistent with the implication of this hypothesis, that the relative demand for educated workers declines as the ages of plant and (particularly) of equipment increase, especially in R&D-intensive industries.

504.   Bryant, Miles T. 1989. "Education and Rural Revitalization: A Study of the Link Between Education and Economic Development," pp. 21-37 in *Nebraska Policy Choices*, M. T. Bryant, P. O'Connell, and C. M. Reed, eds. Omaha, NE: University of Nebraska at Omaha, Center for Public Affairs Research.

Analyzes the relationship of Nebraska schools to rural economic development. Schools are viewed as vital both in attracting new residents and businesses to a community and in retaining existing residents. Quality of schools is seen as essential if a community is to attract new residents; and aspects of education that need to be interrelated with rural development strategies are consolidation, distance learning, educational service units, school board development, and educational opportunity. To retain existing residents, the authors recommend that communities seek to involve students in community development projects and activities.

505.   Chapman, Robert E., Marianne K. Clarke, and Eric Dobson. 1990. *Technology-Based Economic Development: A Study of State and Federal Technical Extension Services*. NIST Special Pub. 786. Washington, D.C.: U.S. Department of Commerce, National Institute of Standards and Technology, 159 pp.

Presents the findings of a nationwide study of state and federal organizations providing business and technology assistance to small and medium-sized businesses. The purpose of this report is twofold. First, it summarizes the recent literature on technology transfer and technology extension. Included in the literature survey is a review of selected federal technology transfer programs, a review of state technical outreach and economic development activities, and an analysis of state efforts in the key areas of program implementation and program evaluation. Second, it summarizes the results of a nationwide survey of state and federal technology extension services.

506. Corsten, Hans. 1987. "Technology Transfer From Universities to Small and Medium-Sized Enterprises--an Empirical Survey From the Standpoint of Such Enterprises." *Technovation* 6:57-68.

Describes an investigation during which 225 small and medium-sized enterprises were asked about their experience of cooperation with universities in dealing with scientific and technical problems. About a quarter replied that they had had such experience in the last ten years. These were asked the following questions (1) Were they satisfied with the cooperation? (2) What were the arguments against cooperation? (3) What especially important factors facilitated cooperation? The results show that companies, in practice, ascribe the highest significance to factors quite different from those which are emphasized in theoretical literature.

507. Dalton, I. G. 1985. "The Objectives and Development of the Heriot-Watt University Research Park," pp. 231-237 in *Science Parks and Innovation Centres: Their Economic and Social Impact*, J. M. Gibb, ed. Amsterdam, The Netherlands: Elsevier Science Publishers B.V.

Reports that Heriot-Watt University established the first science park in the U.K. in 1972 with the prime objective of encouraging the transfer of academic research into marketable industrial processes, products, and services. In particular, the Research Park seeks to encourage the specific activities of research, development, design, engineering, and prototyping by individual company staffs in close proximity to the facilities and the academic community of the University. The Park, which is financed solely by the University, is an integral part of the campus of Heriot-Watt and provides particularly favorable opportunities for close collaboration between companies and University departments. The author reviews the objectives of the Park; its role within the wider scope of collaboration with industry; its resources and facilities; the source and nature of the companies which have located there; and University encouragement of academic members of the staff to form "spin-off" companies.

508. Economic Research Service. 1991. *Education and Rural Economic Development: Strategies for the 1990s*. ERS Staff Report No. AGES 9153. Washington, D.C.: USDA, Economic Research Service, Agriculture and Rural Economy Division, 162 pp.

Examines the education crisis, the relationship between the education shortfall and rural economic stagnation, the importance of local workforce education levels for local area growth, and the options for upgrading the skills of the rural workforce. The central conclusion is that education's potential as a local area rural development strategy is probably quite limited, but that the need to raise education and training levels for rural youth, wherever they will work, is critical.

509.   Feller, Irwin. 1990. "University-Industry R&D Relationships," pp. 313-343 in *Growth Policy in the Age of High Technology*, J. Schmandt and R. Wilson, eds. Winchester, MA: Unwin Hyman, Inc.

Offers a different perspective on the emergent patterns of university-industry collaboration. The author focuses less on the generic reasons for collaboration and more on the characteristics of the firms and universities that enter into alliances. The chapter's unifying theme is that of search. The "new alliances" of recent years are frequently described as "experiments" to highlight the perception that the character of these relationships differs in a meaningful manner from the long-standing pattern by which firms contract for performance of faculty research, and also to suggest the problematic and yet-to-be solidified character of recent forms of collaboration.

510.   Fossum, Harold L. 1993. *Communities in the Lead: The Northwest Rural Development Sourcebook.* Seattle, WA: University of Washington, Northwest Policy Center, 215 pp.

Seeks to improve access to ideas and assistance for community leaders as a way of empowering community-based revitalization efforts in rural areas of the Northwest. Two areas are emphasized--capacity building and value-added enterprise development. Capacity building strives to improve the ability of community groups to shape practical goals from the dreams and opportunities of local people, to effectively marshal resources from within and outside the community in pursuit of these goals, and in time to evaluate and redirect their efforts. Value-added enterprise development strategies attempt to maximize the local benefits captured through design, processing, and marketing of products.

511.   Freier, S. 1985. "Parks of Science-Based Industries in Israel," pp. 107-110 in *Science Parks and Innovation Centres: Their Economic and Social Impact*, J. M. Gibb, ed. Amsterdam, The Netherlands: Elsevier Science Publishers B.V.

Reports that universities and research institutes can become the center of science-based industries, without altering their character. In Israel, it was the Weizmann Institute of Science which first posed the question squarely, of how it could best contribute to the rapid development of science-based industry, without any industrial expertise. The Institute realized that it could give substantial aid during the initial high risk phase of an enterprise. It put at the disposal of such entrepreneurs 300 sq. meters each for 3 years, as well as scientific advice and all its facilities and amenities, for a nominal fee. It also established simple criteria in order to assess a candidate's prospects and admissibility under this program. The risks for the investors were thereby greatly reduced, and this caused an influx of entrepreneurs. Land was set aside next to the Institute and developed to accommodate fledgling industries which had successfully passed the incubatory period at the Institute, had shown promise and found investors to sustain their prospect. This became the first park for science-based industries in Israel, with 30 firms employing 3,000 people at the end of 15 years. The example was successfully copied by the major universities in Israel.

512. Grubb, W. Norton. 1990. "Simple Faiths, Complex Facts: Vocational Education as an Economic Development Strategy," pp. 254-282 in *Growth Policy in the Age of High Technology*, J. Schmandt and R. Wilson, eds. Winchester, MA: Unwin Hyman, Inc.

Presents a series of conditions under which education, and vocational education in particular, would be effective as a mechanism of economic development. Then, the author examines a series of issues that must be faced by states thinking of using their vocational education systems as mechanisms of economic development: (1) the balance between vocational education at the high school level and at the postsecondary level, (2) the development of planning and evaluation mechanisms to keep education and training programs in line with market opportunities, and (3) the balance between general and specific training in vocational education.

513. Jones, A. D. W., and K. E. Dickson. 1985. "Science Parks in Europe-- United Kingdom Experience," pp. 32-36 in *Science Parks and Innovation Centres: Their Economic and Social Impact*, J. M. Gibb, ed. Amsterdam, The Netherlands: Elsevier Science Publishers B.V.

Reports that the association of high technology-based industry with universities is a relatively recent development in the United Kingdom. University-based science parks have expanded rapidly in the past few years and have occurred as a result of pressure on the universities and through initiatives from property developers and local authorities. Economic and political considerations have forced universities to undertake such commercial ventures. Developers have seen opportunities in a growth market and are able to provide much needed expertise while local authorities have been eager to encourage industrial regeneration. University-based science parks in the U.K. are not yet significant generators of new employment, and are not occupied by many companies which have emerged from their associated universities.

514. Kemna, R. B. J., A. P. C. van Duijn, and J. Eekels. 1985. "Delft Innovation Centre--A Feasibility Study," pp. 76-80 in *Science Parks and Innovation Centres: Their Economic and Social Impact*, J. M. Gibb, ed. Amsterdam, The Netherlands: Elsevier Science Publishers B.V.

Reports that the establishment of an innovation center is not an overnight decision. Any university or government wanting to employ this instrument has to go through a process of careful planning and design. This article deals with a feasibility study for an innovation centre, recently conducted at Delft University in The Netherlands, and describes the methodology applied in the research.

515. Levitt, Rachelle L., ed. 1985. *Research Parks and Other Ventures: The University/Real Estate Connection*. Washington, D.C.: ULI--the Urban Land Institute, 113 pp.

Contains seven major chapters that deal with various questions and issues associated with university-affiliated research parks. Topics which constitute focus areas for specific chapters include the university and land development, the high-tech market for university research parks, the developer's role in structuring the development approach, the university's role in structuring the development approach, the financial and legal aspects of project development, market and feasibility concerns, and the development of university-affiliated research parks. Some specific parks that are selected for detailed examination include the Princeton University Forrestal Center, the Research Triangle Park, the MIT Simplex Development Area, the University of Wisconsin-Madison Research Park, and the Stanford Research Park.

516. Mayo, Marjorie, Peter B. Meyer, and Susan B. Rosenblum. 1992. "Workplace-Based Education and Economic Development." *Economic Development Quarterly* 6(4):444-453.

Reports that increased international competition has placed a premium on the quality of the labor force in a local economy. The authors examine the forces shaping worker-employer joint education and training efforts, and the roles local development organizations can play in promoting such investments in local human capital. Cases involving public and private sector employers in Britain and the United States are examined, so as to assess the ways in which union militancy and forms of worker organization may affect efforts at cooperation. As may be expected, the authors find that successful programs depend on shared management and labor objectives. Local development groups can shape those objectives by providing information to both businesses and workers. Thus development organizations can invest their industrial recruitment and business retention data in improving the quality of local labor forces by promoting workplace-based joint education and training programs.

517.   Miller, Robert W., and Frederick A. Zeller. 1988. "Initiating Local Action to Meet the Global Economic Challenge: A Case Study of a University-Assisted Effort to Develop an Area Labor-Management Committee." *Journal of the Community Development Society* 19(2):73-92.

Examines labor-management committees, which have been formed in many communities in response to economic difficulty resulting from increased foreign and domestic competition, as a community development tool. Information about the process and results of working with labor-management committees is provided by an evaluation of a West Virginia University effort to develop such a group. The West Virginia committee, now in its third year, has filled an educational role, opened communications between labor and management at the community level, and facilitated union-management cooperation at the plant level. Analysis of the development process suggests that more training and involvement of committee board members would have been desirable.

518.   Paget, Karen M. 1990. "State Government-University Cooperation," pp. 344-380 in *Growth Policy in the Age of High Technology: The Role of Regions and States*, J. Schmandt and R. Wilson, eds. Boston, MA: Unwin Hyman Inc.

Argues that contemporary demands for access to university knowledge and research constitute distinctly new pressures on universities, creating changes we are only just beginning to see, let alone understand. Patent offices, technology transfer centers, joint ventures with industry, faculty-owned biotechnology companies, and new political alliances between business and higher education are just of few of the manifestations of this new "competitiveness" pressure.

519. Ranney, David C., and John J. Betancur. 1992. "Labor-Force Based Development: A Community-Oriented Approach to Targeting Job Training and Industrial Development." *Economic Development Quarterly* 6(3):286-296.

Reports that efforts of community groups and local governments to gain jobs for a specific pool of unemployed workers often suffer from a limited and fragmented approach that does not give sufficient priority to the unique conditions, skills, and experience of the workers themselves. The authors suggest a remedy. They document the shortcomings of traditional frameworks for addressing the employment needs of specific pools of labor such as dislocated workers or segregated communities. In addition, the authors report on methods and strategies they are developing that enable policymakers and community groups to use skills and available training resources as an anchor for community economic development strategies. Three brief case studies that illustrate different applications of the methodology and strategic approach are also presented.

520. Redman, Susan, Toby Sticka, Doni Spooner, Curt Carlson, Sharon Haugen, Ron Newman, Ken Quamme, and Larry Weil. 1990. *Williston Area Business Retention and Expansion Program Final Report.* Fargo, ND: North Dakota State University, Center for Rural Revitalization, 86 pp.

Provides an example of the business retention and expansion (R&E) programs that have been conducted by the NDSU Extension Center for Rural Revitalization at numerous locations around the state. The report provides background concerning the R&E program, presents a synopsis of recent trends in Williams County, and summarizes findings of an extensive survey of businesses in Williston and Williams County. Major issues identified by the study included skills of the local workforce, needs of firms for a variety of forms of information and technical assistance, need for improvements in transportation services (especially air passenger service and highways), and need for more economic development efforts overall.

521. Root, Ken, Judy Heffernan, Gene Summers, and Julie Stewart, eds. 1992. *Conference Proceedings, "The Rural Family, The Rural Community, and Economic Restructuring."* RRD 159. Ames, IA: Iowa State University, North Central Regional Center for Rural Development, 217 pp.

Contains 10 papers presented at a conference designed to provide new ideas, material, and programs to practitioners who help workers, families, and communities adapt to economic restructuring. The contributors address a variety of topics including coping with economic change, displaced workers and rural entrepreneurship, farm women in rural labor markets, and community support systems.

522. Rosenfeld, Stuart A., and Robert D. Atkinson. 1990. "Engineering Regional Growth," pp. 283-312 in *Growth Policy in the Age of High Technology*, J. Schmandt and R. Wilson, eds. Winchester, MA: Unwin Hyman, Inc.

Examines the importance of science, engineering, and technical education to economic capacity and development from national and regional perspectives. The authors review the demand, supply and quality of the national and regional scientific and technical workforces and then examine the effects of educational institutions on business investment decisions.

523. Smith, Eldon D., and Alan J. DeYoung. 1992. *Exploratory Studies of Occupational Structure of the Workforce and Support of Public Education in Rural Appalachia*. SRDC No. 160. Mississippi State, MS: Southern Rural Development Center, 39 pp.

Focuses on the political economy of public education in depressed rural regions of the United States. The general hypothesis which is explored is that the occupational composition of the community workforce and associated educational requirements for employment have significance as elements of the socio-political environment for public education. The personnel requirements of employers of a community affect the articulated public demand for good schools, that is, schools which are adequately financed and efficient in building human capital. Employers with limited requirements for educated personnel have hypothetically limited demands for high quality schools.

524. Smith, Tim R., Mark Drabenstott, and Lynn Gibson. 1987. "The Role of Universities in Economic Development." *Economic Review* (Federal Reserve Bank of Kansas City) 72:3-21.

Summarizes a survey of 11 major universities in the Tenth Federal Reserve District to determine the nature and effectiveness of these institutions' initiatives in fostering economic development.

525. Steinnes, Donald N. 1987. "On Understanding and Evaluating the University's Evolving Economic Development Policy." *Economic Development Quarterly* 1(3):214-224.

Presents evidence that the university has evolved in recent years into an active player in local economic development. The author then attempts to explain this evolution in university policy on the basis of political and economic events during 1980s. Finally a model is specified and estimated for a sample of cities to evaluate the effectiveness of university economic development policy. The results, while not definitive, do suggest that the university can be a positive influence on economic development in a city and that some of the most explicit policies, including the Small Business Development Centers (SBDCs), have the most significant impact on local job growth.

526. Torok, Steven J., and Alan Schroeder. 1992. "A Comparison of Problems and Technical Assistance Needs of Small Agribusiness and Nonagribusiness Firms." *Agribusiness* 8(3):199-217.

Observes that agribusiness professionals have claimed that the agribusiness complex is unique within the business world. However, little empirical research exists to support this conclusion. This article analyzes Wyoming and Montana data, using the Fischer's exact and chi-square tests. The results indicate that serious business problems and critical technical assistance needs vary significantly within the agribusiness complex and between the agribusiness and nonagribusiness sectors.

527. Woods, Mike D., Gordon R. Sloggett, Gerald A. Doeksen, and Larry D. Sanders. 1989. *Guidebook For Rural Economic Development Training.* Mississippi State, MS: Southern Rural Development Center, 68 pp.

Is intended for Extension workers or economic development specialists for use in designing workshops for local leaders who are seeking help to increase economic activity in their community. Contents of the guidebook are divided into eight sections: (1) rural economic development overview, (2) building an economic development strategy, (3) economic development alternatives, (4) financing economic development, (5) impact analysis, (6) infrastructure, (7) public policy, and (8) bibliography.

Innovation

528. Acs, Zoltan J., and David B. Audretsch. 1988. "Innovation in Large and Small Firms: An Empirical Analysis." *The American Economic Review* 78(4):678-690.

Presents a model suggesting that innovative output is influenced by R&D and market structure characteristics. Based on a new and direct measure of innovation, the authors find that (1) the total number of innovations is negatively related to concentration and unionization and positively related to R&D, skilled labor, and the degree to which large firms comprise the industry and (2) these determinants have disparate effects on large and small firms.

529. Acs, Zoltan J., and David B. Audretsch. 1991. *Innovation and Technological Change: An International Comparison.* New York, NY: Harvester Wheatsheaf, 208 pp.

Examines the subject of innovation and technological change from a multinational perspective. The book contains 11 chapters which are based on papers presented at a conference held in Berlin in 1989. The focus is on those conditions and market environments that are conducive to innovation activity and those conditions that retard it. The work has five distinctive aspects: (1) most of the chapters are empirically oriented, (2) measurement issues are a major focus, (3) several chapters explore the manner in which certain aspects of market structure, and in particular firm size, influence innovative activity, (4) several authors examine the impact of innovation activity in shaping market structure, and (5) the book contains chapters summarizing research from several countries. A major conclusion is that, in order to better understand the relationships between firm size, market structure, and innovative activity, new and alternative measures of technological change must be developed.

530. Ascione, L. 1985. "Science Parks in Europe--Italy," pp. 48-57 in *Science Parks and Innovation Centres: Their Economic and Social Impact,* J. M. Gibb, ed. Amsterdam, The Netherlands: Elsevier Science Publishers B.V.

Reports that science parks can play an important role in the post industrial era and the birth of Technopolis Novus Ortus near Bari has marked their introduction in Italy. This pioneering venture is described, as are others, like Technocity (Turin). Somewhat different projects, on the border line between science parks and innovation centers, are also evaluated to assess their impact upon the industry to university relationship. Some ventures show an orientation toward the vocational instruction of technicians working in their home districts, like Genoa and Naples, while all generally foster a basic aim, such as stimulation of technological entrepreneurship.

531. Britton, J. N. H. 1989. "Innovation Policies for Small Firms." *Regional Studies* 23(2):167-173.

Examines the effectiveness with which small and medium-sized enterprises (SMEs) overcome disadvantages associated with their small size, and of the form of new policy initiatives that are directed towards improving their performance, especially their ability to innovate. The author first outlines the nature of incremental innovation as a logical goal of progressive SMEs. Then the need for pertinent outside expertise is described thus defining the transactional nature of the information economy of small firms. The problems encountered by SMEs in acquiring information so as to produce new designs, for example, are identified; and the article seeks to show that transaction costs which impede effective assembly of relevant information can be offset by appropriate policy instruments. Finally, it is argued that central government policies designed to encourage innovation compare favorably with local and regional alternatives, as do specialized rather than broad networking ventures.

532. Campbell, Adrian, Wendy Currie, and Malcolm Warner. 1989. "Innovation, Skills, and Training: Micro-electronics and Manpower in the United Kingdom and West Germany," pp. 133-154 in *Reversing Industrial Decline? Industrial Structure and Policy in Britain and Her Competitors*, P. Hirst and J. Zeitlin, eds. Oxford, U.K.: Berg Publishers, Ltd.

Argues that the responses of industrial societies to technical and economic challenges differ significantly along national lines. In particular, the authors address the variation between the strategies adopted in the engineering industries of the United Kingdom and West Germany. Their main contention is that the education and training systems of a given country will inform work organization patterns and hierarchial structures within industry. Depending on how these patterns and structures "fit" with technical and economic exigencies, there will be a significant effect on the performance of that country's industry. The authors argue that among the reasons for the continuing poor performance of British manufacturing is not only the country's parsimony regarding training in general, but also the form that its training takes.

533. Dosi, Giovanni. 1988. "Sources, Procedures, and Microeconomic Effects of Innovation." *Journal of Economic Literature* 26:1120-1171.

Analyzes the determinants and effects of innovative activities in contemporary market economies. The author analyzes the processes leading from national technological opportunities to actual innovative efforts and, finally, to changes in the structures and performance of industries. He discusses the sources of innovation opportunities, the role of markets in allocating resources to the exploration of these opportunities and in determining the rates and directions of technological advances, the characteristics of the processes of innovative search, and the nature of the incentives driving private agents to commit themselves to innovation.

534. Drucker, Peter F. 1985. *Innovation and Entrepreneurship Practice and Principles.* New York, NY: Harper and Row, 269 pp.

Examines innovation and entrepreneurship from a number of dimensions. Seven sources of innovation are discussed: (1) the unexpected, (2) incongruities, (3) process need, (4) industry and market structures, (5) demographic, (6) changes in perception, and (7) new knowledge. The author develops principles of innovation and then examines the practice of entrepreneurship. Dimensions of entrepreneurial practice that are examined include entrepreneurial management, the entrepreneurial business, entrepreneurship in the service institution, and the new venture. A discussion of entrepreneurial strategies concludes the work.

535. Kraft, Kornelius. 1989. "Market Structure, Firm Characteristics, and Innovative Activity." *The Journal of Industrial Economics* 37(3):329-336.

Investigates the determinants of product innovation by West German firms operating in the metal industry. A strong positive impact of imperfect competition on innovative activity is estimated. Aside from competition and barriers to entry, factors like the ownership structure of a firm, internal finance, and the skill level of the workforce are considered. One result is that firms led by hired managers tend to innovate less intensively than owner-managed enterprises.

536. Krist, H. 1985. "Innovation Centres as an Element of Strategies for Endogenous Regional Development," pp. 178-188 in *Science Parks and Innovation Centres: Their Economic and Social Impact,* J. M. Gibb, ed. Amsterdam, The Netherlands: Elsevier Science Publishers B.V.

Reports that a major feature of the strategies for endogenous regional development worked out in the early 1970s is the enlargement of the regional stock of innovative and adaptable undertakings from the existing local potential. Innovation centers can make a positive contribution to that end if they are based on local/regional initiatives which bring together key economic forces and combine single-site groupings of young companies with advisory, intermediary and information services. Given the relatively high level of technology demanded, the number of potential candidates for innovation centers will be relatively low. If the current demands for that high level continue, a subsidy race may result.

537. Rhodes, Ed, and David Wield, eds. 1985. *Implementing New Technologies: Choice, Decision and Change in Manufacturing.* Oxford, England: Basil Blackwell, Ltd. 416 pp.

Is a collection of readings directed towards a concept of implementing new technologies that includes study of decision forming and decision taking (including feasibility studies and pilot projects), project planning, the "conversion" or application of plans, and consolidating the change after insertion of new technologies. The readings also deal with the product market, financial and other environments within which implementation takes place and with the mediating influence of corporate strategy between these environments and individual projects. While the book includes material on innovation in the sense of "first commercial transaction involving new products or processes," it is more concerned with the consequences of technology diffusion and technology transfer, concentrating on the adoption within production units of technologies which are novel to the unit.

538. Suarez-Villa, Luis. 1988. "Innovation, Entrepreneurship, and the Role of Small and Medium-Sized Industries: A Long-Term View," pp. 21-43 in *Small and Medium Size Enterprises and Regional Development*, M. Giaoutzi, P. Nijkamp, and D. Storey, eds. London: Routledge.

Relates the broader and most significant aspects of entrepreneurial innovation and its diffusion by considering the role of small and medium-sized industrial enterprises in product and process development. A survey of historical literature is used to define the major innovative entrepreneurial roles, followed by a discussion of the role of small and medium-sized industries in the long-term process of industrialization and economic development. The relationship between the entrepreneurial roles, innovation diffusion, product and process development, and firm size are then explored in the final section.

539. Thomas, Morgan D. 1988. "Innovation and Technology Strategy: Competitive New-Technology Firms and Industries," pp. 44-70 in

Small and Medium Size Enterprises and Regional Development, M. Giaoutzi, P. Nijkamp, and D. Storey, eds. London: Routledge.

Represents a response to the growing recognition that there are very important reasons why a better understanding is needed of the way in which the process of technical innovation shapes the competitive environment of firms and industries. The author's response, largely conceptual in form, primarily focuses attention on selected relationships between innovation and technology strategy development within competitive 'new technology' firms and industries.

ECONOMIC DEVELOPMENT

POLICIES

540. Atkinson, Robert. 1988. "State Technology Development Programs."
      Economic Development Review (Spring):29-33.

      Describes and summarizes state technology policy efforts. The author
      points out that state governments in the United States have become
      increasingly involved in promoting technological innovation in an effort
      to stimulate economic growth. The article summarizes results of a survey
      of state technology development programs.

541. Atkinson, Robert D. 1991. "Some States Take the Lead: Explaining the
      Formation of State Technology Policies." *Economic Development
      Quarterly* 5(1):33-44.

      Points out that the focus on economic development has been largely
      substantive. Researchers have sought to determine what policies states
      are employing, which are most effective, and which policies work best in
      which types of regional economies. Procedural questions regarding how
      state political and institutional arrangements affect the funding and design
      of these policies have been virtually ignored. This article presents results
      of a research project that examined the policy-making processes of six
      states to determine the factors that contributed to more or less effective
      state technology policy efforts. A number of policy-making factors were
      found to have a significant influence on the effectiveness of state
      technology efforts. States which relied on an "active stewardship" mode
      of policy making were able to develop more effective policy efforts than
      states which relied on the "business as usual" mode.

542. Baker, M. Duane. 1993. "An Industrial Policy Framework for Ontario."
      Economic Development Review 11(1):21-23.

Reports that the Province of Ontario is refocusing its economic development activities towards promoting higher value-added activities. The focus on higher value-added activities will be but a process, not an ultimate destination. The long-term success of Ontario's economy will be determined by increasing productivity and innovation. The Ontario Government is taking an active role in the process, but is relying on market-led forces to create opportunities and capabilities.

543. Bartik, Timothy J. 1990. "The Market Failure Approach to Regional Economic Development Policy." *Economic Development Quarterly* 4(4):361-370.

Argues that regional economic development policies should aim to correct failures of private markets to achieve efficiency. Market failures that may rationalize regional economic development policies include involuntary unemployment, involuntary underemployment, fiscal benefits, agglomeration economies, research spillovers, imperfect human capital markets, imperfect information markets, and imperfect financial markets. Development policies to correct market failures may be evaluated by the nonmarket benefits created for society. The market failure approach focuses policymakers' attention on areas where private market performance is weakest and allows comparisons of development policies.

544. Bartik, Timothy J. 1991. *Who Benefits From State and Local Economic Development Policies?* Kalamazoo, MI: W.E. Upjohn Institute for Employment Research, 354 pp.

Evaluates the effects of state and local economic development policies. The author examines the criticisms commonly raised against such policies, which are (1) local and state economic development efforts have little effect on the growth of a small region, (2) even if such policies could affect job growth, an influx of inmigrants would cause the local unemployment rate to return to its original level, and (3) if local growth lowered unemployment in one area, the benefits would be offset by increased unemployment in other areas. The author presents evidence that counters these criticisms; he argues that economic development programs can significantly affect the growth of a state or metropolitan area, that increases in the growth of a local economy can benefit its unemployed, and that state and local development efforts can benefit the overall national economy. In addition to reviewing previous research, the author presents new empirical research on how metropolitan growth affects the unemployed, workers, and property owners.

545. Bartik, Timothy J. 1992. "The Effect of State and Local Taxes on Economic Development: A Review of Recent Research." *Economic Development Quarterly* 6(1):102-110.

Summarizes recent research on the effects of state and local taxes on state and local business activity. Contrary to previous research, this recent research indicates that state and local taxes have statistically significant negative effects on the economic growth of a state or metropolitan area. However, the range of plausible tax effects is large, implying that the annual costs of creating one job could vary from $2,000 to $11,000. For small suburban jurisdictions, taxes have more powerful effects on business growth than is true for metropolitan areas or states.

546. Bergman, Edward M. 1990. "State Innovation Policies and Regional Restructuring of Technologically Dependent Industry," pp. 127-145 in *Growth Policy in the Age of High Technology*, J. Schmandt and R. Wilson, eds. Winchester, MA: Unwin Hyman, Inc.

Begins by reviewing three definitions of Technologically Dependent Industry (TDI), which is the author's term for high-tech industry, that are often used in policy research and discusses their relationship to economic restructuring. The effects on TDI expected from traditional state policies for higher education and transportation are posed as significant in pursuing technology objectives. An exploratory investigation of TDI restructuring and these traditional state policies is conducted for all metropolitan region counties in 13 southern states using data for 1977 and 1984. The concluding section identifies early opportunities for fine-tuning and refocusing these important policy elements.

547. Bonnet, Thomas W. 1993. *Strategies for Rural Competitiveness: Policy Options for State Governments.* Washington, D.C.: Council of Governor's Policy Advisors, 176 pp.

Describes the economic challenges facing rural economies because of global competition and national economic restructuring, addresses the rationale for public interventions to enhance the vitality of rural economies, summarizes trends in state economic development policies, and suggests several broad strategies that state policymakers may wish to consider that hold some promise of providing a healthy and prosperous future for rural communities. The author also describes the process used by 15 states that participated in the 1990 and 1992 CGPA State Policy Academies in developing public policies to advance rural competitiveness strategies. The focus is on the strategies that can be employed by state governments, working in concert with community leadership, to improve rural competitiveness.

548. Boyle, M. Ross. 1990. "An Economic Development Education Agenda for the 1990s." *Economic Development Quarterly* 4(2):92-100.

Points out that economic development has evolved as a legitimate professional discipline, but a profession is only as good as the educational foundation upon which it rests. The author sets forth an agenda for strengthening the economic development education network. He calls for actions to (1) modify the curriculum for practitioners, (2) alter the education delivery system, and (3) expand the audience for economic development education. Advanced technologies must be employed to deliver educational offerings more efficiently to rural economic developers. Universities must be encouraged to offer more degree programs in economic development.

549. Brown, David L., and Kenneth L. Deavers. 1989. "The Changing Context of Rural Economic Policy in the United States," Vol. 4., pp. 255-275 in *Research in Rural Sociology and Development.* W. W. Falk and T. A. Lyson, eds. Greenwich, CT: JAI Press, Inc.

Reviews recent changes in rural economic conditions and suggests their implications for rural economic policy in the 1980s. The authors' general conclusion is that if rural revitalization was the theme of the 1970s, structural adjustment accompanied by economic dislocation and stress is the overriding nonmetro issue of the 1980s. Accordingly, the context for rural policy has been dramatically altered in the 1980s.

550. Carroll, John J., Mark S. Hyde, and William E. Hudson. 1987. "State-Level Perspectives on Industrial Policy: The Views of Legislators and Bureaucrats." *Economic Development Quarterly* 1(4):333-342.

Reports that economic development has emerged as a major function of state government in recent years. Using a nationwide mail survey, the authors examine the economic development views of both legislators and bureaucrats in the states. They test the role-convergence hypothesis that states that, because of institutional changes such as the growing professionalism of legislatures, legislators and bureaucrats are likely to have similar policy views. The hypothesis is confirmed in regard to conventional "smokestack chasing" economic development policies and also for some "industrial policy" proposals, but legislators are found to be more supportive of the more "innovative" policies.

551.   Clarke, Marianne K. 1990. "Recent State Initiatives: An Overview of
       State Science and Technology Policies and Programs," pp.149-170
       in *Growth Policy in the Age of High Technology*, J. Schmandt and
       R. Wilson, eds. Winchester, MA: Unwin Hyman, Inc.

Reports that, although state activities to promote the development and
application of science and technology and the formation of technology-
based businesses have been widely documented, questions remain
regarding the level of state commitment to these efforts. For example,
how significant are state investments in research and development? Are
states likely to maintain and/or increase their involvement in science and
technology policy? How widespread are state technology development
programs? What are the objectives of state science and technology
policy, and how successful have the states been in achieving their
objectives? The author argues that state science and technology programs
are becoming more widespread and that states are indeed making long-
term, and in some cases substantial, commitments to the promotion of
science and technology. Few data to evaluate the effectiveness of these
programs are available, however.

552.   Coffey, William J., and Mario Polese. 1985. "Local Development:
       Conceptual Bases and Policy Implications." *Regional Studies*
       19(2):85-93.

Reports that, although local development is frequently cited as an option
within the broader context of regional policy, the concept remains vague.
The bases of the local development approach lie in its complementarity
with three traditional pillers of regional theory and policy: (1) capital and
infrastructure policies, (2) migration as an adjustment mechanism, and (3)
growth center strategies. In examining the potential utility of local
development as an effective element of regional development policy, the
authors emphasize the emergence of local entrepreneurship and the role
of the state in stimulating local initiatives. Local development policy may
be generalized in terms of three options involving financial assistance,
access to information, and social animation.

553.   Daniels, Thomas L., and Mark B. Lapping. 1987. "Small Town Triage:
       A Rural Settlement Policy for the American Midwest." *Journal of
       Rural Studies* 3(3):273-280.

Reports that the American Midwest of the 1980s has suffered from a
depressed farm economy which has led to rural depopulation. Small
towns with fewer than 2,500 population have been especially hard hit.

States like Iowa face the choice of spreading limited public resources among many towns or concentrating the resources on a relative few. A key settlement policy, which involves the selection of certain villages where public and private investment and population growth will be concentrated at the expense of other rural settlements, may be emerging as a means to create growth centers in rural areas and thus limit depopulation and promote economic diversification. Such policies have been central to much rural planning and settlement policy in Great Britain.

554. Dewar, Margaret E. 1992. "Loans to Business to Encourage Rural Economic Development." *Policy Studies Journal* 20(2):230-240.

Examines a business loan program (Minnesota's Small Cities Economic Development Program) in detail in order to understand how such programs succeed or fail. The program has been successful in some respects, and it could be more effective with feasible reforms. The program's results suggest directions other business loan programs should take to have greater effects on state and local economies.

555. Doeringer, Peter B., and David G. Terkla. 1992. "Japanese Direct Investment and Economic Development Policy." *Economic Development Quarterly* 6(3):255-272.

Reports that the increasing number of Japanese manufacturing plants locating in the United States presents new opportunities for state and local economic development policy. This article compares the location decisions of Japanese startups in manufacturing with counterpart domestic industry and concludes that there are substantial distinctions between Japanese and American firms. Except for a few industries, Japanese firms are not locating in those states that are most attractive to counterpart domestic industries, but are more often choosing average to low-growth states. Interviews with a small sample of Japanese plants and industrial recruiters indicates that their decisions are based on a set of intangible considerations that differ from those that are important to domestic firms.

556. Drabenstott, Mark, and Lynn Gibson, eds. 1988. *Rural America in Transition.* Kansas City, MO: Federal Reserve Bank of Kansas City, 91 pp.

Explains the fundamental economic transition underway in the rural economy and discusses the important policy questions related to that transition. The contributors highlight serious problems of rural America, including the plight of displaced rural workers and the crumbling infrastructure and eroding tax base of rural areas. Major chapters summarize the economic history of rural America in the 20th century, discuss the changing composition of the rural economy, examine factors crucial to economic growth in rural areas, and outline major policy choices. The authors feel that a major choice is the one between a rural transition policy aimed at easing the reallocation of rural resources to more productive uses and a rural development policy designed to stimulate long-run economic development in rural areas.

557. Drabenstott, Mark, and Charles Morris. 1991. "Financing Rural Businesses," pp. 22-35 in *Rural Policies for the 1990s*, C. Flora and J. Christenson, eds. Boulder, CO: Westview Press.

Examines the questions of (1) where rural businesses will find financing in the 1990s and (2) what public policy options, if any, should be considered to encourage rural capital formation. The authors conclude that commercial banks will remain the dominant source of financing, although their role may wane somewhat. Rural capital flows will be quite efficient, as a result of deregulation. Most rural businesses will have ready access to debt financing, but they must be prepared to pay market interest rates. Venture capital, the key to startup businesses, does appear to merit some public policy emphasis.

558. Eisinger, Peter K. 1988. *The Rise of the Entrepreneurial State.* Madison, WI: The University of Wisconsin Press, 382 pp.

Explores the modern origins of government efforts to encourage private investment in particular locales, the justifications for such intervention, and the changing mode of government involvement over the past decade. The author traces the growth among the states of supply-side devices designed to reduce the costs of capital, land, buildings, taxes, and labor as a way to create a comparative location advantage. These policy initiatives, which put a premium on bidding for footloose industry, have recently begun to give way to demand-oriented or market-sensitive efforts where the emphasis is on capital formation. In these efforts, states and localities are seen to be acting as entrepreneurs, seeking new or expanding market opportunities for local producers or even trying to stimulate new demands altogether. The result of these efforts is that individual states are developing industrial policies in which investment and production decisions are often led by government rather than the private sector.

559. Falk, William W., and Thomas A. Lyson. 1991. "Rural America and the Industrial Policy Debate," pp. 8-21 in *Rural Policies for the 1990s*, C. Flora and J. Christenson, eds. Boulder, CO: Westview Press.

Seeks to bring rural America into the industrial policy debate which has been predominately urban in tone. The authors focus on three distinct dimensions along which a federally directed rural development effort should turn: (1) human resources versus available jobs, (2) a national industrial policy versus state and local initiatives, and (3) national planning (steered economy approach) versus free market principles (*laissez faire* approach).

560. Ferguson, Ronald F., and Helen F. Ladd. 1988. "Massachusetts: State Economic Renaissance," pp. 21-32 in *The New Economic Role of American States: Strategies in a Competitive World Economy*, R. S. Fosler, ed. New York, NY: Oxford University Press.

Discusses the role of state economic policy in enhancing economic growth in Massachusetts during the 1970s and 1980s. The authors point out that two special achievements in the state have attracted national attention: (1) the unemployment rate fell from 12 percent in 1975 to under 4 percent in 1985 and (2) innovative civic and political leadership has made the state a national leader in creating new roles for the states to play in economic policy. Many public officials are trying to learn from the "Massachusetts miracle," but the authors believe that they must be careful what lessons they draw. The Massachusetts experience shows that the short-term impact of state policy can be positive on the firms and geographic areas directly affected. With time, these effects may diffuse through the state's economy and accumulate, but state-sponsored economic initiatives are neither quick fixes for weak economies nor certified elixirs for healthy ones.

561. Flora, Cornelia B., and James A. Christenson, eds. 1991. *Rural Policies for the 1990s*. Boulder, CO: Westview Press, 347 pp.

Contains 27 chapters addressing a wide variety of policy issues affecting rural areas of the United States. The chapters are grouped into three areas: jobs and the economy, people and services, and the environment. In the first area, the authors address major problems of capital and economic organization that have particular impacts for rural people. In the second, the services needed by rural people and special populations in rural areas, such as the aged, the poor, and minorities, are discussed.

The third set of chapters discusses the environment, focusing on land and water in its national and international context.

562. Fosler, R. Scott. 1992. "State Economic Policy: The Emerging Paradigm." *Economic Development Quarterly* 6(1):3-13.

Discusses the evolution of state economic development policy. The conventional paradigm focused on the attraction of firms from outside the state. Over the last two decades, states have expanded their concern and have engaged in a variety of ad hoc experimental efforts. Out of that experience is emerging a new paradigm of state economic development policy with three principal elements. The first is a concept of economic development as a process rooted in a market-driven private sector. The second is a new set of state responsibilities, including a wide range of public actions that affect the process of development. The third is a set of new institutional capacities required for shaping and carrying out those new responsibilities. During the 1980s, states attempted to devise economic strategies that accounted for their new responsibilities, which had been only dimly defined. In the 1990s, states also will need institutional change strategies required to develop the capacity to more sharply define and carry out those responsibilities.

563. Fox, William F., and Matthew N. Murray. 1991. "The Effects of Local Government Public Policies on the Location of Business Activity," pp. 97-119 in *Industry Location and Public Policy*, H. Herzog and A. Schlottmann, eds. Knoxville, TN: The University of Tennessee Press.

Presents results of an analysis designed to determine the importance of local public policy structure on the location of existing or startup businesses and, by implication, identifies what local governments could do to enhance the rate of business startups and to attract firms. The analysis is somewhat unique in that it focuses on the effects of differing public policies within one state (Tennessee). As such, state government policies are not examined since they have similar effects, regardless of where a firm locates within the state. Perhaps the most important finding is that the influence of any single local government policy on the startup or location of firms is, in general, very small in any given year. Many local policies were found to affect the entry of firms into counties, but the effects of each one are so small that a local government could expect to influence its economic development noticeably only over a long period of time, and then only through changes in many policies. Another conclusion is that firms of different sizes, and firms in different industries, respond in different ways to the mix of public policies and other locational factors in a county. This suggests that no single set of policies can broadly attract firms of all types.

564.   Fox, William F., and Matthew N. Murray. 1993. "State and Local Government Policies," pp. 223-245 in *Economic Adaptation: Alternatives for Nonmetropolitan Areas*, D. L. Barkley, ed. Boulder, CO: Westview Press.

Reviews how effectively various state and local government policies promote economic development. First, the role of state and local fiscal policies is examined. The emphasis is on the way in which the broad structure of taxes and expenditures influences economic growth and development. The following section explores public infrastructure, including transportation and communications networks, water and sewer systems, and electricity. The focus in this context is whether infrastructure can promote (as opposed to accommodate) growth and which types of infrastructure are most conducive to promoting rural development. The discussion then turns to policies that might be employed to overcome human resource constraints (such as inadequate job skills) that confront rural economies. State technology policies are presented next. The final section of the chapter integrates the literature review to provide policy prescriptions for a limited set of specific rural scenarios, including declining manufacturing regions and growing communities near metro areas.

565.   Furuseth, Owen. 1992. "Uneven Social and Economic Development," pp. 17-28 in *Contemporary Rural Systems in Transition: Volume 2, Economy and Society*, I. R. Bowler, C. Bryant, and M. Nellis, eds. Wallingford, Oxon, U.K.: CAB International.

Examines rural social conditions in the U.S. during the past decade, with an assessment of likely conditions in the future. This period has been marked by significant economic restructuring in the global economy which has given rise to major impacts on the American countryside. The events of the past decade have accelerated the pattern of uneven social development between rural and urban areas of the U.S. More significant, however, is the evidence of a growing uneven development within rural America. While some rural communities have benefitted from the restructuring process, others have been adversely affected. The author suggests that the current pattern of uneven social development begun in the 1980s will continue through the 1990s, resulting in even further differentiation in rural America by the end of the century.

566. Giloth, Robert P. 1992. "Stalking Local Economic Development Benefits: A Review of Evaluation Issues." *Economic Development Quarterly* 6(1):80-90.

Points out that widespread concern exists concerning the gap between local economic development promises and outcomes, particularly for business incentives made available by local jurisdictions. The author examines how this problem results from the design limitations of local economic development policy, the typical result being vaguely designed programs with multiple goals. A case study of Industrial Development Bonds (IDBs) in Chicago between 1977 and 1987 is used to show how this failure in design results in selection bias in which firms obtained IDBs. He finds that research about how governments operate IDB programs, how firms use IDBs, and how interurban competition influences program operations are neglected topics in the evaluation literature concerning business incentives. Two shortcomings of IDB research are the lack of control groups to isolate IDB effects and the over-reliance on jobs as a measure of program success.

567. Green, Roy E., ed. 1991. *Enterprise Zones: New Directions in Economic Development.* Newbury Park, CA: Sage Publications, 266 pp.

Presents recent empirical analyses focusing on the status and impacts of state enterprise zones in the United States. The book is composed of four parts. The first, Urban Development and the Concept and Design of Enterprise Zones, provides an analytical overview and a historical context to the economic, political, and programmatic policy streams from which the American experience with enterprise zones emerged. The second part, the Practice of Enterprise Zones, includes (1) three of the most recent case studies of state enterprise zone programs and (2) two comparative analyses of state enterprise zone programs. The third part of the volume offers chapters that summarize three nondomestic sets of governmental arrangements, all of which have been referred to by various advocates and analysts as sources of continuing influence on the path of enterprise zone experience in the United States. The final part presents two concluding essays that review the methodological and policy issues raised by the analyses presented earlier.

568. Hadwiger, Don F. 1990. *Helping Those Who Venture: Iowa's Rural Economic Development Measures.* ERS Staff Rpt. No. AGES 9047. Washington, D.C.: USDA, Economic Research Service, 38 pp.

Provides an example of a state's involvement in rural economic development. A survey of state agency heads and budget officers in Iowa identified 82 rural development measures, which account for about one-fourth of the state budget. A majority of the measures are aimed at community and business development. State and local efforts have increased in recent years, partly in response to a declining federal effort.

569.   Hansen, Niles.   1988.   "Economic Development and Regional Heterogeneity: A Reconsideration of Regional Policy for the United States." *Economic Development Quarterly* 2(2):107-118.

Points out that national policies and programs that implicitly treat the United States as a homogeneous area or that are oriented toward some "average" situation thereby fail to take into account the fact that the nation is a collection of heterogeneous regions with differing problems and opportunities. Issues concerning the competitiveness and adaptability of the U.S. economy have often been addressed in sectoral terms, even though the more fundamental matter is one of regional development in the broadest sense. Some suggestions are made concerning factors that could be considered in the formulation of a comprehensive federal regional policy. These deal with the appropriate geographical framework, the role of the federal system, and relevant program issues.

570.   Hansen, Niles, Benjamin Higgins, and Donald J. Savoie. 1990. *Regional Policy in a Changing World*. New York, NY: Plenum Press, 311 pp.

Argues that geographic space is an essential element in the performance of any economy. The authors point out that, whereas policy-oriented regional economics recognizes the importance of efficient markets, it also seeks to diagnose the causes of significant spatial disequilibrium and to use regional analysis as a tool to diagnose malfunctioning of the economy as a whole. It then tries to find appropriate policies (cures) and to implement them in an efficient manner. The comparative method is used in this volume to ascertain if there are certain empirical regularities that can be observed in the postwar period in different countries with respect to the evolution of regional economies, the nature of regional problems, the policies intended to deal with those problems, and the consequences of these policies.

571.   Hansen, Susan B.   1991.   "Comparing Enterprise Zones to Other Economic Development Techniques," pp. 7-26 in *Enterprise Zones:*

New Directions in Economic Development, R. Green, ed. Newbury Park, CA: Sage Publications.

Provides a historical and comparative perspective on enterprise zones. The author points out that state and local government involvement in the economy is hardly novel, but the rationale for such involvement has varied greatly across time and across jurisdictions. The choice of specific policy tools has also changed over time. Enterprise zones have much in common with several recent approaches to economic development, yet they are unique in one major aspect: policies to encourage economic development are limited to particular geographic areas. This salient feature has little precedent in American political economy, but has profound implications for trends in investment and job creation.

572.   Herzog, Henry W., Jr., and Alan M. Schlottmann, eds. 1991. *Industry Location and Public Policy*. Knoxville, TN: The University of Tennessee Press, 299 pp.

Contains 12 papers originally developed for a "Symposium on Industry Location and Public Policy," held at the University of Tennessee in 1988. The contributors address the spatial determinants of industrial location, the efficacy of public policy in the location process, and the outcomes of such initiatives on local economic well-being.

573.   Higgins, Benjamin, and Donald J. Savoie. 1987. *Regional Economic Development: Essays in Honour of Francois Perroux*. Boston, MA: Unwin Hyman, 415 pp.

Aims to assist in the process of defining new approaches to regional development. The book is divided into five parts. The first part, on Perroux and his work, is followed by a discussion of methods and approaches. Part III deals with experiences of regional development in Canada, and the next part with regional development experiences elsewhere. The concluding chapter presents an overview of the regional development experience.

574.   Hirst, Paul, and Jonathan Zeitlin, eds. 1989. *Reversing Industrial Decline? Industrial Structure and Policy in Britain and Her Competitors*. Oxford, U.K.: Berg Publishers, Ltd., 295 pp.

Reports that policies for industrial renewal are now an important feature of political debate in advanced industrial countries such as the United Kingdom and the United States, where they have been proposed as a response to fundamental failure in the performance of the manufacturing sector. This book is concerned both to diagnose the sources of industrial failure of nations such as the U.K. and U.S. in the prevailing patterns of international competition, and to prescribe new policy instruments in order to respond to these patterns. Four major themes are considered: (1) the emergence of new patterns of international competition centered on market fragmentation and productive flexibility; (2) the British economy's response to international pressures and explanations for the competitive failure of its manufacturing sector; (3) the evaluation of strategies for the regeneration of regional and local economies; and (4) the macroeconomic and political requirements for industrial renewal at the national level. Ten major chapters address these topics.

575.   Honadle, Beth Walter. 1993. "Rural Development Policy: Breaking the Cargo Cult Mentality." *Economic Development Quarterly* 7(3):227-236.

Reports that a comprehensive national rural development policy has been thwarted by at least five factors: inaccurate rural stereotypes, perceived conflicts between urban and rural interests, competition among rural development advocacy groups, declining rural population, and fragmentation of rural development within Congress. Rather than formulate a coherent strategic policy for rural development, the last several presidential administrations have substituted rhetoric and procedural changes for real action. They have cut programs and slashed technical assistance efforts in the name of efficiency and used terms like coordination, targeting, and improved access to make existing programs more responsive. Despite the clear focus of federal policymakers on urban and international issues, rural development advocates behave like cargo cults, religious sects that wait for material goods to be brought by magic by the spirits of their ancestors in cargo ships. This article offers some suggestions for how rural development advocacy groups might better serve rural people.

576.   Huillet, Christian, Pieter VanDijk, and Theodore Alter. 1990. *Partnerships for Rural Development.* Paris, France: Organisation for Economic Co-operation and Development, 155 pp.

Reports that one of the most striking trends in OECD member countries' recent efforts to address structural changes in rural areas is the trend towards more comprehensive, integrated policies. Such approaches necessarily bring together not only many sectoral departments, but also different levels of government and a wide spectrum of private sector economic and social interests. In many countries the ultimate viability of comprehensive rural policymaking is seen to depend on the capacities of a considerable number of heterogeneous institutions to work out together durable forms of cooperation that go beyond mutual consultation in the policy formulation phases, and provide for actual risk- and responsibility-sharing arrangements during the implementation phase. Partnership arrangements turned out to be the mechanism most OECD-member countries had overall experience with, although the administrative, legal, and political contexts vary widely within the membership. This report has two parts. Part I describes the organizational and policy aspects that are important for partnership machinery to operate. It presents information on various kinds of institutional partnerships, and the prospects they hold out for successful implementation of rural development programs. Part II summarizes particular examples of institutional partnerships set up in 16 OECD member countries.

577.   James, Franklin J. 1984. "Urban Economic Development: A Zero-Sum Game?" pp. 157-174 in *Urban Economic Development*, R. Bingham and J. Blair, eds. Beverly Hills, CA: Sage Publications.

Examines available evidence to assess whether economic development programs for distressed communities have an important role to play in a national industrial policy aimed at enhancing the economic strength of the nation or whether they serve merely to redistribute economic activity. The author concludes that the theoretical foundations for targeted economic development policies are ambiguous and evidence of their effectiveness is scant. Advocates of such programs must develop more convincing evidence of the efficacy of such programs if further cutbacks of federal support are to be avoided.

578.   Kenyon, Daphne A. 1990. "Reassessing Competition Among State and Local Governments." *Intergovernmental Perspective* 16(1):32-35.

Reports on a recent study by the Advisory Commission on Intergovernmental Relations that examined the issues associated with tax and policy competition among jurisdictions. The author concludes that the issues involved are complex, as state and local governments can compete in taxation, service, and regulatory dimensions, and tax competition cannot be divorced from service competition. Further, interjurisdictional competition serves as a regulator of the federal system and does not necessarily depress state and local service or revenue levels. Overall, recent analyses have indicated that there are some benefits associated with interjurisdictional competition.

579. Law, C. M. 1985. "Regional Development Policies and Economic Change," pp. 219-248 in *Progress in Industrial Geography*, M. Pacione, ed. London: Croom Helm.

Defines regional development policy (RDP) as policies operated by the state or state agencies which seek to influence economic development as between the major regions of a country. The author discusses (1) why governments choose to have RDPs and what objectives they seek to achieve when such policies are adopted, (2) the types of policies that have been employed or considered, (3) approaches to delineation of regions, and (4) assessing the impacts of the policies to see to what extent the objectives have been achieved.

580. Ledebur, Larry C., and Douglas Woodward. 1990. "Adding a Stick to the Carrot: Location Incentives with Clawbacks, Recisions, and Recalibrations." *Economic Development Quarterly* 4(3):221-237.

Addresses clawback provisions associated with state incentive awards. The authors indicate that clawbacks provide recourse to reclaim all or some of a financing package when a firm fails to meet performance requirements but that such provisions have been a largely neglected part of the bargaining process between governments and businesses. The authors contend that policymakers can avoid expensive mistakes if they tie incentives to written guarantees of job creation and other benefits.

581. McGahey, Richard. 1986-87. "State Economic Development Policy: Strategic Approaches for the Future." *Review of Law and Social Change* (New York University) 15(1):43-77.

Examines the growing role of state government in economic development. The author points out that, to achieve the dual goals of development and equality, state policy makers will have to coordinate myriad existing state and local policies with future policies. Creating specific initiatives, even those that recognize the importance of structural factors, will do little good if the effects of one policy cancel out those of another. Adaptive and structural policies alike affect a variety of socioeconomic factors, including capital, labor, technology, education and training, and social welfare. Specific policies will have to be coordinated among government, business, labor and community groups to produce an efficient and flexible overall strategy for the future. Discussion focuses on the states of New York and Massachusetts.

582. Osborne, David. 1989. *State Technology Programs: A Preliminary Analysis of Lessons Learned.* Washington, D.C.: The Council of State Policy and Planning Agencies, 73 pp.

Examines state-sponsored programs designed to spur technological development in an attempt to provide a focus for future research and analysis. The paper (1) provides a brief discussion of the nature of technological innovation and failures of the current "innovation system," (2) offers a typology of state technology programs, (3) outlines a series of lessons learned from the state technology programs, and (4) suggests major flaws that appear to hinder state technology strategies.

583. Peters, Alan H. 1993. "Clawbacks and the Administration of Economic Development Policy in the Midwest." *Economic Development Quarterly* 7(4):328-340.

Reports that clawbacks have been proposed as a way of imposing controls on the provision of state economic development subsidies. Clawbacks stipulate that a publicly subsidized firm not achieving agreed-upon employment performance targets must pay back a portion of the subsidy it received. This article reviews the arguments made in favor of clawbacks and presents new data on clawback usage in major midwestern grant and loan incentive programs that indicate clawback provisions are reasonably widely used. However, there is considerable divergence in the operation and organization of clawbacks across programs, and there appears to be little agreement on how firm employment performance should be evaluated. Most directors of state grant and loan programs feel that the inherent riskiness of business should be taken into account when deciding whether clawback sanctions should be applied to underperforming firms.

584. Pigg, Kenneth E., ed. 1991. *The Future of Rural America: Anticipating Policies for Constructive Change.* Boulder, CO: Westview Press, 285 pp.

Seeks to provide, first, a broadening of perspectives for the future basis of rural policy and, second, to provide a beginning point for rethinking the rural problem that confronts policy makers. Fourteen papers address three major themes. The first theme addresses the question of the essential elements of "ruralness." The second theme is a critique of commonly accepted remedies for rural problems, namely economic development and technological change. The third theme has direct programmatic implications, calling for institutional restructuring. The contributors provide a rich set of concepts and practical approaches to addressing the future of rural America in constructive ways.

585. Plosila, Walter H., and David N. Allen. 1985. "Small Business Incubators and Public Policy: Implications for State and Local Development Strategies." *Policy Studies Journal* 13:729-734.

Places the business incubator concept into an economic development, public policy context and discusses issues unique to publicly supported incubators, as opposed to those that are privately supported. Public policy approaches to the design and operation of incubators are the main focus of the article.

586. Popovich, Mark. 1988. *New Businesses, Entrepreneurship, and Rural Development: Building a State Strategy.* Washington, D.C.: National Governors' Association, 34 pp.

Indicates that between 1980 and 1984, new businesses accounted for 46 percent of all net new jobs in the United States and 88 percent of job growth in nonmetropolitan areas. The report addresses the impact and characteristics of new rural businesses, barriers to new business formation in rural areas, and potential state policies to encourage new business formation. Barriers to rural business formation that were identified include smaller population and economic scale, lower educational and skill levels, concerns about essential inputs (financing, workforce, and infrastructure), poor local economic conditions, and lower wealth. State program alternatives discussed include investments in human capital, technical assistance (including incubators and market information), financing assistance, incentives to involve the poor and dislocated, easing of regulatory constraints, building community leadership, and investments in public facilities.

587. Portz, John. 1993. "State Economic Development Programs: The Trials and Tribulations of Implementation." *Economic Development Quarterly* 7(2):160-171.

Reports that, during the 1980s, state governments initiated an array of economic development policies and programs. Although plans were numerous, obstacles to implementation were equally evident. This article considers such obstacles by focusing on three programs in Massachusetts and Michigan--the Massachusetts Social Compact and the Re-employment Assistance Benefits Program and the Michigan Modernization Service. An implementation framework that includes four elements (problem definition, program capacity, political support, and state ecology) is used to analyze the trials and tribulations that led to the demise of these programs. The Massachusetts and Michigan experiences are also placed in the broader context of distributive, redistributive, and regulatory policies. As these case studies demonstrate, each policy type poses a different set of challenges for public policymakers and administrators.

588. Premus, R. 1988. "U.S. Technology Policies and Their Regional Effects." *Environment and Planning C* 6:441-448.

Contains an examination of the changes in U.S. science and technology policies in response to the recently increasing international competition and worldwide economic restructuring. Although historically these policies have been the responsibility of the Federal Government, in recent years the states and local governments have emerged as important partners in efforts to bridge the gap between science and industry. The central focus is on overcoming technical, financial, labor market, and community locational barriers to high-technology expansion. The old practice of "smoke stack chasing" has given way to inward-looking policies that encourage business startups and expansions. Key objectives of state and local government policies are to increase the flow of new ideas into the innovation process, to shorten the time for its initial introduction into a new product or process technology, and for a more rapid assimilation of new technology throughout the regional industrial structure.

589. Randall, J. N. 1985. "Economic Trends and Support to Economic Activity in Rural Scotland." *Scottish Economic Bulletin* (1985):10-20.

Discusses the relative economic performance of rural Scotland and of three subareas: (1) the Highlands and Islands, (2) the rest of Northern Scotland, and (3) Southern Scotland. Trends during the 1970s and more recently are generally more favorable in rural Scotland than in Scotland as a whole, although population has declined in many of the smallest settlements. Estimates are then presented of government expenditure in Scotland which can be identified as being in direct support to the major sectors of economic activity. Per capita expenditures of this type in rural Scotland compare favorably to those for Scotland as a whole. The extent of assistance to rural areas reflects both preferential assistance to particular areas and the rural incidence of national policies towards particular industrial sectors, particularly agriculture.

590. Redwood, Anthony. 1987. "Job Creation in Nonmetropolitan Communities--Issues for State Policy," pp. 32-52 in *Rural Economic Development--The States Agenda*. Lexington, KY: Council of State Governments.

Identifies state policy issues that are crucial to nonmetropolitan business development and job creation. The author identifies five foundations on which development is based and the primary issues of state policy related to each. These foundations are (1) infrastructure, (2) innovation, (3) commitment (i.e., leadership), (4) financial capital, and (5) human capital. Particular attention is paid to the human capital dimension because many see it as critical to success, and states have considerable influence over it.

591. Reeder, Richard J., Mary Jo Schneider, and Bernal L. Green. 1993. "Attracting Retirees as a Development Strategy," pp. 127-144 in *Economic Adaptation: Alternatives for Nonmetropolitan Areas*, D. L. Barkley, ed. Boulder, CO: Westview Press.

Provides a review of the potential for and problems with attracting retirees as a rural development strategy. The author's overview begins with background information on migration trends and factors responsible for these trends. Next, the economic and community impacts of retiree attraction are presented. The chapter concludes with a discussion of policies used to enhance retiree attraction.

592. Reid, J. Norman, and Thomas D. Rowley. 1990. *Future Directions in Rural Development Policy: Findings and Recommendations of the National Commission on Agriculture and Rural Development Policy*. Washington, D.C.: National Commission on Agriculture and Rural Development Policy, 29 pp.

Points out that generally the 1980s were much harder on rural areas than on their urban counterparts. The problems of rural America are not homogeneous, however, and so neither farm policy nor any other single-issue policy can sufficiently address them. The Commission believes that the following principles should guide rural development: (1) rural areas and people must be economically self-reliant, (2) rural areas and people must be able to adapt, and (3) the rural physical and cultural environment must be protected.

593. Schmandt, Jurgen, and Robert Wilson, eds. 1990. *Growth Policy in the Age of High Technology*. Winchester, MA: Unwin Hyman, Inc., 470 pp.

Deals with the new activism of state governments that is evident in the area of economic development, which has become closely linked to technology policy in recent years. While some state efforts date from the end of the 1970s and early 1980s, although many are more recent, detailed knowledge about what types of initiatives have been effective and which have not is still limited. This book attempts to fill this gap. Part I examines the political and intergovernmental aspects of the renewed policy activism of state government, especially in terms of development policy. Part II assesses the contribution theory and empirical studies can make for assessing state actions aimed at influencing regional growth. Part III evaluates alternative action strategies, and Part IV discusses the implications of state policy for institutional innovation and issues of governance.

594. Silver, Hilary, and Dudley Burton. 1986. "The Politics of State-Level Industrial Policy: Lessons from Rhode Island's Greenhouse Compact." *Journal of the American Planning Association* 52(3):277-289.

Evaluates Rhode Island voters' rejection of the Greenhouse Compact, a $750 million, seven-year, comprehensive economic development plan designed to create 60,000 new jobs and increase wages statewide. After describing the proposal and examining criticisms to it, the authors argue that the defeat of the Greenhouse Compact was a consequence of its procedures as much as its content. Voters rejected the distribution of costs and benefits under the plan and its elitist, exclusionary characteristics. The authors conclude with suggestions for planners, based on the principle that economic development planning or industrial policymaking must be as concerned about how a program is designed, publicized, and implemented as about the substance of the plan itself.

595. Smith, Tim R., and William F. Fox. 1990. "Economic Development Programs for States in the 1990s." *Economic Review* (Federal Reserve Bank of Kansas City) 75(4):25-35.

Describes the broad range of traditional state recruitment programs that states have implemented in the attempt to create jobs. Then the authors examine how well traditional state recruitment programs have met the goal of creating jobs. The third section outlines strategies for refocusing existing programs and adopting new programs aimed at indigenous businesses. The authors conclude that states stand a better chance of boosting employment if they move aggressively to shift the focus of their efforts from recruiting large manufacturing businesses to providing a more favorable economic environment for all businesses.

596.   Strange, Marty, with P. E. Funk, G. Hansen, J. Tally, and D. Macke. 1990. *State Economic Development Policies and the Small Agricultural Communities of the Middle Border.* Walthill, NE: Center for Rural Affairs, 130 pp.

Reviews the economic development policies of six states in the nation's mid-section that embrace 277 counties whose economies are heavily dependent on agriculture. The states are Iowa, Kansas, Minnesota, Nebraska, North Dakota, and South Dakota. The counties analyzed all had 30 percent or more of their nonretail and nonservice workers employed in farming or ranching, and none had a town of 20,000 or more.

597.   Wilson, Robert. 1990. "Structural Economic Change and the Powers of State Government: The Viability of Regional Development Strategies," pp. 39-63 in *Growth Policy in the Age of High Technology*, J. Schmandt and R. Wilson, eds. Winchester, MA: Unwin Hyman, Inc.

Seeks to identify the means by which state government affects the economy of the state and to determine the potential effectiveness of these means in a period of structural change. Do states have the capabilities (i.e., powers and resources) to significantly affect their economies? Or do other factors, such as the existing levels of the factors of production, federal macroeconomic policy, and the forces of structural change and international competition, predominate and diminish the effectiveness of state actions? If state actions can be effective, which of the wide range of activities are most important? Can "beggar thy neighbor" policies be avoided by state government or is one state's gain another state's loss? The author first briefly examines history to identify instances where state action has been important, if not decisive, in economic development. Then the contemporary role of state government is examined. He concludes by assessing the potential of current state strategies to promote development given the forces of structural change.

598.   Wolf, Michael Allan. 1990. "Enterprise Zones: A Decade of Diversity." *Economic Development Quarterly* 4(1):3-14.

Reviews the U.S. experience with enterprise zones as an economic development policy tool. The author traces the origins of the enterprise zone concept, and the attempts by various states to implement the concept. Then the experience of one state (Maryland) is discussed in detail. Conclusions are presented regarding the strengths and weaknesses of the enterprise zone concept, and suggestions for further analysis are presented.

599. Wolman, Harold, and Gerry Stoker. 1992. "Understanding Local Economic Development in a Comparative Context." *Economic Development Quarterly* 6(4):406-417.

Provides a contextual framework for understanding local economic development policymaking and policy in Britain and the United States. The article is aimed at readers familiar with local economic development in one country (particularly the United States) who wish to gain an understanding of local economic development policymaking, policy, and politics in the other. The authors examine a series of differences between the two countries as they relate to local economic development. They then describe and discuss differences in national governmental structure and intergovernmental relations, local government structure and politics, local finance, the national policy framework, and the role of local interests (particularly local business) in local economic development. In each case, the authors analyze the consequences of those differences for local economic development policy.

600. Woods, Mike D., and Larry D. Sanders. 1989. "Rural Development: A Critical Oklahoma Issue." *Oklahoma Current Farm Economics* 62(3):3-16.

Reviews issues and options related to rural development in Oklahoma. Specifically, the authors (1) provide an overview of Oklahoma demographics and discuss general definitions regarding rural development; (2) review specific issues regarding rural development; (3) summarize various types of policies which are available; and (4) discuss types of rural development assistance offered by Oklahoma State University.

INCENTIVES

601. Alderman, Neil, Pooran Wynarczyk, and Alfred T. Thwaites. 1988. "High Technology, Small Firms, and Regional Economic Development: A Question of Balance?" pp. 104-121 in *Small and Medium Size Enterprises and Regional Development*, M. Giaoutzi, P. Nijkamp, and D. Storey, eds. London: Routledge.

Reports that policymakers are placing increasing reliance on assistance to small and medium-sized firms and on specific developments in new technological systems such as microelectronics and biotechnology. The authors draw upon research undertaken at the University of Newcastle and elsewhere to question some of the assumptions underlying these particular policy emphases and to draw attention to potential implications for regional economic development.

602.   Alexander, Donna. 1992. "Incentives as Economic Development Tools."
       Economic Development Review 10(4):64-66.

Examines the use of economic development incentives nationally. Current literature regarding the use of incentives was used as background. A survey was utilized to quantify and qualify the use of incentives. The results of the survey are outlined and incorporated into the conclusion. The author's intent is to illustrate national trends regarding the use of incentives. Following the discussion of trends, recommendations are provided for future use of incentives.

603.   Bachelor, Lynn W. 1991. "Michigan, Mazda, and the Factory of the
       Future: Evaluating Economic Development Incentives." *Economic
       Development Quarterly* 5(2):114-125.

Examines the considerations that guided the deliberations of Michigan officials in determining the incentives to be offered to attract Mazda to locate an auto assembly plant at Flat Rock, Michigan. State officials examined the project's impact on state employment and revenues and on transformation of the state's economic base before arriving at a multi-faceted incentive package, comprised of job training, infrastructure improvements, and loans worth almost $49 million. The city of Flat Rock granted property tax abatements worth $87 million. The author finds that the validity of quantitative measures of project impact was limited by incomplete data and differences between state-and-local-level impacts and concludes that future economic development policies should be guided by criteria based on review of both qualitative and quantitative impacts of past policies.

604.   Bender, Lloyd D. 1989. *Community-Based Small Business Start-Up
       Funds*. WREP III. Corvallis, OR: Western Rural Development
       Center, 11 pp.

Provides guidance to communities considering startup funds to foster the development and retention of small businesses. A building block approach is suggested for communities starting such a fund. First is to initiate a small business planning assistance program. The second step is to help provide financial and service resources to small businesses. The third and final step is management oversight through each phase of a business' growth.

605. Blair, John P., Rudy H. Fichtenbaum, and James A. Swaney. 1984. "The Market for Jobs: Location Decisions and the Competition for Economic Development." *Urban Affairs Quarterly* 20(1):64-77.

Discusses the market for industrial locations in which cities, states, and other governmental units compete to attract firms to locate in their area. The authors first examine the evolution of this market for jobs, then explore the economic efficiency of the market, explaining how the market can capture or internalize effects that were previously external to it, and finally discuss the practical limitations on the efficiency of the market for jobs. The authors indicate that economic development subsidy programs have, to a large extent, replaced wage rate differentials and labor mobility as the means by which labor surpluses and deficits are corrected.

606. Broadway, Michael. 1991. "Economic Development Programs in the Great Plains: The Example of Nebraska." *Great Plains Research* 1(2):324-344.

Reports on Nebraska's experience with state programs to stimulate economic growth and development. The Nebraska Employment and Investment Growth Act of 1987 provides various tax incentives to businesses that make investments in the state or create "new jobs." The majority of these "new jobs" have been in metropolitan counties, but the facility responsible for the largest number of jobs to result from the legislation was Iowa Beef Packers (IBP) beefpacking plant in Lexington. Previous studies of the impact of beefpacking on small towns found high levels of social disruption associated with the arrival of the workers. Lexington, by contrast, has so far been able to avoid many of the adverse social impacts associated with sudden population growth by a defacto policy of restricting new housing construction in the community.

607. Burnier, DeLysa. 1992. "Becoming Competitive: How Policymakers View Incentive-Based Development Policy." *Economic Development Quarterly* 6(1):14-24.

Examines the question of why local politicians and officials decide to offer development incentives to firms when the literature challenges the economic rationality of such decisions. Previous studies have concluded that very little systematic information exists on how public officials think about local economic development and how they make policy decisions in that realm. The author's purpose is to supply the kind of systematic information about economic development that has heretofore been lacking. Interview data is used to examine how one group of officials explain their decisions to offer firms tax abatements through Ohio's enterprise zone program.

608. Dabney, Dan Y. 1991. "Do Enterprise Zone Incentives Affect Business Location Decisions?" *Economic Development Quarterly* 5(4):325-334.

Concludes that financial incentives, such as tax refunds, credits, and abatements, that are offered to new businesses through enterprise zone programs only marginally affect the firm's location decision and are not a major location factor. Enterprise zones generally do not fare well in terms of either classical or nontraditional location factors, causing enterprise zone incentives to be unable to offset the deficiencies of major location factors in zones. Examples of traditional factors that are often not favorable in zones are transportation, insurance costs, and access to raw materials; examples of nontraditional factors include amenities. The author concludes that whether the enterprise zone incentives can be a pivotal factor in the location decision is highly dependent on the percentage of the financial incentive to the initial investment of the new firm.

609. Dommel, Paul R. 1984. "Local Discretion: The CDBG Approach," pp. 101-113 in *Urban Economic Development*, R. Bingham and J. Blair, eds. Beverly Hills, CA: Sage Publications.

Examines the community development block grant (CDBG) program, administered by the U.S. Department of Housing and Urban Development (HUD). The author concludes that, since the program began in 1984, a relatively small percentage of the funds have been allocated to economic development. Rather local officials have preferred to channel most of the resources into revitalization of residential neighborhoods, public services, and general public improvements that might normally be funded from local tax revenues.

610. Drabenstott, Mark, and Charles Morris. 1989. "New Sources of Financing for Rural Development." *American Journal of Agricultural Economics* 71(5):1315-1323.

Examines recent developments in rural financial markets and evaluates proposed rural capital programs. The authors conclude that, while rural lending has slowed in the 1980s, most of the slowdown is caused by the weak rural economy, not by excessive caution on the part of lenders. Nevertheless, an uneven rural economy has given rise to great geographic variation in the availability of funds to rural businesses.

611.　Economic Research Service. 1990. *Financial Market Intervention as a Rural Development Strategy.* ERS Staff Rpt. No. AGES 9070. Washington, D.C.: USDA, Economic Research Service, Agricultural and Rural Economy Division, 93 pp.

Is concerned with the usefulness of Federal intervention in rural financial markets as a mechanism for fostering rural development. The chapters in this report describe the financial system serving rural America, assess the adequacy of this system at meeting the financial needs of rural businesses and governments, and examine the effectiveness of previous federal "credit" programs of special concern to rural America.

612.　Florida, Richard L., and Martin Kenney. 1988. "Venture Capital, High Technology, and Regional Development." *Regional Studies* 22(1):33-48.

Explores the role of venture capital in technological innovation and regional development. Both aggregate data and a unique firm-level data base are employed to determine the location of major centers of venture capital in the U.S., flows of venture capital investments, and patterns of investment syndication or coinvestment among venture capital firms. Three major centers of venture capital were identified (California, New York, and New England), as well as three minor centers (Illinois, Texas, and Minnesota). Venture capital firms were found to cluster in areas with high concentrations of financial institutions and those with high concentrations of technology-intensive enterprises. Venture capital firms which are based in financial centers are typically export-oriented, while those in technology centers tend to invest in their own region and attract outside venture capital. Venture capital investments flow predominately toward established high technology areas, and venture investing is characterized by high degrees of intra- and inter-regional syndication or coinvestment.

613.　Florida, Richard, and Donald F. Smith, Jr. 1990. "Venture Capital, Innovation, and Economic Development." *Economic Development Quarterly* 4(4):345-360.

Reports findings from a two-year study that resulted in a new data base on venture capital supply and investment. The findings indicate that venture capital is not sufficient to stimulate high-technology development. In fact, U.S. venture capital exhibits a strong flow from such capital centers as New York and Chicago toward established high-technology regions such as the Silicon Valley and Route 128. The authors conclude that venture capitalists are proficient in locating high-technology investment opportunities where they exist and that, as such, capital gaps are a reflection of underlying structural weaknesses in an area's technology base.

614. Frederic, Paul. 1992. "Economic Development Versus Land Use Regulation," pp. 225-241 in *Contemporary Rural Systems in Transition: Volume 2, Economy and Society*, I. R. Bowler, C. Bryant, and M. Nellis, eds. Wallingford, Oxon, U.K.: CAB International.

Examines the relationship between nonmetropolitan and metropolitan economic trends relative to development incentives and environmental land use regulation in the United States. The author reports that over the past two decades most rural regions and small towns have continued to trail metropolitan communities in economic opportunities. During this same period, a wide variety of rural-oriented economic and environmental protection programs have been enacted by individual states.

615. Grady, Dennis O. 1987. "State Economic Development Incentives: Why Do States Compete?" *State and Local Government Review* 19:86-94.

Examines three hypotheses offered in the literature to explain why states compete among themselves for economic growth by providing business inducements. The analysis begins with the premise that these inducements have little, if any, impact on job creation yet states continue to enact incentives. Using a measure of incentive effort employed in previous research, the analysis assesses whether or not increases in incentives can be attributed to economic conditions, political subsystems, or innovation diffusion theory. The paper concludes that diffusion or the "arms race" hypothesis accounts for the incentive competition and suggests that states call off such competition and focus on nurturing indigenous business and industry by concentrating on improving traditional state services for the benefit of all citizens.

616. Howland, Marie, and Ted Miller. 1990. "UDAG Grants to Rural Areas: A Program That Works." *Economic Development Quarterly* 4(2):128-136.

Uses data from the U.S. Department of Housing and Urban Development (HUD) Urban Development Action Grant (UDAG) grant agreement data base and a survey of 169 rural UDAG projects to evaluate the job-creation success of rural UDAG projects. The authors draw the following conclusions. First, the rural component of the UDAG program has created the number of jobs promised in the original grant agreements. Second, there is little evidence that UDAG projects have resulted in job creation outside of the UDAG recipient firms. Finally, the federal cost of creating a rural manufacturing job through the UDAG program is approximately $5,546.

617. Humphrey, Craig R., and Kenneth P. Wilkinson. 1993. "Growth Promotion Activities in Rural Areas: Do They Make a Difference?" *Rural Sociology* 58(2):175-189.

Examines whether leaders in small towns can actually influence local economic and demographic growth. The authors report that competing views but few studies of this issue characterize recent debates about the effects of "growth machines" in rural areas. In this paper, the authors use alternative indicators of growth during the 1980s for a sample of local areas in rural Pennsylvania to examine the effects of development efforts, controlling ecological and structural characteristics. The analysis considers local participation in state programs and maintenance of a favorable business climate as well as measures of local growth promotion for business and industry, recreation and tourism, development of forest products, and services development. Hierarchial regressions, taking account of the statistically dominant effects of ecological and structural variables, show that local efforts can influence local growth.

618. Jones, Susan A., Allen R. Marshall, and Glen E. Weisbrod. 1985. *Business Impacts of State Enterprise Zones.* Prepared for the U.S. Small Business Administration. Cambridge, MA: Cambridge Systematics, Inc., 157 pp.

Examines eight enterprise zones in different states and provides a preliminary analysis of enterprise zone impacts. The eight zones were all located in metropolitan areas, ranging in population from about 93,000 to 1,688,000. The area of the zones varies from 40 acres to 9.3 square miles. All had been in operation for at least two years at the time of the study. Dun's (Dun and Bradstreet) market identifiers data were used to assess changes in the number of firms, business mix, and total employment in each of the zones.

619. Lansford, Notie H., and Lonnie L. Jones. 1991. "Tax Abatement as a Development Incentive: Economic Impact on Rural Communities." *Impact Assessment Bulletin* 9(3):31-42.

Presents a computerized, interactive model that can be used to analyze the economic and fiscal impacts of industrial development. The model's applications are illustrated through analysis of projected impacts of alternative development incentives considered in connection with a specific industrial development proposal in Texas.

620. Lyman, David. 1992. "California Cities' Use of Incentives." *Economic Development Review* 10(4):67-68.

Reports that most California cities use incentives and the incentives that are used the most are below-market rate loans and amendments to the general plan. The incentives are used for revitalizing specific areas within the community. Local lender home loan approval and historical tax credit and other tax-related incentives are the least used. The incentives used most frequently are not those with the greatest results nor the highest return on investment, but rather are the easiest to use.

621. Marlin, Matthew R. 1990. "The Effectiveness of Economic Development Subsidies." *Economic Development Quarterly* 4(1):15-22.

Makes use of data recently compiled by the U.S. Treasury Department to analyze the relationship between one form of economic development subsidy, Industrial Development Bonds, and Gross State Product during the years 1983-1986. The results provide evidence that those states that used the subsidy more intensively than others tended to have greater increases in Gross State Product.

622. Marvel, Mary K., and William J. Shkurti. 1993. "The Economic Impact of Development: Honda in Ohio." *Economic Development Quarterly* 7(1):50-62.

Addresses the knowledge gap that exists regarding the effectiveness, efficiency, and equity of state industrial location incentives, such as tax incentives, technological assistance, subsidized loans, tax exempt bonds, and direct loans. The costs and benefits of the state of Ohio's investment in Honda are calculated to provide an assessment of that seminal initiative. In addition, the analysis considers the portability of the findings to other economic development programs. Direct benefits to the state of Ohio and to local governments directly attributable to the Honda plants clearly exceed direct investment of tax dollars. Indirect effects are much more difficult to measure; however, it is clear that both indirect benefits and indirect costs are significant. The portability of the Honda experience to other venues should proceed with caution.

623. Milward, H. Brinton, and Heidi Hosbach Newman. 1989. "State Incentive Packages and the Industrial Location Decision." *Economic Development Quarterly* 3(3):203-222.

Provides an analysis of the industrial location process. Recent literature on the topic is reviewed, and six case studies of auto plant location decisions are examined. A trend toward increasing cost per worker of the state incentive packages is noted.

624. Oates, Wallace E., and Robert M. Schwab. 1988. "Economic Competition Among Jurisdictions: Efficiency Enhancing or Distortion Inducing." *Journal of Public Economics* 35:333-354.

Explores the normative implications of competition among "local" jurisdictions to attract new industry and income. Within a neoclassical framework, the authors examine how local officials set two policy variables, a tax (or subsidy) rate on mobile capital and a standard for local environmental quality, to induce more capital to enter the jurisdiction in order to raise wages. The analysis suggests that, for jurisdictions homogenous in workers, local choices under simple-majority rule will be socially optimal; such jurisdictions select a zero tax rate on capital and set a standard for local environmental quality such that marginal willingness-to-pay equals the marginal social costs of a cleaner environment. However, in cases where jurisdictions are not homogenous or where, for various reasons, they set a positive tax rate on capital, distortions arise not only in local fiscal decisions, but also in local environmental choices.

625. Reeder, Richard J. 1993. *Rural Enterprise Zones in Theory and Practice: An Assessment of Their Development Potential.* Staff Report No. AGES 9305. Washington, D.C.: USDA, Economic Research Service, 52 pp.

Reports that state enterprise zone programs use tax incentives and other forms of assistance to encourage business development in distressed areas. Research suggests that enterprise zones have been fairly successful in generating jobs, and the cost per job created appears reasonable when compared with other job creation programs. Although enterprise zones may not be appropriate for all rural areas, most rural zones appear to be doing as well as or better than urban zones in creating jobs. Zone performance might be improved by screening out potentially unproductive sites, by providing more hands-on technical assistance, and by modifying program incentives.

626. Rich, Michael J. 1992. "UDAG, Economic Development, and the Death and Life of American Cities." *Economic Development Quarterly* 6(2):150-172.

Reports that the Urban Development Action Grant (UDAG) program awarded $4.6 billion to assist about 3,000 economic development projects in more than 1,200 cities during its 12 years of operation (1978-1989). The author examines data from a variety of sources to assess the UDAG experience. Topics addressed include the program's legislative history, characteristics of participant cities and the distribution of UDAG projects and funds, public-private partnership composition and fiscal strategies in selected cities, and an assessment of UDAG program impacts. The article concludes that UDAG made several important contributions to local economic development in addition to the federal aid that was targeted to distressed cities. The program's most important contribution was its role in transforming local economic development policy from one based primarily on a donor mentality that emphasized tax abatements and infrastructure improvements to a more entrepreneurial approach that emphasized the recapture of public funds.

627. Robinson, Kenneth L., and Richard J. Reeder. 1991. "State Enterprise Zones in Nonmetro Areas: Are They Working?" *Rural Development Perspectives* 7(3):30-35.

Reports that state enterprise zone programs appear to be successful economic development tools in nonmetro areas. The programs have created jobs for disadvantaged residents, but most of the jobs are in low-paying, traditional manufacturing industries. Furthermore, many rural areas are excluded from zone participation, either directly through population and area limitations, or indirectly through competitive application processes. The effectiveness of zone programs might be improved by changes that would increase rural participation and provide a better mix of jobs.

628. Stinson, Thomas F., and Andrea Lubov. 1993. "Minnesota's Nonmetro Cities Use Revolving Loans as a Development Tool." *Rural Development Perspectives* 8(2):12-15.

Reports that nearly 100 of Minnesota's nonmetro towns use revolving loan funds as a way to spur local economic development. Here's how they work: a town makes the initial loans to qualified businesses, and as the loans are repaid, the money is loaned out again and again to other businesses. A few problems need to be worked out: default rates somewhat higher than those experienced by other lenders, slow accumulation of funds needed to make second-generation loans, and slow turnover in "revolving" the funds to the next round of businesses. In city-based programs, there is also the risk that viable projects are going unfunded in towns without access to a revolving fund.

APPROACHES/STRATEGIES

629. Barkley, David L., ed. 1993. *Economic Adaptation: Alternatives for Nonmetropolitan Areas.* Boulder, CO: Westview Press, 298 pp.

Is primarily concerned with the ability of small, isolated, limited resource areas to function and prosper in the new global economy. Fifteen chapters examine factors contributing to a widening economic gap between metropolitan and nonmetropolitan areas in the United States. The authors also discuss potential solutions and strategies to reverse the losses of jobs and income in rural areas. The work aims to provide regional scientists, practitioners, and students with an appreciation for the opportunities and problems facing nonmetropolitan areas as they adapt to the new economic environment.

630. Bartsch, Charles, and Diane DeVaul. 1992. *Utilities and Industries: New Partnerships for Rural Development.* Washington, D.C.: The Aspen Institute, 87 pp.

Reports that utilities are becoming actively involved in the economic development process and are serving as catalysts for technology transfer. In partnerships with local and state officials, utilities offer hope to small towns and rural areas that are least able to muster the resources to cope with economic change. This book and the policy workshop that preceded it provide a rationale for utilities to stimulate economic development activities. The authors outline a process for designing and implementing cooperative relationships between utilities, state governments, and industry to improve competitiveness, increase the pace of technological modernization, enhance efficiency, reduce wastes, and stimulate economic growth. They also suggest ways to strengthen ties between utilities and state economic development officials to support a utility-based, energy efficiency-economic development strategy.

631. Bayne, J. Nick. 1993. "A Comprehensive Approach to Economic Development: The BIDCO Example." *Economic Development Review* 11(2):22-27.

Reports that economic growth is highly dependent on an area's competitiveness and capacity for such growth. Moreover, to facilitate desired economic growth, local economic development organizations must broaden the definition of their "customer" base and ensure the quality delivery of services and products to their "customers." In effect, the need is for a comprehensive approach to economic development.

632. Beauregard, Robert A., Paul Lawless, and Sabina Deitrick. 1992. "Collaborative Strategies for Reindustrialization: Sheffield and Pittsburgh." *Economic Development Quarterly* 6(4):418-430.

Reports that governmental actors in regions faced with stagnant or declining economies often involve various groups in the common pursuit of a reversal of fortunes. Such collaborations recognize that economic development is as much an organizational and political as an economic activity. This article reviews the economic development collaborations that formed in Sheffield (England) and Pittsburgh (United States) during the 1980s in order to turn those regional economies away from reliance on a rapidly disappearing dominant industry. The purpose of this comparative analysis is to develop lessons for policymakers who are contemplating or currently undertaking such approaches to regional economic development.

633. Benington, John, and Mike Geddes. 1992. "Local Economic Development in the 1980s and 1990s: Retrospect and Prospects." *Economic Development Quarterly* 6(4):454-463.

Suggests that local economic development in the 1990s is facing a very different economic and political context from that of the 1970s and 1980s, and that this requires the development of very different paradigms and strategies. In particular, the authors argue that the transition from a Fordist to a post-Fordist economy, and the process of economic and political integration in the European Community confront local economic development agencies with a fundamentally new set of challenges in both the United Kingdom and the United States. This also means that the focus of comparative study of local economic development needs to be shifted to recognize the European context within which British localities increasingly operate.

634.   Bingham, Richard D., and John P. Blair, eds. 1984. *Urban Economic Development* Vol. 27, Urban Affairs Annual Reviews. Beverly Hills, CA: Sage Publications, 283 pp.

Provides a broadly-based review of economic development strategies for urban areas. The chapters cover four major areas: (1) economic development paths, (2) analysis and evaluation of federal economic development programs, (3) state and local approaches to economic development, and (4) case studies of local economic development.

635.   Blakely, Edward J. 1989. *Planning Local Economic Development: Theory and Practice.* Newbury Park, CA: Sage Publications, 307 pp.

Intended primarily for persons studying to become professional practitioners of local economic development at the local agency, city or county government, and neighborhood levels. This book may also serve as a reference for professional practitioners and economic development or planning specialists as they carry out their responsibilities. In addition, the book is intended to provide guidance for community-based organizations and their client groups engaged in the struggle to find viable means to develop the economic base of their communities.

636.   Blakely, Edward J., and Nancy Nishikawa. 1992. "Incubating High-Technology Firms: State Economic Development Strategies for Biotechnology." *Economic Development Quarterly* 6(3):241-254.

Reports that state economic development agencies are engaged in a variety of efforts to increase the capacity of the state to attract or create new biotechnology firms. Some states have established well-endowed organizations dedicated to promoting biotechnology whereas others have adopted more modest programs or have incorporated biotechnology issues into other policy areas, such as education or agriculture. Despite the range of organizational forms and purposes, there is evidence of a common paradigm, "the incubator model," being used by state policymakers with respect to biotechnological economic development activity. The thrust of this strategy is to create a set of conditions that will nurture technological innovation and the formation of indigenous firms. The incubator model provides a coherent conceptual framework for policymakers to pursue a slate of recognizable programs. Changes in the structure of commercial biotechnology, particularly increasing fragmentation and externalization of productive relations, suggest that the local resources identified as the incubation base may provide regions with a competitive edge.

637. Burchell, Robert W., and David Listokin. 1981. "The Fiscal Impact of Economic-Development Programs: Case Studies of the Local Cost-Revenue Implications of HUD, EDA, and FmHA Projects," pp. 163-229 in *New Tools for Economic Development: The Enterprise Zone, Development Bank, and RFC*, G. Sternlieb and D. Listokin, eds. New Brunswick, NJ: Rutgers University, Center for Urban Policy Research.

Investigates the local fiscal impact of federal economic development programs. The authors compare the costs incurred by the municipality in providing public services and other development accommodations to the revenues garnered as a result of development through the property tax, local income/sales taxes, and such other local revenues as user charges and miscellaneous revenues as well as intergovernmental transfers from both state and federal governments. They then offer conclusions with respect to (1) the federal and local costs and benefits of urban and rural economic development efforts, (2) the types of projects and the fiscal environments that tend to yield either the greatest or the least fiscal benefits, (3) the appropriateness of the structure and form of federal allocation programs, and (4) the capacity of current evaluation methods to accurately chart cost and revenue flows for a number of projects in a variety of settings.

638. Butler, Stuart M. 1981. "Enterprise Zones: Pioneering in the Inner City," pp. 25-42 in *New Tools for Economic Development: The Enterprise Zone, Development Bank, and RFC*, G. Sternlieb and D. Listokin, eds. New Brunswick, NJ: Rutgers University, Center for Urban Policy Research.

Examines the rationale supporting the concept of urban enterprise zones and traces the evolution of the concept from its inception in England to its initial implementation in proposed legislation in the United States.

The author identifies the key features of enterprise zones as first proposed in the United States to be (1) suspension of minimum wage laws, (2) a turnover trigger point to prevent tax shelter abuse by large companies, (3) free trade zones, (4) innovative action on housing, including reducing property taxes and increasing capital gains deductions, and (5) a general philosophy of experimentation that would allow the enterprise zones to be used as laboratories to test a variety of policy alternatives.

639.   Canada, Eric P. 1993. "TQM Benchmarking for Economic Development Programs: Good is Not Good Where Better is Expected." *Economic Development Review* 11(3):34-38.

Argues that a properly executed "total quality management" (TQM) program within an economic development organization can create a sustainable competitive advantage for funding and/or industrial investment. Quality improvement in economic development hinges on understanding customer expectations for each customer group, then exceeding expectations. To satisfy increasing expectations, the business practice of "benchmarking" (finding, documenting, and analyzing best practices of others against current practices and customer needs) adapted to economic development is an extremely useful tool.

640.   Christenson, James A., Thomas W. Ilvento, Kim Fendley, and Timothy Collins. 1987. "Jobs, People, and Toyota: A Study of North Central Kentuckians Conducted in 1979 and 1986." *Community Issues*, Vol. 9, No. 1. Lexington, KY: University of Kentucky, Department of Sociology, 11 pp.

Reports on the results of surveys conducted in 1979 and 1986 in a 41-county area of north central Kentucky. Responses of 2,271 people who participated in both surveys constitute the data base of the study. A large manufacturing plant being built by Toyota Motor Company in Scott County was a major focus of the study. The authors report that between 1979 and 1986, the number of respondents who felt that unemployment was a serious problem rose from 41 to 65 percent. Four out of five people wanted more industry in their community in 1986, a 21 percent increase since 1979. Although the support for state funding for industrial development increased slightly between 1979 and 1986, less than half of the respondents favored this type of funding in either year. Only one out of three people surveyed in 1986 supported state funding for the Toyota plant. Few people felt that continued growth in their county would adversely affect their quality of life, and there was little concern for problems specifically associated with industrial development.

641. Clarke, Susan E., and Gary L. Gaile. 1992. "The Next Wave: Postfederal Local Economic Development Strategies." *Economic Development Quarterly* 6(2):187-198.

Reports that in the absence of significant federal economic development resources, local officials face complex choices about both the level and the orientations of their policy efforts. A national study of local economic development officials indicates that cities in this postfederal period are characterized by increased local economic development activities even when relying on own-source revenues, by risk-taking rather than risk-aversive approaches, and by more diverse policy orientations emphasizing indigenous growth and job creation strategies. Cities using more entrepreneurial tools that demand active city roles appear to be more likely to have higher average job and firm growth rates than cities never using these tools.

642. Cole, Barbara A. 1988. *Business Opportunities Casebook.* Washington, D.C.: U.S. Small Business Administration, 54 pp.

Presents examples of communities that improved their local economies by using local skills and resources more effectively to support and expand existing businesses and encourage the development of new business.

643. Cook, Annabel Kirschner. 1990. "Retirement Migration as a Community Development Option." *Journal of the Community Development Society* 21(1):83-101.

Reports that one recent focus of community development efforts has been to attract retirees to rural areas. Emphasizing nonmetropolitan retirement migration in the Pacific Northwest, this paper discusses net migration trends and shifts in these trends and explores the types of rural counties that are most attractive to retired migrants. It then examines the relative ability of three models (using amenities, service availability, and cost-of-living factors, respectively) to explain nonmetropolitan retirement migration between 1980 and 1985. The findings are interpreted to imply that community developers in communities seeking to attract retirees may want to highlight what the area has to offer, rather than how inexpensive it might be to live there, in their promotional efforts.

644. Cornell-Ohl, Susan, Patrick M. McMahon, and John E. Peck. 1991. "Local Assessment of the Industrial Development Process: A Case Study." *Economic Development Review* 9(3):53-56.

Describes the planning and assessment process used in economic development by South Bend, Indiana. The planning process was initiated early in the 1980s in response to substantial losses of manufacturing jobs; some 25,000 manufacturing jobs had been lost in the county from 1950 to 1980. A major result of the planning process was creation of Project Future, a well financed and well staffed community economic development entity. During the 1980s, Project Future and the local economic development community united efforts to finalize development projects with capital investment in excess of $1 billion. Employment in the county increased by 14,000 jobs and population by 6,000.

645. Danz-Hale, Dawn, Dennis R. Domack, and Glen C. Pulver. 1989. *Community Economic Analysis: A Case Example, Mt. Horeb, Wisconsin.* Madison, WI: Madison Gas and Electric Company, 72 pp.

Provides an example of the Community Economic Analysis process developed by University of Wisconsin-Extension specialists. Major sections deal with (1) the community economic analysis process, (2) national, regional, and local trends, (3) strategies for improving jobs and income, and (4) developing a plan of action.

646. Dewar, Margaret E. 1993. "Minnesota's Economic Recovery Fund: Positive Results, Room for Improvement." *Rural Development Perspectives* 8(2):16-21.

Reports that, since 1984, Minnesota has been channeling $8-9 million per year in loans and grants to businesses through a fund that aims to stimulate state and local economic growth, aid distressed areas, and help low- and moderate-income people. The program sends 90 percent of its funds to nonmetro areas, with moderate success. Forty percent of the nonmetro projects appeared to contribute to economic growth within the state (during the period 1984-88), and the most economically distressed counties received more than their share of projects. However, most of the jobs created paid lower wages than the local average.

647. Doeringer, Peter B., David G. Terkla, and Gregory C. Topakian. 1987. *Invisible Factors in Local Economic Development.* New York, NY: Oxford University Press, 144 pp.

Examines the prospects for economic growth and development in local economies that are dominated by mature, and frequently stagnant, industries. The authors look beyond the traditional explanations of growth based on industry mix and quantifiable production costs and argue for the importance of less visible factors that contribute to industrial growth and decline, such as corporate practices and strategies, the quality of the work force, entrepreneurial skills, and the local labor-management environment. The focus of the study is on Worcester County, Massachusetts, but the authors believe that the findings can be applied to a wide variety of local economies. Of particular importance are local business strategies, particularly those that emphasize product specialization and flexibility in production. The authors conclude that revitalized mature industries offer an important complement to emerging industries as a source of sustained growth in the American economy.

648. Doescher, Tabitha, Robert Dauffenbach, and Larkin Warner. 1986. "Identification of Target Industries for Industrial Recruiting in a Nonmetropolitan Area." *Review of Regional Economics and Business* 11:3-12.

Identifies target industries for a small town located in a nonmetropolitan area of northern Oklahoma. Because the project was conducted for a local industrial foundation, the methodology for identifying target industries had to be easily understood by the client, and at the same time be thoroughly grounded in both location theory and rural development theory. The resulting Industrial Development Screening System is a step-by-step screening model which first identifies industries with a strong potential for growth and then screens these industries in accordance with community strengths and weaknesses. The result is a list of target industries for the community to use in its industrial recruiting and marketing efforts.

649. Edgington, David W. 1993. "The Globalization of Japanese Manufacturing Corporations." *Growth and Change* 24(1):87-106.

Discusses recent shifts in the overseas investment strategies of Japan's major multinational manufacturing companies (MNCs). Based on a survey of 20 corporations, it is postulated that the move towards globalization of these companies has taken place in three distinct but overlapping phases: (1) a linear link-up to Japan, (2) a transition phase based on international specialization and "mesh" strategies, and (3) a tetra-polar strategic division of the world. The paper commences with a discussion of recent trends in MNC behavior, and then shows how overseas corporate organization has changed the Japanese firms surveyed, especially after 1985. The implications of these changes among the major global regions is examined. The paper concludes with an assessment of

whether the strategies of Japanese MNCs have converged with those of
the United States or European MNCs, and to what degree they have
retained their own distinctive attributes.

650. Eisinger, Peter. 1991. "The State of State Venture Capitalism."
      Economic Development Quarterly 5(1):64-76.

Reports that state governments have become increasingly visible players
in the venture capital arena, allocating an estimated $192 million in tax,
bond, and other revenues and perhaps a billion dollars in pension trust
funds to a variety of public and quasi-public venture capital arrangements.
The author offers a review of the variety of arrangements at the beginning
of the 1990s by attempting a census of such programs, an estimate of
their financial dimensions, and some preliminary observations regarding
their impact. The review concludes by suggesting that state venture
capitalism, although an established feature in state economic development
strategy, represents a very small commitment of capital compared, for
example, to private venture investment. Economic development results
of such programs, therefore, tend to be modest.

651. Eisinger, Peter K. 1993. "State Venture Capitalism, State Politics, and
      the World of High-Risk Investment." *Economic Development
      Quarterly* 7(2):131-139.

Reports that state venture capital programs, using public money to make
high-risk equity investments in innovative firms in order to generate jobs,
proliferated in the 1980s. A state by state follow-up survey of an earlier
effort reveals that by the beginning of the 1990s, however, there was a
shakeout in the ranks of these programs. Some lost political support;
others could not be justified in economic hard times; still others could not
operate effectively under the constraints of open democratic government
norms. Although the theory of state venture capitalism suggests that there
is a continuing role for such programs, there are sufficient inherent
contradictions to make their long-term survival a highly uncertain
proposition.

652. Ekstrom, Brenda L., and F. Larry Leistritz. 1988. *Rural Community
      Decline and Revitalization: An Annotated Bibliography.* New York,
      NY: Garland Publishing, Inc., 203 pp.

Contains 670 references dealing with socioeconomic consequences of
economic decline in rural areas and strategies for the economic
revitalization of the affected communities. The scope of the book has

been further narrowed by examining problems of decline and revitalization only within the world's industrialized countries. The compilers have concentrated on North American, European, and Australian literature written in English. The compilers concentrated their literature review on the period 1975-1987, although salient works written prior to 1975 were reviewed if they were deemed of enduring interest or formed the basis of later research.

653. Farley, Josh, and Norman J. Glickman. 1986. "R&D as an Economic Development Strategy: The Microelectronics and Computer Technology Corporation Comes to Austin, Texas." *Journal of the American Planning Association* 52:407-418.

Evaluates the effects of the location of the Microelectronics and Computer Technology Corporation on Austin's economy and land use. The results of the analysis provide qualified support for the state's economic development strategy, which is based on science and technology. The results confirm the importance of an excellent research university and attractive quality of life in supporting an emerging technology strategy.

654. Feldman, Richard J. 1993. "Economic Development on Purpose: The Role of TQM." *Economic Development Review* 11(3):10-13.

Argues that total quality management (TQM) applied to economic development involves the organization and optimal use of internal resources to meet the challenges of a rapidly changing external world. TQM in economic development requires a committed, serious, and full-range implementation emphasizing outcomes and mission accomplishments rather than activity inputs. A set of basic TQM operating guidelines for economic development practitioners is presented.

655. Feller, Irwin. 1991. "Do State Programs on Technology Work?" *Forum for Applied Research and Public Policy* 6(3):69-72.

Contends that state technology development and modernization programs have reached a point where the lack of systematic and external evaluations has added to their political vulnerability. Inadequate data, the absence of standardized measures of success, and the difficulty of assessing responsibility for a program's impact all stood in the way of objective evaluations. New pressures on state budgets, coupled with changes in political leadership in many states, have placed many of these programs under increased scrutiny, which in turn heightens the demand for more formal and quantitative evaluations.

656. Fields, W. Calvin. 1992. *Using Business Consultants to Expand Small Rural Firms.* Rural Research Report Vol. 3, Issue 6. Macomb, IL: Western Illinois University, Illinois Institute for Rural Affairs, 6 pp.

Identifies specific ways in which business consultants assist small firms. Data are presented to indicate which types of assistance are most beneficial and which have the least influence. This analysis compares the performance of the Illinois firms that improved after obtaining assistance (successful firms) with those that did not improve (unsuccessful firms). These data are a subanalysis of a broader study that examined the satisfaction levels of firm owners after receiving assistance. Data come from a questionnaire mailed to a random sample of 3,000 small, rural Illinois firms in 1991. The average number of employees of these firms was 39, and 62 percent of the firms were in areas with a population less than 10,000.

657. Finsterbusch, Kurt, and Daniel Kuennen. 1992. "A Look at Business Recruitment as a Rural Development Strategy: Some Previous Findings on Business Recruitment Results in Rural Areas." *Policy Studies Journal* 20(2):218-229.

Examines the role of business recruitment in efforts to generate jobs by 15 rural counties in the Delmarva Peninsula and Southern Maryland. The article is based on a study conducted in 1988 which looked at a wide range (38) of job generating activities that were employed in seven different economic development strategies. These strategies were guided by six different economic development policies (economic development policies refer to the extent that county authorities promote or limit economic development). The study found business recruitment to be the most emphasized and effective strategy on average according to evaluations by county leaders. While the informants may have had a biased view of the effectiveness of business recruitment and may have overlooked some other options, the record of reported events in the study counties and the meager results of most other job-generating activities that were tried support the conclusions of the informants.

658. Finsterbusch, Kurt, Cecelia Formichella, Daniel Kuennen, and Meredith S. Ramsay. 1992. "An Evaluation of a Wide Range of Job-Generating Activities for Rural Counties." *Journal of the Community Development Society* 23(1):103-122.

Examines the job-generating activities of governments and civic groups in 15 rural counties on the Delmarva Peninsula and southern Maryland through analysis of more than 175 informant interviews and related field work. The 15 counties engaged in a wide range of job-generating activities, and many of these were directed toward business recruitment. When community leaders ranked activities for their impact on jobs, industrial parks received the highest ranking, economic development units second, and tourism promotion third. Special financial arrangements for relocating or new businesses were evaluated as very important on average to economic development, and grantsmanship was a successful activity in all counties though it never ranked as the first or second most productive job generating activity. Guidance on economic development strategies for rural counties is derived from the findings.

659. Fisher, Peter S. 1988. "State Venture Capital Funds as an Economic Development Strategy." *Journal of the American Planning Association* 54(2):166-177.

Examines state venture capital funds that provide financing for new and small businesses, generally in technology-based industries. The experience of the oldest state venture fund, the Massachusetts Technology Development Corporation (MTDC), indicates that a state can successfully operate such a fund with an expectation of eventual profit and limited employment impact. However, state venture funds modeled after MTDC are unlikely to make a significant contribution to state economic development in broader terms, considering such issues as the structure and stability of the economy or the quality of the jobs they create.

660. Flora, Jan L., James J. Chriss, Eddie Gale, Gary P. Green, Frederick E. Schmidt, and Cornelia Flora. 1991. *From the Grassroots: Profiles of 103 Rural Self-Development Projects.* Staff Rpt. No. 9123. Washington, D.C.: USDA, Economic Research Service, 109 pp.

Reports on a study of self-development projects in rural communities. The authors define self-development activities as ones that result in the generation of jobs and/or income in rural communities and also (1) actively involve local organizations, (2) involve the investment of substantial local resources, and (3) result in an enterprise that is locally controlled. Through a survey, information was obtained from 103 self-development projects that had been implemented since 1980. The profiles for each project include name and location, a brief project description, involvement of local organizations, an estimate of the amount of income and/or number of jobs generated, and the means by which the project was financed. Types of projects include (1) community-based development (community-owned and worker-owned firms, agricultural marketing organizations, community finance institutions, community-based service firms, etc.), (2) local business and industrial development (locally owned industrial and value-added firms, business incubators, retention and expansion programs), and (3) tourism and historical development (recreational development, festivals, craft fairs, downtown revitalization). A comprehensive index is included.

661.   Fosler, R. Scott. 1984. "Tailoring Economic Development Efforts to Meet Specific Needs." *National Civic Review* 73(10):497-502.

Points out that the goals of economic development efforts should be carefully defined and that programs should be designed specifically to meet those goals. Two examples of development efforts targeted to specific needs are presented. Job Creation Limited is a British firm established specifically to create jobs, often in areas affected by plant closings. The Corporation for Technological Training is a nonprofit organization recently established in Montgomery County, Maryland, to link labor needs of high-technology firms with the current and potential skills of the labor force.

662.   Fosler, R. Scott, ed. 1988. *The New Economic Role of American States: Strategies in a Competitive World Economy.* New York, NY: Oxford University Press, 370 pp.

Examines the new activism of the states in economic development and asks whether it is significant. Case studies conducted in seven states (Massachusetts, Michigan, Tennessee, California, Arizona, Indiana, and Minnesota) suggest that it is. The general finding is that, while the state role is limited, it is increasingly important and in certain instances may be decisive. The authors find that the emerging state role is substantially different from the conventional one in three important ways: (1) in the conventional role, economic development is viewed as a government function whose primary mission is to recruit industry to the state, but in the new role, economic development is conceived as a process that occurs primarily in the private sector but is affected in all phases by a wide range of state actions; (2) in the conventional role, the state passively accepts prevailing economic forces, but in the new role the state employs an active strategy to improve its competitiveness; and (3) in the conventional role, institutional responsibility for economic policy is consigned to a line agency of the state government, but in the new role a fundamentally different set of institutional arrangements is used to accommodate the new strategic orientation--institutions that are more versatile and flexible in permitting the state to anticipate, specialize, experiment, integrate, evaluate, and adjust in dealing with new and changing economic forces.

663. Fosler, R. Scott. 1990. "State Strategies for Business Assistance," pp. 171-193 in *Growth Policy in the Age of High Technology*, J. Schmandt and R. Wilson, eds. Winchester, MA: Unwin Hyman, Inc.

Discusses seven strategies that are currently employed by states to foster business and economic growth. These strategies are (1) improving the general economic or business climate of the state, (2) strengthening the process of economic development, (3) providing support appropriate to the variable life-cycle needs of the firms, (4) tailoring economic programs to the needs of different-sized firms, (5) strengthening the competitive advantage of the state in the global economy, (6) identifying and promoting those industries, firms, or technologies that are thought most likely to offer growth in the future, and (7) fostering synergistic relationships among interdependent but isolated economic resources.

664. Friedli, Eric. 1988. "Interstate Competition for Economic Development Opportunities." *Pacific Northwest Executive* 4(4):20-22.

Examines recent trends in economic development activities of the states. The focus is on the state of Washington. A 1986 survey of Washington state policymakers and economic development officials revealed that 75 percent of respondents believed it is important for the state to have programs that are equal to or better than programs in other states. Respondents also identified Massachusetts and North Carolina as the states with the best economic development programs. The author identifies three models for state economic development activity: (1) the grab-it model, (2) the efficiency model, and (3) the no-deal model.

665. Glasgow, Nina L. 1990. "Attracting Retirees as a Community Development Option." *Journal of the Community Development Society* 21(1):102-114.

Compares recent trends in population and employment growth in nonmetropolitan retirement counties with those in other types of nonmetropolitan counties. The retirement counties number 481 out of approximately 2,400 nonmetropolitan U.S. counties. Since 1980, nonmetropolitan retirement counties have accounted for over half of all nonmetropolitan population growth, and they have grown at a rate over four times greater than the remaining counties. Post-1980 employment in these counties also far outstripped that for the remaining counties.

666. Goode, Frank M., and Steven E. Hastings. 1989. *Northeast Industrial Targeting (NIT) and Economic Development Database (EDD) System, Users Manual, Version 1.1.* Staff Paper 162. University Park: Pennsylvania State University, Department of Agricultural Economics and Rural Sociology, 46 pp.

Describes the structure and potential applications of a microcomputer-based information system that has been created to help elected officials and leaders of rural and small metropolitan communities identify their potential to attract new employers. The system provides economic development information for nearly 1,098 nonmetropolitan and small metropolitan communities with populations of 1,000 to 100,000. The system assesses a community's chances of attracting up to 69 manufacturing industries and enables the user to identify those industries that are most likely to be looking for the particular characteristics that the community offers. The system also allows the user to compare the community with 1,100 other communities in the Northeast in relation to 118 economic development variables, including labor force, tax rate, highway access, and proximity to markets.

667. Green, Gary P., and Kevin T. McNamara. 1988. "Traditional and Non-traditional Opportunities and Alternatives for Local Economic Development," pp. 288-303 in *The Rural South in Crisis: Challenges for the Future*, L. J. Beaulieu, ed. Boulder, CO: Westview Press.

Discusses various traditional economic development strategies and their potential for stimulating future rural development. Then, the authors focus on new institutional arrangements that can be utilized to improve local development opportunities by increasing access to debt and equity capital and fostering ownership structures to maintain manufacturing facilities. These strategies can improve a community's ability to sustain or expand its economy in the short run. Improving access to debt and equity capital also can complement long run strategies to stimulate economic growth through human capital investment and development of entrepreneurs.

668. Green, Gary P., Jan L. Flora, Cornelia Flora, and Frederick E. Schmidt. 1990. "Local Self-Development Strategies: National Survey Results." *Journal of the Community Development Society* 21(2):55-73.

Evaluates local self-development strategies among nonmetropolitan communities. It analyzes the characteristics of these projects, their benefits and costs, and the obstacles facing self-development communities. Based on a survey of more than one hundred communities, it was found that most self-development projects in the 1980s were initiated because of the depressed rural economy. Self-development efforts do not appear to replace traditional rural economic development activities; instead, they appear to complement them. Self-development activities produce a wide variety of jobs that are taken primarily by local residents. Informants reported that the cost and availability of credit are major obstacles for self-development projects. In terms of benefits, local business/industrial development projects tend to produce the most jobs and to produce them at the least cost.

669.   Hanratty, Patricia. 1990. "Massachusetts Industrial Services Program: A State Economic Adjustment Strategy," pp. 106-108 in *Plant Closure and Community Recovery*, J. E. Lynch, ed. Washington, D.C.: National Council for Urban Economic Development.

Reports on the accomplishments of the Massachusetts Industrial Services Program (ISP), a quasi-public agency created legislatively in 1984 to address the problems of industrial competitiveness and job loss. The ISP works with management and labor to help prevent plant closings or layoffs and to respond to plant closures if and when they occur. The ISP's preventative strategies focus on improving the competitive position of manufacturing companies by helping them improve their business planning, marketing, production management, and financial position. This is done by providing management and financial consulting as well as high risk loans and equity investments from a state funded capital pool. When major plant closings or layoffs occur, the ISP establishes and funds Worker Assistance Centers.

670.   Hanson, Gordon S. 1993. "Evaluation of State Lender Commitment Programs." *Economic Development Quarterly* 7(3):255-266.

Reports that states have been adopting a variety of economic intervention strategies intended to stimulate growth in the small business sector. This study uses an interrupted time-series analysis to test the hypothesis that growth in the small business establishment sector of a state's economy can be stimulated and sustained when lender commitment programs are in effect. These state-initiated loan packages are designed to extend the availability of capital to potential employment-generating enterprises by diffusing the risk among lenders and having the state assume a share of it. The findings provide only mixed support for this hypothesis. There is evidence that the programs do raise the level of economic activity in the short run, but a diminished rate of growth in small business establishments over time is also observed.

671. Harrison, David S., ed. 1989. *A Northwest Reader: Options for Rural Communities.* Seattle, WA: University of Washington, Northwest Policy Center, 95 pp.

Is a collection of readings on an important policy issue: revitalizing the nonurban expanse of the Pacific Northwest. The authors define revitalization of rural economies to include those steps that will narrow the widening gap between urban and rural per capita personal income levels and decrease rural underemployment and unemployment. The authors focus on strategies for revitalization which appear to be underutilized. They contend that for new development initiatives to have much impact on smaller rural communities, they must be accompanied by changes in educational and transfer payment programs and by renewed commitments to extending telecommunications infrastructure into rural areas and strengthening economic linkages between rural and urban areas.

672. Hawker, Chris, and Niall MacKinnon with John Bryden, May Johnstone, and Alison Parkes. 1989. *Factors in the Design of Community Based Economic Development Initiatives in Europe.* Enstone, Oxon, England, U.K.: The Arkleton Trust (Research) Ltd., 86 pp.

Examines the experience of local self-help activity directed toward employment creation in rural areas of Europe. The particular focus of interest is the work of locally based development agents and their organizations which have served as catalysts and enablers of the local employment initiatives. The main characteristics of 27 case studies from 12 countries are analyzed and summaries are presented. On the basis of the analysis, a framework for the design of local employment initiatives is proposed. The focus is on two project dimensions: the nature and role of local development agencies, and the characteristics and mode of operation of individual agents working in the local communities.

673. Henshall Hansen Associates. 1988. *Small Towns Study in Victoria.* Horsham, Victoria, Australia: Victorian Department of Agriculture and Rural Affairs, 218 pp.

Seeks to identify the possible responses which may be necessary to ensure that the economic and social well-being of small towns and their communities are maintained and, if possible, enhanced. The specific aims of the study are (1) to examine the nature of economic linkages between the government, commercial, and farming sectors and to identify the key sectors influencing the viability of country towns, (2) to analyze the perceptions, attitudes, and behavior patterns of people in small towns as they respond to changing economic circumstances, (3) to identify items of a strategic nature to be taken into account in examining prospects and problems for small towns, and (4) to prepare an agenda for continuing Government and community involvement in small town development. The general approach involved an overview of the general situation of small towns in rural Victoria and more detailed case studies for individual towns.

674.   Henton, Douglas C., John Melville, and Steven A. Waldhorn. 1988. *Connecting Rural Economies: Strategies for Coping with Western Rural Economic Development Issues.* Denver, CO: Western Governor's Association, 92 pp.

Aims to provide state policy makers with new tools for diagnosing state rural economies and developing new strategic directions for better connecting rural areas to the state or regional economy. The guide is designed to help policymakers analyze the forces affecting rural areas and devise appropriate rural strategies depending on their state of readiness. The guide provides examples from other states that can help in developing new strategic directions.

675.   Hoppe, Robert A. 1991. *The Role of the Elderly's Income in Rural Development.* Res. Rpt. No. 80. Washington, D.C.: USDA, Economic Research Service, 23 pp.

Reports that the elderly receive substantial property income (interest, dividends, and rent) and transfer payments (mostly from Government programs, such as Social Security), which if spent locally, can create jobs and help stabilize local economies. Some rural development specialists advocate attracting older migrants to stimulate local economies. However, the author finds that the elderly's income is not a panacea for rural economic development. While elderly migrants have contributed to economic growth in some nonmetro areas, a rural development strategy based on attracting them is limited by the number of elderly of adequate means who are willing to move. Providing the local elderly poor with services may be a more pressing issue for some nonmetro areas than attracting more elderly. In addition, development strategies that rely on the income of the elderly must also consider the future of the Social Security Program, which provides about one-third of that income.

676. Jackson, N. B., M. O'Connell, and S. Williams. 1987. *Rural Local Employment Initiatives: A Self-Help Manual For Rural Communities.* Armidale, N.S.W., Australia: University of New England, The Rural Development Center, 166 pp.

Aims to foster employment creation in rural areas by the organization of community groups. Rural is used to mean nonmetropolitan, including country towns, forming communities, and larger regional centers. Major sections of the report deal with (1) explaining the current situation in rural communities and the need for local employment initiatives (LEI), (2) explaining the concept of a local development agency (LEDA) and the ways that such an agency can combine different LEI tools into an integrated strategy, (3) outlining issues related to managing a LEDA, and (4) describing the various LEI tools, discussing how each can be used, and providing examples of communities that have used that particular tool.

677. John, De Witt, Sandra S. Batie, and Kim Norris. 1988. *A Brighter Future for Rural America? Strategies for Communities and States.* Washington, D.C.: National Governors' Association, 115 pp.

Outlines the competitive challenge facing rural America and reports on signs of hope for the rural economy. The authors discuss the "secrets of success" in sixteen rural counties in the Farm Belt states of Iowa, Kansas, Missouri, Nebraska, and North Dakota which have gained employment at the same time that most rural areas were losing jobs. It also describes new state initiatives and lists six "operating principles" to guide state efforts to help rural communities.

678. Kraybill, David S., and Thomas G. Johnson. 1989. "Value-Added Activities as a Rural Development Strategy." *Southern Journal of Agricultural Economics* 21(1):27-36.

Focuses on the role of value-added activities in rural economic growth and development. Examples of effective institutional support for value-added development are drawn from current programs in several states. These include programs instituted in Texas, Illinois, and Mississippi. The importance of incentives for collaboration between entrepreneurs and university researchers is emphasized. The paper concludes by outlining the elements of a value-added program that meets a broader set of rural development objectives than have been met in the past by business development programs.

679. Lambright, W. Henry, and Dianne Rahm. 1991. "Science, Technology, and the States." *Forum for Applied Research and Public Policy* 6(3):49-60.

Reports on the development of state science and technology programs aimed at enhancing economic development. In 1980, only 9 states had technology innovation programs but by 1988, 45 states had developed these programs. The authors review the states' experience with such programs and observe that state science and technology-based economic development policies have evolved in stages. These stages are (1) policy initiation, (2) early implementation, (3) later implementation, and (4) consolidation/modification. The authors report that state programs have displayed two distinct but increasingly linked aspects (1) an internal aspect concerned with state research and development investments in particular technologies, and (2) an external dimension concerned with competitions designed to place national facilities within a given state (e.g., the Superconducting Super Collider).

680. Lapping, Mark B., Thomas L. Daniels, and John W. Keller. 1989. *Rural Planning and Development in the United States*. New York, NY: The Guilford Press, 353 pp.

Is a text designed for use both for teaching and as a practical reference for rural planning. The work includes chapters on the history of federal rural planning and development programs, planning law and the regulation of rural land and water, agriculture, forestry, recreation, natural areas, land markets, and rural economic development. Also included is a chapter on the needs of special populations--the poor, the elderly, and native people.

681. Laszlo, Andrew P. 1984. "A Survey of Techniques Employed by State and Local Governments for the Promotion of Foreign Direct Investment." *George Washington Journal of International Law and Economics* 18(1):155-181.

Surveys trends in state and local promotional activities to encourage foreign direct investment (FDI) (defined as the ownership by a foreign entity of 10 percent or more of the voting securities of an incorporated business or an equivalent interest in an unincorporated business). First, the author provides general information regarding FDI in the United States, such as its rate of growth, the predominant forms and implementations of FDI, the leading investing countries, and the major reasons prompting foreign investors to locate FDI in the U.S. Then, he reports on state and local promotion of FDI, including the structural organization and the interrelation of state and local bodies responsible for the promotion of FDI, community self-assessment studies, strategies for enhancing a community's attractiveness to potential foreign investors, dissemination of information to these investors, and incentive packages.

682. Leaman, Sam H., Thomas J. Cook, and Leslie S. Stewart. 1992. "Rural Economic Development: Learning From Success." *Economic Development Review* 10(4):27-33.

Is designed to help local officials and business people interested in rural economic development learn from success. The Research Triangle Institute conducted detailed statistical analyses of economic data on nonmetropolitan counties to select 12 counties that had successfully generated strong overall economic growth during the 1982-1986 period. Ten of these counties also ranked high in employment growth derived from small, local businesses. Excluded from analysis were any rural counties adjacent to large metropolitan areas and any counties that had large tourist attractions. Both elected officials and business owners in these counties were contacted through site visits and telephone interviews to determine the steps they took to create employment growth in their counties. This paper presents these steps and the local characteristics that lead to successful rural economic development.

683. Leaman, Sam H., Thomas J. Cook, Leslie S. Stewart, and Alan B. Sprayt. 1990. *Rural Economic Development: Learning From Success.* Research Triangle Park, NC: Research Triangle Institute, 80 pp.

Analyzes the strategies used for successful rural economic development in 12 counties around the U.S. These counties all had strong employment growth relative to other rural counties in the 1980s. The report is intended for the use of officials and businessmen interested in economic development in rural counties and towns. On the basis of case studies in each of the 12 counties, the authors outline 12 key steps in a strategy for successful rural economic development and suggest three predictors of economic success. The programs that the selected counties used include financial assistance, technical and managerial assistance, job training, location assistance, and innovative programs such as enterprise zones and regional marketing. The report discusses the most useful programs and the infrastructure important for rural development in selected counties, such as schools and highways.

684. Loveridge, Scott, and Thomas R. Smith. 1992. "Factors Related to Success in Business Retention and Expansion Programs." *Journal of the Community Development Society* 23(2):66-78.

Uses a survey of local coordinators of business retention and expansion (R&E) programs to determine factors associated with successful programs. The most successful R&E programs go beyond short-term goals of solving firms' immediate problems, and begin a process of dialogue and coalition building among community leaders from various disciplines. The vehicle for this consensus for development is the written community action plan based on overall results of the survey of local businesses. The most successful coordinators in this survey resisted the temptation to do everything themselves and worked closely with a task force of local leaders in developing community recommendations.

685. Loveridge, Scott, Thomas R. Smith, and George W. Morse. 1991. "What Does it Take to Run a Local Business Retention and Expansion Program? A Six State Survey." *Economic Development Review* 9(1):12-22.

Reports on the results of a survey of 158 persons managing local business retention and expansion (R&E) programs in 6 states. The intent is to provide information about the resources used by local R&E coordinators and thus help development professionals determine the resources required to undertake such a program. The authors found that the average coordinator contributes about 90 hours over 2 to 18 months in order to implement an R&E program. The coordinators were enthusiastic about the value of the program--almost 90 percent of the respondents would recommend the program to other communities. The R&E programs reached an average of 39 firms and resulted in about 10 recommended courses of action for improving the community's business climate.

686. Lyman, Theodore R., et al. 1987. *New Seeds for Nebraska: Strategies for Building the Next Economy.* Menlo Park, CA: SRI International, 189 pp.

Examines Nebraska's capacity to adapt to the macroeconomic forces shaping today's economy. Major sections examine (1) the state's economy in the context of global change, (2) the dynamics of four key economic sectors (agriculture, food processing, other manufacturing, and services) and their future opportunities, (3) the state's capacity to adapt in the face of the challenges confronting it, and (4) a multidimensional strategy for building Nebraska's future economy.

687. Lynch, John E., ed. 1990. *Plant Closures and Community Recovery.* Washington, D.C.: National Council for Urban Economic Development, 208 pp.

Describes and illustrates how communities can respond to plant closures and major dislocations. The book draws from the recovery experiences of 28 communities nationwide in an attempt to summarize the best economic development practices today and help future communities recover from plant closures and place dislocated workers. The study is organized into seven parts treating the plant closure environment, previous community recovery efforts, state-federal adjustment programs, recovery planning, reusing and financing industrial plants, worker placement experience, and an overall conclusion--involving a composite community recovery approach for future plant closures. The work contains 64 separate articles and represents contributions by 82 authors and joint authors.

688.   Mangum, Stephen L., and Judith W. Tansky. 1993. "Displaced Workers Turned Small Business Operators: A Viable Economic Development or Reemployment Strategy?" *Economic Development Quarterly* 7(3):243-254.

Sets small business startup training initiatives within the context of other strategies used to serve displaced workers, and then proceeds to describe and evaluate a recent programmatic effort of this type. The evaluation is based on a two-year postprogram follow-up of participants in an Ohio pilot project funded through Job Training Partnership Act (JTPA) funds. Comparisons of business starts, longevity of operation, employment generation, and income generation are made to U.S. businesses in general, European programs of similar philosophy, and to the experience of displaced worker programs in general. Implications are then drawn for managers of this type of employment and training program.

689.   Martin, Stephen. 1992. "Local Economic Initiatives in Rural Areas of the U.K.," pp. 254-264 in *Contemporary Rural Systems in Transition: Volume 2, Economy and Society*, I. R. Bowler, C. Bryant, and M. Nellis, eds. Wallingford, Oxon, U.K.: CAB International.

Examines the impacts of local economic initiatives undertaken in rural areas of the U.K. since the mid-1970s on employment levels and labor markets. One of the most widely adopted local initiatives has been the public sector provision of business premises. The author finds that premises provision has helped to increase the number and range of job opportunities in rural areas. The provision of new job opportunities in turn has helped to alleviate the three main employment problems facing rural areas: unemployment, underemployment, and low activity (participation) rates, particularly among women.

690. McBeth, Mark K. 1993. "How-To ... Using a Survey in the Rural
      Planning Process." *Economic Development Review* 11(2):76-80.

      Reports that rural communities are increasingly implementing citizen-
      based economic development efforts. Such efforts require substantial and
      substantive amounts of public input. The survey is the primary method
      by which economic development professionals assist the rural community
      in securing such citizen data. Surveys, however, often become little more
      than bureaucratic reports that do not effectuate citizen input in the
      planning process. This article suggests a method of using a survey to
      both give the public voice and then use that voice to guide the planning
      process.

691. McLaughlin, Robert T. 1987. *Making Connections in the Heartland: An
      Educator's Case Study of a Local Business Retention and Expansion
      Program.* Ames, IA: Iowa State University, North Central Regional
      Center for Rural Development, 51 pp.

      Evaluates a recent innovation in local economic development technique--
      business retention and expansion programs. The author evaluated one
      such program conducted in Ohio, conducting participant and non-
      participant observation and interviewing persons who implemented the
      program. This information was complemented by data drawn from
      telephone and personal interviews with coordinators of similar programs
      elsewhere in Ohio and in five other states. The primary research
      questions were (1) how do the participants themselves define program
      effectiveness? and (2) what factors do they, and the researchers, identify
      as enhancing or impeding effectiveness? The author concludes that
      retention and expansion programs have substantial potential as a local
      economic development technique because (1) they involve minimal
      expense, (2) they increase rapport and networking among program
      participants, (3) they help address conflicts and problems that may be
      generated by the conventional economic development strategy of
      attracting new firms, and (4) they appear to improve significantly the
      capacity of local leaders, *as a group*, to respond efficiently and
      concertedly to barriers to local firm retention and expansion.

692. Miller, Wayne P., and Edward O. Fryar. 1990. *Expanding Export
      Industry Employment in the Lower Mississippi Delta.* Fayetteville,
      AR: University of Arkansas, Department of Agricultural Economics
      and Rural Sociology, 56 pp.

      Defines the issues surrounding economic development in the Lower
      Mississippi Delta region. The authors present an analysis of employment

data from 1969 to 1986 for 32 industries in the 190 nonmetropolitan counties of the Lower Mississippi Delta to identify industries that have contributed the most jobs and the greatest stability of employment to the region. Finally, they recommend a series of steps that will enable the Lower Mississippi Delta Commission to develop a 10-year plan that targets resources for industrial development on the industries that have the greatest potential to increase jobs and improve the stability of employment in the Delta.

693. Morrison, Hugh. 1987. *The Regeneration of Local Economies.* Oxford, England: Clarendon Press, 212 pp.

Discusses ways in which the central government and local authorities in Great Britain have sought to stimulate economic activity in urban areas of high unemployment over recent years and particularly during the period 1979-1983. Major chapters address (1) an overview of tools for economic regeneration, (2) the role of the private sector in development, and (3) the new approach represented by enterprise zones and freeports. Three additional chapters describe specific development initiatives, including the Merseyside Task Force (Liverpool), the Glasgow Eastern Area Redevelopment Project, and the Glengarnock and Clydebank Task Forces.

694. Morse, George W., ed. 1990. *The Retention and Expansion of Existing Businesses.* Ames, IA: Iowa State University Press, 195 pp.

Describes the theoretical foundations, educational programs, and practical applications of the business retention and expansion (R&E) program. The intended audience includes state development officials, local practitioners, and community economics academics. Contributors include James P. Miller, Daniel Otto, Ellen Hagey, John D. Rohrer, William Gillis, Robert McLaughlin, and Marion Bentley.

695. Morse, George W., John D. Rohrer, and Sam J. Crawford. 1985. *Retention and Expansion Business Visits: A Guide for an Effective Economic Development Program.* Bulletin 728. Columbus, OH: Ohio State University, Ohio Cooperative Extension Service, 52 pp.

Is designed for Extension specialists, development educators, and local leaders initiating or strengthening a retention and expansion (R&E) visitation program. The program outlined is based on the experiences of 33 Ohio communities as well as information received from programs in New Jersey, Wisconsin, and Michigan. In 1983-84 an extensive research project examined the Ohio programs and the factors that influenced their effectiveness in job creation. In 1984-85, pilot programs were conducted in four communities to test this program.

696. Morse, George W., Kathryn Wilson, and Steven I. Gordon. 1985. *Local Industry Visitation Programs: Policy Research and Recommendations.* Columbus, OH: Ohio State University, Rural Community Economics Program, 38 pp.

Analyzes the effectiveness of alternative local development programs that focus on the retention and expansion (R&E) of existing firms. Specific objectives were to (1) identify contact persons involved in existing R&E programs, (2) describe local industry visitation programs in terms of their objectives, resources, procedures, and impacts, (3) examine factors affecting success of local industry visitation programs, and (4) recommend state and local policies to strengthen local visitation teams. Surveys of organizations conducting visitation programs in Ohio provided the data base for the study. The authors conclude that visitation programs provided annual net benefits that averaged over $26,000 and that the benefit-cost ratio for such programs was, on average, quite favorable.

697. Murphy, Terry. 1993. "A Comprehensive Approach to Economic Development: The Muncie-Delaware County, Indiana Chamber of Commerce Horizon '96 Program." *Economic Development Review* 11(2):28-31.

Reports that the Muncie-Delaware County Chamber of Commerce's "Horizon '96" economic development effort is a five-year program designed to create and retain jobs, address infrastructure needs, and promote visitor and convention business. The program was the first to use a local economic development income tax (EDIT) to address the comprehensive economic development needs of a county in Indiana.

698. Northdurft, William E. 1992. "Strategies and Conditions Needed for the Promotion of Rural Entrepreneurship," pp. 61-74 in *Local Initiatives for Job Creation: Businesses and Jobs in the Rural World.* Paris, France: Organisation for Economic Co-operation and Development.

Describes the strategies and conditions needed to enable rural communities to respond to threats and seize the opportunities presented by change. The paper draws upon the author's experience in the United States and a recent survey of United Kingdom rural development organizations, but the strategic approach is believed to have wider applicability.

699. Organisation for Economic Co-operation and Development. 1992. *Local Initiatives for Job Creation: Businesses and Jobs in the Rural World.* Paris, France: Organisation for Economic Co-operation and Development, 203 pp.

Argues for an approach to economic development using local initiatives to create new enterprise and thus expand the range of economic activities. Eleven papers present analyses of the requisite conditions for such development and reflect the growing awareness that solutions to rural problems can be found within local economies themselves. The mechanisms examined include bringing together local actors to form new partnerships, developing an entrepreneurial climate, and utilizing the full range of resources available, particularly human resources. Establishing rural economies able to generate wealth and maintain their social and economic vitality and capacity to adapt is a necessary precondition. The report provides an overview of this approach and suggests components for a successful strategy.

700. Otto, Daniel M., and Gary W. Williams. 1989. "Value-Added Research as a State Economic Development Strategy," pp. 1-11 in *Value-Added Research Investments: Boon or Boondoggle?*, G. Williams, ed. College Station, TX: Texas A&M University, Department of Agricultural Economics

Indicates that value-added research generally is aimed at expanding the market share of existing value-added products or at developing and marketing new value-added commodities. The authors discuss both types of research, define the role of economists, and offer some thoughts for policymakers and research administrators for developing the value-added research agenda. They suggest that (1) the agenda must go farther in bridging the gap between the research laboratory and the consumer table and (2) administrators should broaden the set of criteria for promotion and tenure.

701. Pankratz, John. 1989. *Job Creation in Rural Areas: A Select Annotated Bibliography.* WRDC 37. Corvallis, OR: Western Rural Development Center, 38 pp.

Contains 120 annotated entries and is designed to assist rural leaders who are seeking ways to effectively structure job development projects. The selections are grouped into eight major categories: (1) education, job training, skill level improvement, (2) industrial recruitment, (3) capitalizing on existing resources and businesses, (4) adding value to existing products, (5) rural leadership development, (6) grantsmanship and financing, (7) new and innovative concepts, and (8) general. A subject index is provided as well as a short summary of findings.

702. Persky, Joseph, David Ranney, and Wim Wiewel. 1993. "Import Substitution and Local Economic Development." *Economic Development Quarterly* 7(1):18-29.

Reports that import substitution deserves more consideration as a theoretical basis for local economic development policies. Its role in promoting local growth is theoretically well-founded. Less clear is the extent to which public policies can promote it. In order to facilitate experimentation, the article discusses several examples of analyses and programs that can be used to select target industries for import substitution policies. One approach uses changes in location quotients to identify potential targets; another approach focuses on the potential impact of redirecting purchases by local governments to targeted industries.

703. Plugge, Patricia L. 1993. "Self-Help Strategic Planning for Small Communities." *Economic Development Review* 11(2):14-17.

Argues that strategic planning is a valuable tool for communities wishing to engage in economic development. This article describes the nature of strategic planning in selected Nebraska communities and focuses on a program called S.T.A.R.T. (Strategic Training and Resource Targeting), which is largely a self-help approach for communities interested in starting or upgrading their economic development programs.

704. Pulver, Glen, and David Dodson. 1992. *Designing Development Strategies in Small Towns*. Washington, D.C.: The Aspen Institute, 59 pp.

Reports that rural America is seriously lagging behind urban America in personal income, health, and education. If rural people are to have any hope of achieving a level of living approximating that of their urban neighbors, local leaders must become very adept at identifying the most effective strategies for community development. The best hope for improvement is a combination of well-informed action by local leaders and supportive state and national policy. Because the dynamics of rural economies are neither simple nor uniform, community assessment (the careful analysis by local people of their current and prospective challenges and opportunities) is thus fundamental to effective planning and informed action. When a strong assessment process is tied to sound strategic planning, chances increase that the actions a community chooses will fit its circumstances and abilities. Without careful analysis provided by a thorough assessment process, communities risk making ill-considered choices about the future; failure and frustration are much more likely to result.

705.   Reed, B. J., and David F. Paulsen. 1990. "Small Towns Lack Capacity for Successful Development Efforts." *Rural Development Perspectives* 6(3):26-30.

Based on a survey of 135 small towns in Nebraska, the authors report that residents put a high priority on the need for economic development efforts, yet most feel that their towns' efforts fall short. Communities appear to need a critical mass of leadership, skills and knowledge, financial resources, etc., in order to generate successful development projects. Further, many communities that had undertaken development activities believed that these efforts had not been successful in terms of generating jobs or retaining and expanding businesses. State programs that help communities build local capacity can be useful in resolving the development dilemmas facing local communities.

706.   Reeder, Richard J., and Kenneth L. Robinson. 1992. "Enterprise Zones: Assessing Their Rural Development Potential." *Policy Studies Journal* 20(2):264-275.

Uses state experience with enterprise zones (EZs) to critically examine the theoretical and empirical support for using EZs to create jobs and other benefits in distressed rural areas. The authors focus on two empirical questions: (1) how effective are state EZs in general, and (2) how effective are rural EZs in particular? Originally conceived in England in the late 1970s, the enterprise zone approach immigrated to the United States in the early 1980s, where it was extensively modified and adopted by state governments. By the end of the 1980s, 38 states had enterprise zone programs. About half of the state-designated EZs were in rural (nonmetropolitan) areas.

707.   Reese, Laura A. 1992. "Local Economic Development in Michigan: A Reliance on the Supply Side." *Economic Development Quarterly* 6(4):383-393.

Reports that recent research on local economic development policies suggests that the types of techniques employed by cities are changing as they move into the 1990s. Specifically, some authors posit that cities and states are increasingly moving to embrace demand- rather than supply-side economic development incentives as questions over the efficacy of the latter mount. Cities in the "rust belt" state of Michigan do not appear to be moving in that direction and still rely heavily on traditional supply-side inducements such as tax incentives, infrastructure investment, and marketing strategies. In the face of numerous questions about the effectiveness of supply-side incentives and the promise suggested by demand-side activities, it is a matter of concern that cities appear to continue to widely embrace such supply-side initiatives.

708. Reid, J. Norman. 1988. "Entrepreneurship as a Community Development Strategy for the Rural South," pp. 325-343 in *The Rural South in Crisis: Challenges for the Future*, L. J. Beaulieu, ed. Boulder, CO: Westview Press.

Evaluates the potential of local development through entrepreneurship as an economic development strategy for rural areas of the southern United States. The author reports that entrepreneurship has become a topic of great interest in recent years and that some have come to regard entrepreneurship as a means for restoring the "competitiveness" of the American economy. He then addresses a number of questions related to assessment of entrepreneurship as a rural development strategy. What is an "entrepreneur" and how does entrepreneurship contribute to community economic development? Is it realistic to expect entrepreneurial growth to be a major creator of jobs in rural America? What community factors affect the chances for successful enterprise development? Is there a useful role for governments and public service organizations in encouraging it? Will the benefits of entrepreneurial strategies outweigh their costs? And how does the rural South compare with the rest of the country in its chances for growth through entrepreneurship?

709. Robertson, Robert W. 1993. "Local Economic Development and the Total Quality Management Revolution." *Economic Development Review* 11(3):14-16.

Describes an improvement program called Total Quality Management (TQM) that has been sweeping the world business community. TQM promises to increase the productivity of a company's resources and competitive position by reducing its waste and developing methods and programs for constant improvement. As a mechanism to improve the competitive position of business, TQM is a subject which requires the attention of the economic development professional. Indeed, the principles of TQM can be applied to the day-to-day operations of an economic development function to improve efficiency and effectiveness.

710. Robinson, Carla Jean. 1989. "Municipal Approaches to Economic Development: Growth and Distribution Policy." *Journal of the American Planning Association* 55(3):283-295.

Discusses ways in which administrations in large cities participate in the planning and implementation of economic development activities. The author focuses on the extent to which efforts are made to direct some of the economic development benefits created to black, Hispanic, low income, and other economically disadvantaged residents. While some of the administrations examined follow a "corporate-center" policy approach emphasizing the promotion of growth and real estate development, most combine elements of this approach with elements of a more distributive approach emphasizing the creation of benefits for economically disadvantaged residents.

711. Rosenfeld, Stuart A. 1990. *Technology, Innovation, and Rural Development: Lessons From Italy and Denmark.* Washington, D.C.: The Aspen Institute, Rural Economic Policy Program, 39 pp.

Examines development policies in less urbanized but industrialized and industrializing regions of two European countries to find out more about the successes and failures of science and technology in promoting rural development, the ways in which local and state governments and European Community programs have contributed, and the conditions that have impeded or spurred development. The two regions studied, north-central Italy and northern Jutland in Denmark, were until recently quite poor by European standards. However, relying heavily on technological innovation, the strength of their small firm and artisan sector, and local leadership, they have been transformed into healthy and growing industrial economies. The common features of economic development in Italy and Denmark include first, and perhaps most importantly, a strong reliance on cooperative ventures and integrated phases of production among small-and medium-sized enterprises (SMEs). Second, both regions look to what are called Centers for Real Services to support critical needs that the market can not support. Finally, each region considers the world, not the region or state, as its market area.

712. Rubin, Barry M., and Craig M. Richards. 1992. "A Transatlantic Comparison of Enterprise Zone Impacts: The British and American Experience." *Economic Development Quarterly* 6(4):431-443.

Reports that since the late 1970s, over 20 enterprise zones have been designated and are operating in Great Britain. In the United States, over

35 states have implemented an enterprise zone program. Even though some work has been done comparing the concept of enterprise zones as implemented in the United States and the United Kingdom, no research has examined the comparative impacts of enterprise zones in these two contexts. This article analyzes the available research on zone impacts, and concludes that the U.K. zones have been largely unsuccessful in meeting program goals. In contrast, some of the state-sponsored zones in the United States have achieved a moderate degree of success. The article specifies several primary factors that help explain the moderate success of these U.S. zones. The absence of these factors in the U.K. program's structure and implementation appears to be the major determinant of the failure of the British zones.

713. Rubin, Barry M., and C. Kurt Zorn. 1985. "Sensible State and Local Economic Development." *Public Administration Review* 45(2):333-339.

Evaluates the economic development initiatives that have become common in recent years as states and localities have sought to attract jobs and economic activity. Despite the popularity of industrial location incentives among state and local policy makers, it is not clear that current policies are either efficient or effective. Acknowledging that states and localities are not likely to cease offering economic development incentives, an alternative approach is presented by the authors. By first determining how they fare in terms of uncontrollable business costs (transportation, energy, and labor costs), states and localities can better focus their use of industrial location incentives.

714. Saskatchewan Rural Development. 1989. *Economic Development and Diversification in Rural Saskatchewan.* Proceedings of conference sponsored by Saskatchewan Rural Development and University of Saskatchewan. Saskatoon, Saskatchewan, Canada: University of Saskatchewan, 252 pp.

Contains summaries of a number of talks addressing economic development experiences and initiatives both within Saskatchewan and in other regions.

715. Schneider, Mary Jo, and Bernal L. Green. 1989. *Retirement Counties: A Development Option for the Nineties.* Special Report 134. Fayetteville, AR: Arkansas Agricultural Experiment Station, 23 pp.

Examines the changing nature of rural economies and the changing role of retirees in those economies. The authors examine the location and characteristics of destination-retirement (D-R) counties (defined as those in which the number of persons 60 years and over increased at least 15 percent through immigration from 1970 to 1980) on a nationwide basis. They then examine the location of D-R counties in Arkansas and the role of retirement migration in economic and population growth. To obtain insight into the attributes that made certain counties attractive to retirees, the authors focus on the 171 fastest growing D-R counties nationwide and compare their attributes with those of other D-R counties and other nonmetropolitan counties.

716. Schoening, Niles C., and Larry E. Sweeney. 1992. "Proactive Industrial Development Strategies and Portfolio Analysis." *The Review of Regional Studies* 22(3):227-238.

Reports that many communities have become interested in creating a targeted industrial list to guide their industrial recruitment efforts. The targeted industry list is generally based on the locational advantages offered by the community (transportation services, labor skills, prevailing wages, and local taxes) as well as on the targeted industry's compatibility with the community's existing industrial base. The authors point out that the analytical concepts of security portfolio theory can be applied to measure a targeted industry's compatibility with the community's existing industrial base. The model introduced in this paper allows for measurement of the trade-off between employment growth and employment stability. The basic premises underlying this application are that employment and income instability in a region are analogous to risk in securities markets and that economic growth is similar to the return on a security portfolio.

717. Scott, David, Fern K. Willits, and Donald M. Crider. 1991. *Public Opinions About Economic Development Options: Data From a Pennsylvanian Survey.* AE & RS 225. University Park, PA: Pennsylvania State University, College of Agricultural Sciences, 26 pp.

Was designed to provide policy makers, educators, local leaders, and the citizenry with up-to-date information concerning the priority Pennsylvanians place on various economic development strategies. The analysis addressed two research questions: (1) What priority does the citizenry give to different economic development strategies? and (2) What social and economic characteristics of Pennsylvanians are associated with the priorities among different economic development strategies? The data were drawn from a statewide mail survey; 3632 useable questionnaires were returned, which represented 55 percent of the valid addresses. Overall, the respondents expressed considerable support for the economic development activities included on the questionnaire. The most obvious exception was an item which asked about lowering pollution standards to keep or attract business and industry. Pennsylvanians were more likely to support giving direct financial aid to communities facing economic hardship than they were to endorse technical assistance to aid communities in their economic development efforts. Small businesses were endorsed more than large businesses. Respondents felt that greater priority should be devoted to promoting traditional industries (coal, agriculture, and lumber) than to promoting either rural or urban tourism.

718. Scott, R. Douglas, Mark Cochran, and Donald E. Voth. 1988. "The Effect of Self-Help Community Development Programs on Rural County Development in Arkansas." *Journal of the Community Development Society* 19(2):56-72.

Evaluates the effects of community development programs in 73 nonmetropolitan counties in Arkansas for the periods 1960-70 and 1970-80. The evaluation focused on the impacts that the programs had upon net migration of youth, unemployment, and employment in retail and wholesale trade and in manufacturing. Regression analysis was used, and two basic analytical models were employed. The results showed that either the community development inputs had no positive impacts or that their effects were opposite of what local leaders desired. Migration, in particular, tended to be affected by community resource development inputs in a way that was not desired.

719. Sears, David W., and J. Norman Reid. 1992. "Rural Strategies and Rural Development Research: An Assessment." *Policy Studies Journal* 20(2):301-309.

Evaluates the state of research on rural development strategies. The authors review seven articles dealing with specific rural development strategies (included in the same volume) and draw three major conclusions: (1) no strategy for rural development should be automatically dismissed as inappropriate, (2) there is no magic formula that will produce rural development in all places under any conditions, and (3) patient and careful analysis of each local situation is a necessary prerequisite to effective development programs.

720. Shaffer, Ron. 1990. "Building Economically Viable Communities: A Role for Community Developers." *Journal of the Community Development Society* 21(2):74-87.

Uses three fundamental elements of economic theory to explain the options available to localities that want to alter their economic destiny. The three elements are demand, supply, and institutional forces. An understanding of these forces will increase a community developer's ability to work with community residents attempting to manipulate these same forces to their community's advantage. Demand forces relate to external (export) and internal (consumer) markets. Supply forces incorporate the access to and mobility of capital, labor, and technology for use by the community to produce the economic output desired. Institutional forces represent the "rules of the economic game" and the decision-making capacity of the community. Both are subject to local manipulation but are too often the forgotten elements of a comprehensive community economic development strategy. These elements operate within a context of preconditions or values that influence the extent to which the community chooses to exercise its options. While an understanding of demand and supply forces is a necessity, the involvement of community developers in the institutional component is often the critical difference.

721. Sharp, Elaine B., and David R. Elkins. 1991. "The Politics of Economic Development Policy." *Economic Development Quarterly* 5(2):126-139.

Uses data from a national sample survey of cities to examine the extent to which mechanisms for citizen involvement are in place for economic development decision making. The analysis shows that there is considerable variation in involvement mechanisms and, more importantly, that for cities that are suffering from property tax stress there are interesting and significant implications of citizen involvement in the economic development process. Where tax stress is high, the authors find that higher levels of citizen involvement are associated with greater use of development tools such as loan guarantees that minimize apparent tax costs, as well as development activities that provide credit-claiming opportunities for politicians. However, greater citizen involvement diminishes the likelihood that the city will use tax abatement.

722. Siegel, Paul B., and Frank O. Leuthold. 1992. *Economic and Fiscal Impacts of Tellico Village, Loudon County, Tennessee*. Research Rpt. 92-17. Knoxville, TN: The University of Tennessee, Agricultural Experiment Station.

Reports that in recent years planned residential developments, called recreation and retirement communities (RRC), have proliferated. RRCs have been promoted as a way for some rural regions to develop their economies. RRCs generate new economic activity associated with the construction of infrastructure and homes, lot and home sales, administration, operation and maintenance of the community, and expenditures by residents and visitors. In addition, RRCs generate new sources of tax revenues for local governments and new demands for services provided by local governments. Assessment of the pros and cons of RRCs as a stimulus to rural economic development should consider both economic impacts (change in income and employment) and fiscal impacts (changes in local government revenues and costs). This report presents a case study of the economic and fiscal impacts of Tellico Village on Loudon County, Tennessee. The detailed impact analysis presented in this report should provide a foundation for similar undertakings in the future.

723. Sower, John, and Beverly L. Milkman. 1991. "The Bank Community Development Corporation: An Economic Development Tool for the Nineties." *Economic Development Quarterly* 5(1):3-8.

Reports that with the shift in economic development responsibility away from the federal level in the 1980s, state and local governments have been called upon to join forces with the private sector to plan and finance local development. The Economic Development Administration (EDA) has attempted to help local innovations with substantial private involvement. In this article, an EDA project that tested the widespread utility of the Bank Community Development Corporation (Bank CDC) is described for the purpose of acquainting economic development practitioners with an innovative financing tool.

724. SRI International. 1990. *Nebraska: Leading the Great Plains into the New Economy*. Lincoln, NE: Nebraska Futures, Inc., 23 pp.

Presents an action agenda to advance economic development in Nebraska. Nine major initiatives are suggested: (1) comprehensive educational enhancement, (2) statewide access (to information and education), (3) innovative training partnerships, (4) community partnerships (clusters), (5) cross-state connections, (6) growth of high value-added agriculture and food processing, (7) innovation in diversified manufacturing, (8) expansion of the service economy, (9) commitment to collaboration between higher education and business. Specific recommendations for implementing each initiative are presented.

725. SRI International. 1990. *Vision 2000: An 8-Point Action Agenda for Building a Better North Dakota*. Fargo, ND: North Dakota 2000 Committee, 47 pp.

Presents goals and strategies for a statewide economic development effort. The authors indicate that the two primary economic development goals in the state are improved economic stability and a higher standard of living. Five factors that are viewed as critical to a competitive economy are human capital, financial capital, technology, entrepreneurship, and quality of life. Three additional factors also viewed as important are physical infrastructure (especially highway and water development), state and local government reform, and supportive federal policy.

726. Stark, Joyce C. 1988. *Proceedings of the EDA/MRI Industrial Park Conference.* Kansas City, MO: Midwest Research Institute.

Consists of summaries of presentations from a conference held April 17, 1988, and co-sponsored by the U.S. Economic Development Administration and Midwest Research Institute. Major presentations included (1) a summary of the EDA/MRI industrial park technical assistance project, (2) a presentation on how communities can organize their development future, (3) a paper on recent trends in the rural economy, (4) a review of alternatives for rural industrial parks, (5) a discussion of marketing methods for industrial parks, (6) a review of one community's development program, and (7) a discussion of means for raising private funding for economic development.

727. Sternlieb, George, and David Listokin. 1981. *New Tools for Economic Development: The Enterprise Zone, Development Bank, and RFC.* New Brunswick, NJ: Rutgers University, Center for Urban Policy Research, 230 pp.

Contains six articles that examine the potential of three relatively new mechanisms for promoting economic development: the enterprise zone, the development bank, and the reconstruction finance corporation. These strategies represent different forms of public intervention with one common denominator--not to provide a public dole but to stimulate private initiative and investment. Enterprise zones use preferential regulatory and tax treatment to spur entrepreneurial islands within urban areas, a national development bank could secure financing for capital-short distressed areas, and the reconstruction finance corporation would have the goal of providing financial aid and other support to aging, basic industries.

728. Swager, Ronald J. 1991. "A Prospective View of Economic Development in the 1990s." *Economic Development Review* 9(3):7-10.

Summarizes a study, *Economic Development Tomorrow: A Report to the Profession*, commissioned by the American Economic Development Council. The author outlines some of the major challenges to economic development as a process and as a practice. Challenges to the process of economic development include (1) the changing global economy, including the growing importance of major trading blocs, (2) the changing structure of the domestic economy, marked by declining employment in manufacturing and expansion in service activities, (3) changing social conditions, (4) the leadership crisis, in which government often appears incapable of addressing the major economic development challenges of the 1990s, (5) changing environmental priorities, (6) infrastructure issues, (7) the education and labor crisis, (8) changing sources of capital, and (9) technological progress. Challenges to the practice and profession of economic development include (1) changing organizational structures, with fewer organizations and larger professional staffs, (2) building local capacity, (3) broadening the activities of development agencies, (4) blending traditional economic development practices (e.g., recruitment) with new ones (e.g., tourism, small business development) to achieve a comprehensive strategy, (5) increasing demands for professionalism, (6) need for research and innovation, (7) changing demands on professional organizations, (8) shifting from reactive to proactive approaches, (9) achieving professional recognition, and (10) increasing the professional commitment.

729. Swager, Ronald J. 1991. *Economic Development Tomorrow: A Report From the Profession.* Rosemont, IL: The American Economic Development Council, 62 pp.

Reports on the outcome of a year-long effort which included a Delphi-type survey of leaders in the economic development field, as well as extensive input from all segments of the profession. The report reviews developments of the 1980s and previews trends likely to affect both the process of economic development and the economic development profession for the remainder of the century.

730. Swaim, Paul. 1990. "Rural Displaced Workers Fare Poorly." *Rural Development Perspectives* 6(3):8-13.

Points out that many workers, both rural and urban, were permanently laid off from their jobs between 1981 and 1986. Some found comparable jobs quickly, but others were jobless for six months or more, took a cut in pay to land a new job, or had to move away to find a new job.

Overall, rural displaced workers fared more poorly than urban. Rural communities need to enhance the labor market flexibility of workers displaced by economic change.

731. Thomas, Margaret G. 1990. *Recouple: Natural Resource Strategies for Rural Economic Development.* Report prepared for U.S. Department of Commerce, Economic Development Administration. Kansas City, MO: Midwest Research Institute.

An extensive sourcebook for rural community leaders and rural development specialists as well as natural resource professionals at county, state, and federal levels. There are three sections with guidance on utilizing forest, agricultural, and scenic and wildlife resources for rural economic development. Guidance materials were prepared on (1) forest and wildlife resources in rural economic development; (2) the forest industry park as a rural development strategy; (3) agriculture resources in rural economic development; (4) organizing a food industry association; and (5) developing small-scale aquaculture enterprises. These materials are presented in a question/answer format for use by community leaders in encouraging group discussion. There are also four sections with selected bibliographies on technical assistance materials useful in developing strategies for forest, agricultural, and wildlife resource use, plus a listing of periodicals and newsletters. Over 100 publications are referenced.

732. Thompson, Wilbur R., and Philip R. Thompson. 1993. "Cross-Hairs Targeting for Industries and Occupations," pp. 265-286 in *Economic Adaptation: Alternatives for Nonmetropolitan Areas*, D. L. Barkley, ed. Boulder, CO: Westview Press.

Presents a "cross-hairs" approach to nonmetropolitan industrial targeting based on both industrial and occupational characteristics. This new occupational-functional approach uses a distinctive set of five occupations to identify each of the five basic economic functions of any industry: entrepreneurship, headquarters decision making, research and development, precision operations, and routine work. Next, the profile of local competitive advantage (disadvantage) in key occupations (skills) in each of these five functions (one cross hair) can then be matched against the occupational requirements of each of the separate functions of each prospective new industry (the other cross hair). The authors review the fundamentals of cross hairs targeting and provide examples of its usefulness in rural area and small town development planning.

733. Thornburgh, Dick. 1988. "Commentary: The State's Role in an Era of Economic Transition: The Pennsylvania Experience." *Economic Development Quarterly* 2(3):203-210.

Reports that, as the decade of the 1970s drew to a close, Pennsylvania was in serious economic trouble. The most serious of its problems was its overcommitment to traditional "smokestack" industries, without any strategy for diversification or modernization. The Governor's Office of Policy Development, along with the State Planning Board, developed an economic strategy based on new economic priorities. With this strategy as a starting point, steps were taken to improve the economy and turn Pennsylvania around. The author (a former Governor of Pennsylvania) concludes that the ability to look to the long run is critical for other states that are addressing their own economic problems.

734. Thornton, Linda W., LaDene Morton, Joyce C. Stark, Karen McCarthy, and Craig Cunningham. 1986. *Kansas Development Study Target Industry Analysis.* Kansas City, MO: Midwest Research Institute, 219 pp.

Provides a list of target industries which the state can use in its marketing efforts to attract new industries as well as retain and foster the growth of existing industries. An assessment of the state's economic base, infrastructure, and locational strengths and weaknesses is provided. Locational requirements of various industries are evaluated and compared to the resources of various regions of the state. Strategies and recommendations for legislative action are presented.

735. Tremblay, Gerald D. 1993. "Moving Towards a Value-Added Society: Quebec's New Economic Development Strategy." *Economic Development Review* 11(1):18-20.

Reports that the goal of Quebec's new economic development strategy is to help the province move to a value-added economy. The program proposes to do this through the industrial cluster approach. Thirteen such clusters have been identified, and five are considered currently competitive. Efforts need to be undertaken to retain the competitiveness of the initial five and to improve the competitiveness of the remaining eight.

736. Tweeten, Luther, and George L. Brinkman. 1976. *Micropolitan Development: Theory and Practice of Greater-Rural Economic Development.* Ames, IA: Iowa State University Press, 456 pp.

Presents a comprehensive look at greater rural development and attempts to integrate literature on micropolitan development into a meaningful whole. The definition of micropolitan (or nonmetropolitan) development requires that cities of up to 50,000 population, which serve as centers of trade, services, and jobs, must be included in addition to rural towns when examining rural development.

737. Walton, Marsha, and Robert A. Kraushaar. 1990. "Ideas and Information: The Changing Role of States in Economic Development." *Economic Development Quarterly* 4(3):276-286.

Suggests that the ability of states to adapt successfully to the rapidly changing economic conditions of the 1990s is contingent upon their ability to provide accurate, timely, and accessible information about their local and regional economies to public and business interests. Examples of electronic information systems implemented by states include the Colorado Economic Information System and the Minnesota "DATANET."

738. Walzer, Norman. 1991. *Innovative Economic Development Practices in Small Illinois Communities.* Rural Research Report Vol. 2, Issue 5. Macomb, IL: Western Illinois University, Illinois Institute for Rural Affairs, 8 pp.

Examines economic trends and conditions in small rural Illinois communities and reviews innovative programs or approaches adopted by four small cities, in rebuilding their local economies. The programs presented in this report are only illustrative of options available to small cities and are not meant to be prescriptive for all small Illinois communities. The cities in the study all have agriculturally based economies and none have immediate access to an interstate highway. The four towns ranged in population from about 550 people to about 6,350.

739. Watts, H. D. 1981. *The Branch Plant Economy: A Study of External Control.* New York, NY: Longman, Inc., 104 pp.

Examines the implications when a regional economy has a large part of its employment in establishments owned by firms whose head offices lie outside the region. The author emphasizes externally controlled manufacturing activities. Specific areas addressed include (1) the concept of external control, (2) the extent of external ownership, (3) external ownership and employment characteristics, and (4) external ownership and linkage. The effects of ownership change are examined through a detailed examination of ownership change in the Yorkshire and Humberside brewing industry.

740. Waugh, William L., Jr., and Deborah M. Waugh. 1988. "Baiting the Hook: Targeting Economic Development Monies More Effectively." *Public Administration Quarterly* 12:216-234.

Examines the issue of how state and local governments can target their economic development monies more effectively. Using data from a 1984 mailed survey of firms having high research and development expenditures relative to gross sales, the authors examine the key factors influencing firms' location decisions. Information provided by 65 firms constitutes the data base for the analysis. The authors' major conclusions were (1) for information processing, telecommunications, and semi-conductor firms, the most important considerations are the skills and availability of labor, (2) for many manufacturing firms, the crucial variables are labor costs, tax climate, regulatory practices, and energy costs and availability, (3) light manufacturing firms appear to put greatest emphasis on the skills, availability, and cost of labor, regulatory practices, and tax climate, and (4) the primary industries (e.g., building materials, chemicals, fuels, mining and minerals) would appear to be much less influenced by factors amenable to government manipulation. In general, the most effective strategies for targeting monies would seem to be to focus on programs to develop human resources. Tax and regulatory incentives might also be offered but with care to avoid excessive and unnecessary benefits. Investments in transportation facilities and infrastructure in general are also consistent with the indicated preferences.

741. Weintraub, Donald L. 1993. "Implementing Total Quality Management." *Economic Development Review* 11(3):39-42.

Argues that companies that successfully implement total quality management (TQM) principles focus on customer satisfaction, total involvement, measurement, systematic support, and continuous improvement. The author raises key questions, and suggests implementation strategies, in the areas of leadership and commitment, infrastructures, focus and roll-outs, measurement, education, resources, information, systems alignment, public responsibility, and alignment with customers and suppliers.

742. Wells, Betty L. 1990. "Building Intercommunity Cooperation." *Journal of the Community Development Society* 21(2):1-17.

Indicates that the long-term viability of many rural communities depends on the adoption of innovative institutional arrangements. This paper focuses specifically on the development of multicommunity clusters as an institutional innovation whereby neighboring communities cooperate, rather than compete, with each other. Principles for promoting the growth of cooperation are integrated into the curriculum of a multicommunity leadership program. A combination action-learning/action-research framework is recommended so that community developers can implement multicommunity programs while simultaneously contributing to the knowledge base needed to guide such programs.

743. Wilkinson, Kenneth P. 1989. "Community Development and Industrial Policy," Vol. 4, pp. 241-254 in *Research in Rural Sociology and Development*, W. W. Falk and T. A. Lyson, eds. Greenwich, CT: JAI Press Inc.

Reviews key criticisms of rural industrialization, particularly those identified from a Marxian viewpoint, as background for examining the role of industrialization in an effective rural policy for the United States. A concept of community development is used to address issues raised by these criticisms, and thus suggest the foundations of an effective policy. The discussion is cast as a rural labor market analysis because any effective rural policy must begin with a consideration of labor resources and needs.

744. Wolkoff, Michael J. 1990. "New Directions in the Analysis of Economic Development Policy." *Economic Development Quarterly* 4(4):334-344.

Re-examines economic development research and policy making by focusing on strategic behavior as an important component of the process. In particular, the potential of game theory in explaining economic development decisions is examined. The author reviews the small but emerging game theory literature as it applies to economic development policy. Game theory is shown to be a powerful tool for analyzing such economic development policies as competitive subsidization and urban renewal.

745. Wolman, Harold, and Kenneth Voytek. 1990. "State Government as a Consultant for Local Economic Development." *Economic Development Quarterly* 4(3):211-220.

Examines the experience of the state of Michigan, which in 1987 created the Center for Local Economic Competitiveness (CLEC) within the Michigan Department of Commerce. CLEC was designed to provide consulting services, free of charge, to Michigan communities willing to engage in a strategic analysis of their local economy. The authors discuss the experience of the CLEC, focusing both on the analytic and the political problems it faces and ends by setting forth the benefits to local communities of the analysis it provides as well as lessons other states can draw from the Michigan experience.

746. Wood, William C., Dennis R. Harbaugh, and LaDene H. Bowen. 1993. "Critical Barriers in Total Community Development and Practical Steps to Overcome Them." *Economic Development Review* 11(2):6-13.

Reports that total community development is a process that results in a variety of improvements throughout a community. The process is composed of the three phases of preparing, planning, and implementing and focuses on the major challenges of forming and maintaining the team, forming and maintaining commitment, and forming and maintaining community action. Critical barriers and practical solutions associated with each of the phases and challenges are presented.

747. Yarzebinski, Joseph A. 1993. "Industrial Impact Management." *Economic Development Review* 11(3):43-46.

Reports that active management of the risks and impacts due to job creation and retention is being forced upon the economic development profession. One tool which can help meet this challenge is the Industrial Impact Management process whereby a community can assess the impacts of development and determine what it can do to attempt to avoid or reduce them, or even accept them. With such information, a community is in a better position to determine what it is "paying" for the investment and jobs.

748. Young, Alan Daniel. 1993. "Strategic Planning in a Rural County: The Example of Union County, South Carolina." *Economic Development Review* 11(2):18-21.

Points out that strategic planning, while in vogue, should not be viewed as an overnight cure for the economic ills of a community. Rather it should be viewed as a consensus-building tool for actions needed to strengthen the community's potential for economic growth. Through a case study, the author demonstrates how those principles can be applied in a rural setting.

AUTHOR INDEX

GEOGRAPHIC INDEX

SUBJECT INDEX

competitiveness. *See* Competitiveness
conditions
    global, 31
development
    approaches and strategies, 629-748
    effects of, 120, 287, 322, 543, 710, 718
    factors affecting, 729
    opinions about, 717
    partners in, 630-632
    planning, 644-645, 680, 732
diversification, 4, 12-13, 47, 151, 170, 249, 374, 385, 462, 492, 553, 714, 724, 733
effects, 72, 93, 96, 247-248, 619, 622, 651, 722
growth, 246, 406
regeneration, 693
relations, 470
restructuring, 2, 9, 14, 22-23, 31, 59, 61, 277, 546-547, 556, 565, 584
state's role, 737
    See also Policy, state
structure, 1, 3
Education, 5, 7, 523, 532, 548
    distance learning, 504
    higher education institutions, 68, 462, 501
    need for, 95, 462, 472, 503, 508, 522, 701, 724
    program, 502
    See also Universities
    vocational, 512, 522
Elderly, 5, 148, 174, 675, 680
    retirees, 137, 142-143, 591, 643, 665, 715, 722
Elected officials. *See* Political leaders
Employment
    See also Agriculture, employment
    creation, 62-63, 68, 103, 121, 125-126, 146, 177-178, 204-205, 246-249, 272, 299-301, 305, 323-324, 326, 358, 361, 398, 411-412, 435, 452, 486, 488, 545, 571, 580, 590, 594-595, 606, 615-616, 625, 627, 641, 645-646, 658-659, 661, 672, 676, 682, 692, 695-696, 699, 701, 706, 747
    effects of size of firm, 246, 296, 299-300, 326
    energy industry, 47
    expanding firms, 248

growth, 407
high-tech industries, 225, 229
information-sector, 178
job loss, 450
layoffs, 378
manufacturing, 60, 66, 69, 88, 90, 105, 121-122, 127, 242, 261
new firm, 239, 243, 246-248
occupation structure, 479
off-farm, 16
quality of jobs, 103, 276, 329, 381, 396, 488
racial factors, 428
redundant, 378, 521, 556, 688
rural, 105, 353, 358
self, 308
service sector, 164, 177-178, 184, 191, 193
stability, 121
subcontracting, 83, 97-98, 311
turnover, 381
unemployed, 8, 85
Entrepreneurship, 244, 246, 297, 308, 321, 325, 330-346, 423, 462, 482-483, 485, 511, 534, 538, 552, 558, 586, 641, 678, 698, 708, 732
    high tech, 200, 206, 225, 227, 476, 489, 530
    manufacturing, 131
    minority, 435
    rural, 68, 249-250, 256, 698, 708, 725
Environment
    business, 106, 216, 341, 479, 495, 523, 529, 537
    economic, 110, 117, 290, 595, 629, 637
    impact, 23, 130, 142, 430, 561, 614, 728
    industrial, 115, 228, 243, 366, 481, 687
    issues, 463
    labor, 87, 647
    policy/regulation, 42,113, 270, 294, 351, 614, 624
    rural, 124, 332, 437
    technological, 476, 539, 592
    telecommunications, 287, 444
Expenditures to suppliers, 248-249
Export services 165-166
Exports, 91, 471
    intermediate service sector, 180
    potential of services for, 190, 195
Extension
    industrial, 9
    service, 347, 438, 520, 645

About the Compilers

F. LARRY LEISTRITZ is Professor of Agricultural Economics at North Dakota State University. The author of nine books, he is currently working on a book on the farm crisis in the Heartland.

RITA R. HAMM is a Socioeconomic Research Specialist in the Institute for Business and Industry Development at the North Dakota State University. She is the coauthor of numerous publications.